ALIENS IN THE HOME

ALIENS IN THE HOME

The Child in Horror Fiction

Sabine Büssing

Contributions to the Study of Childhood
and Youth, Number 4

GREENWOOD PRESS
NEW YORK • WESTPORT, CONNECTICUT • LONDON

Library of Congress Cataloging-in-Publication Data

Büssing, Sabine, 1960-
   Aliens in the home.

   (Contributions to the study of childhood and youth,
ISSN 0273-124X ; no. 4)
   Bibliography: p.
   Includes index.
   1. Horror tales—History and criticism.   2. Children
in literature.   I. Title.   II. Series.
   PN3435.B87   1987   809.3'872   86-19389
   ISBN 0-313-25420-6 (lib. bdg. : alk. paper)

Library of Congress Catalog Card Number: 86-19389
ISBN: 0-313-25420-6
ISSN: 0273-124X

First published in 1987

Greenwood Press, Inc.
88 Post Road West, Westport, Connecticut 06881

Printed in the United States of America

∞™

The paper used in this book complies with the
Permanent Paper Standard issued by the National
Information Standards Organization (Z39.48-1984).

10 9 8 7 6 5 4 3 2 1

For David Galloway, teacher and friend

CONTENTS

PREFACE

Within the broad field of contemporary literature horror fiction has, both with regard to quantity and quality, developed into a factor which should no longer be ignored by scholarly criticism. Unlike its predecessor, Gothic literature, this genre has nevertheless been widely neglected up to the present time, which must at least partly be ascribed to the fact that it is still stained with the odor of triviality. On the other hand, science fiction and fantasy literature, which are very closely related to the genre under discussion, appear to have meanwhile attained sufficient "respectability" to rouse critical interest. Although most critics refrain from clearly defining their subject matter (and those definitions that do exist are rather controversial), the mainstream and its varieties are catalogued in a great number of descriptive works.

The average reader of horror fiction may feel able to distinguish his favorite literary field from contiguous genres by mere intuition. Moreover, the fact that the brand "horror" is readily and frequently employed by publishers, editors of anthologies and others engaged in the book market suggests that horror fiction is an uncontested, independent branch of literature and that the productions in question are always unequivocal representatives of this genre only—which, however, they are not. Apart from the counter-argument that many of the very same stories simultaneously appear under the headings "fantasy" and/or "science fiction," the few critics who actually work with the term and phenomenon "horror fiction" tend to categorize their subject as a mere sub-genre within the vast area of fantastic literature. It is notable that the problems of demarcation are not restricted to horror fiction and its "fringeland;" the confusion is complete if one considers that science fiction has repeatedly been regarded as a field of fantasy literature, and vice versa. Hybridizations like "fantasy SF" or "horror SF" (as employed by Horst Schröder in his study Science Fiction-Literatur in den USA) testify to the fact that it is virtually impossible to draw clear lines which would allow unequivocal classifications for each single literary work of art.

Therefore, it cannot be the aim of the following study to venture upon a "foolproof" definition of horror fiction. On the contrary, the examination of a specific literary motif, the image of the child, within this genre will rather give additional evidence of the blurred boundaries that exist between horror fiction and the other genres mentioned above. Starting from the working definition that, roughly speaking, horror fiction can be regarded as "literature of fear," which subsists both on the terrors it describes and the dread and anxiety it evokes within the reader, and which is the rightful successor to the "classic" Gothic mode, this study will include literary representatives that cover one and a half centuries: the period ranging from the definitive decline of the original Gothic romance up to the present time. The method of proceeding, however, will not be a chronological one for the simple reason that the following analysis is intended to demonstrate how—despite gradual developments and the rise of individual trends within the field of horror fiction—a complex literary motif may grow into an essential component of a genre without undergoing any remarkable alteration.

This motif, the image of the child, occupies a peculiar position because a) it is virtually non-existent in the early Gothic representatives (the term "child" as used in the context of this study notably refers to boys and girls up to the age of puberty), b) it fulfills several functions fundamental to horror literature in a manner that predestines it to play a special role, and c) as a result it has, especially within the last decades, become an indispensable ingredient of its genre. Therefore, a phenomenological approach offers the likeliest way of doing justice to this motif, which is restricted in its basic manifestations but which simultaneously carries within itself a multiplicity of "dramatic" possibilities, and of latent but sometimes explicitly revealed meanings. The patterns that underlie its appearance show a remarkable universality and ubiquity. In order to point out this particularity, which partly accounts for the difficulties in demarcation mentioned above, the study deals with several literary examples from countries with a "non-English" background, although the overwhelming majority of texts stem from America and Great Britain. These exceptions are not introduced for the sake of completion (such an attempt will seem presumptuous if one considers that only a limited number of English productions can be examined here); the few foreign works which will be discussed in detail deserve their place because (irrespective of their "nationality") they offer new angles and clues for a well-grounded analysis of the child's functions and meanings. Most of the exceptions are French productions, which is no surprise since the "conte cruel" has a great tradition as an idiosyncratic successor to Gothic literature. It goes without saying that the cross-section which forms the basis of analysis can cover neither every single tendency nor every country where horror fiction has been written. It will suffice to give the reader a notion of the fact that a single motif may well function as a link between related genres and connect representatives from different countries as well.

The admission of non-narrative texts to the corpus must be seen in the same light. Very much like its Gothic predecessor, horror fiction consists almost exclusively of novels and short stories; yet unmistakable specimens like Maxwell Anderson's play <u>Bad Seed</u> demonstrate that drama and poetry fill a special place within the genre, too. Moreover, the Twentieth Century has brought about a decisive change through the rise of the horror film: the frequent dramatization of novels and the new literary form of the screenplay have shown a high degree of interchangeability between narration and drama. For this reason, the study includes a separate chapter on the horror film, which deals (among other topics) with the adaptation of novels and short stories for the screen.

INTRODUCTION

For the modern reader it is difficult to comprehend that, up to the last decades of the 18th century, the theme of childhood was generally neglected in literature. To be sure, the child obviously belonged to the human race and was thus allowed to figure occasionally in poetry and drama, in works from Homer through Shakespeare, just as adult men and women appeared. The child as such, however, did not have the qualities that authors (Greeks and Elizabethans alike) considered important--cognitive faculties, rational conduct, adult passions. Since it could not, in the artist's opinion, present "a suitable medium through which to comment on the conditions of man,"[1] it was depicted in a distorted fashion. It either appeared as a helpless, passive creature that had to remain silent (like Astyanax, Hector's "sweet child" in Euripides' Trojan Women, who witnesses all the cruelties of war and, being torn from his mother's side, does not utter a sound), or it was endowed with adult thoughts and feelings and acted accordingly. It rarely had qualities appropriate to the child's real nature, and it was never rendered as an individual personality.[2] The child was mainly an emblem, a symbol of innocence, an object of compassion-- functions that are especially rooted in the Christian tradition.

The child first appears prominently in Romantic poetry, when poets began to regard not only the adult mind, but also the feelings. Since this period, when childhood came to be treasured as a metaphor for the ideal human condition, a steady development can be observed with regard to the child's role in literature as a whole. William Wordsworth, Charles Dickens, Nathaniel Hawthorne, Mark Twain, Robert Louis Stevenson, Lewis Carroll, Rudyard Kipling and innumerable others all had their share in bringing this development to a point where the child is no longer reduced to a soulless entity. Especially with the consolidation of psychology and psycho-analysis at the turn of the century a new interest in the true nature of the child arose. Writers of fiction grew more and more aware that the child was a personality, a vessel of consciousness worthy of being explored in depth.

In certain aspects the development of the child's representation in horror literature may be compared to that within the "main stream." In such early Gothic novels as The Castle of Otranto, Melmoth the Wanderer, or The Monk, children simply cannot be discovered. One can explain this fact by the original nature of Gothic literature. Initially, its center is occupied by the Gothic hero (or anti-hero), a very special character who in the course of his actions becomes more and more isolated, separated from both God and society. He is not an atheist but a heretic,[3] who finds himself involved in a continual moral and religious struggle. Ambrosio, Melmoth, Schedoni, and their kind are searching for their own ways (just as, later on, Victor Frankenstein and Dr. Jekyll do). Their search is a "matter of metaphysical, even theological concern,"[4] and thus one can easily understand why there is scarcely any room for children; they appear at best incidentally, and once again, as more or less speechless victims. Even Bram Stoker's Dracula, a comparatively late successor to the early Gothic examples, contains a good illustration: Count Dracula brings his evil brides an edible present--a small infant. Significantly, it is stuffed into a bag like an inanimate object, then thrown before the undead

ladies as if it were a dead piece of meat. Above all, the reader has
to guess what is hidden inside the bag and can only identify the creature by its faint wail.[5]

From the early 19th century up to the present a pronounced change
has occurred in the role of the child. It has displayed more and more
activity, developing from a mere victim into a frequent aggressor,
killer, a veritable monster. And even in its initial function as a
victim it meanwhile often occupies a central position. For 20th-cen-
tury horror literature, in particular, the child has become absolutely
indispensable. In another respect, however, the child's role in horror
literature greatly differs from its presentation in fiction as a whole.
The lack of individual traits and qualities, the absence of a personality, which have generally been replaced by a great complexity of
character, continue to appear in horror fiction; indeed, these "deficiencies" have been more and more emphasized and elaborated. The
reader can discern several special devices that help to create and
reinforce the strangely flat impression which the child evokes. These
circumstances might lead the critical observer to conclude that there
is a particular conception implicit in such distortions. The stylized
depiction of the child in fact fulfills requirements essential to the
effectiveness of horror literature.

This pronounced artificiality in the representation of the child
can also be observed quite frequently in the genres closest to horror
fiction, science fiction and fantasy literature. Significantly, the
phenomenon occurs in those individual works which one is almost unable
to classify with absolute certainty, since they show basic traits considered typical of at least two of the genres. Thus, for instance, the
reader may regard a clone child both as a purely scientific "product"
and as an unnatural monster; infants with superhuman abilities are,
strictly speaking, mutants; and hordes of children whose heredity
qualities have changed through atomic radiation can be called
"aliens." The "mad scientist" motif, among many other recurrent images,
appears in horror literature and science fiction alike and is not
clearly attributable to one of the genres--after all, the first great
"unauthorized" obsessed scientist, Victor Frankenstein, has repeatedly
been considered the founder of science fiction.[6] On the other hand,
supernatural creatures like vampires and werewolves are to be found in
fantasy literature as well.[7]

As mentioned before, the three genres are sometimes, at least in
their borderland, hardly distinguishable from each other. The image of
the child as the main motif and dominant factor of the works it appears in is not very "helpful" in this respect, because of its obvious
universality. There does not seem to be much sense in combining the
genres as categories of "fantastic literature," since the definitions
and descriptions of this field are often more confused (and confusing)
than those of its "subspecies."[8] The matter gets completely out of
hand if the term "fantastic" is treated as a synonym of "supernatural":
in this case at least two-thirds of modern horror fiction could no
longer be regarded as such for they do not contain any overtly supernatural creatures or happenings.[9] Like many representatives of Gothic
fiction, horror literature frequently provides the reader with rational explanations of seemingly incomprehensible phenomena. One can
observe that it has more and more developed a semi-realistic mode of
expression.[10] Thus, Rosemary Jackson combines all "uncanny" manifesta-

tions of fantasy in a chapter entitled "Fantastic Realism," whereas Marie-Claire Bancquart, who concentrates on the nature of Maupassant's tales of horror, speaks of "réalités fantastiques"[11]: the supernatural is the inexplicable, but for Maupassant humanity and life themselves are inexplicable phenomena. The French antonyms "fantastique" and "merveilleux" bring in a convenient distinction in this connection, the more since their difference roots in colloquial usage; the connotations of both terms were not artificially ascribed to them in order to attain the basis of a classification. The "spirit of the French language," as Dorothea Schurig-Geick calls it,[12] had coined the word "fantastique" long before, in 1828, the critic Jean-Jacques Ampère employed it as a literary term and epithet for the tales of E. T. A. Hoffmann (which introduced the "peur hoffmannesque" to French literature). In contrast to the word "merveilleux," which has a clearly positive meaning (comparable to the English "miraculous") and which, in literature, is mainly used in connection with the fairytale, "fantastique" has two characteristics which show its obvious relation to horror fiction: the word always expresses fear, and the contact to reality is never fully interrupted: "Le fantastique...ne quitte jamais le réel, il l'élargit."[13]

In order to attain at least one useful criterion for the distinction between horror literature and related genres, one has to fall back upon a "method" brought forward by Roger Caillois,[14] who tries to grasp the nature of fantastic literature by relying on the reader's "impression d'étrangeté irreductible" as the ultimate touchstone. Of course, this approach is determined by subjectivity and emotionality and has roused the indignation of Tzvetan Todorov, whose structural approach for its part is annulled by Stanislaw Lem.[15] Lem defends Caillois, conceding that the humanities are not "conquerable" by logic and objectivity as much as the natural sciences are, and he allows a high degree of personal intuition on the part of the reader/critic. Thus, one must analogously look for the special "impression" which indicates to the reader that he has come across a work of horror fiction. Primitive as it may appear, this clue is without doubt man's strongest emotion: fear.

The fact that the nature of this dread has undergone a change since the days of the English Gothic novel surely partly accounts for the admission of children to the literature of fear and the increasing importance of the child's role in this field. The Gothic romance, the first genre in which fear is the main theme of interest, is considered both a subversive answer to the doctrines of the Enlightenment and an expression of Man's being endangered in a new social and moral situation.[16] Although every frightening incident means a temporal disturbance, the universal order beneath always proves solid and unshakable; the outsider who has tried to defy God and mankind is finally destroyed, peace is restored. The conciliatory basic attitude which underlies the terrors of Gothic fiction has been called a mere preliminary stage to the breakdown of value systems and the Existenzangst which determine the literary products of the Twentieth Century.[17] Moreover, the original numinous fear has been largely extinguished in modern horror fiction; the confrontation between heretic and divine being does not have much room in a literature with an increasingly atheistic background. The fears expressed nowadays are of a more general kind,[18] not always aimed at a special object or situation, since concrete grounds are hard to find. Such a diffuse anxiety (which is nevertheless as much "down-to-earth" as earlier forms) calls for a manifestation which in its universality corresponds to it as a projection and embodiment. The child meets this demand in an ideal manner, for it personifies the future and the hopes of mankind but remains a tangible and (in most cases) perfectly natural member of the human race, omnipresent in everyday life. Thus, it suits the realistic character of contemporary horror literature and, because of its inherent connotations, it may be a vessel for all the fears that concern the existence of Man.

In addition to this, the child has in a way taken over the function of the Doppelgänger. In one of the rare critical works on twentieth-century horror fiction, Danse Macabre, Stephen King states that the myth of Narcissus and his lethal mirror must be considered essential especially to the modern representatives of the genre.[19] The child is such a mirror, a juvenile, beautiful reflection of Man, his plans and desires. It may come to harm through adult man, as William Wilson's Doppelgänger is killed by the irresponsible protagonist in Poe's tale, and it may as well turn on the adults it mirrors. One can easily comprehend that such an idealized image invites a stylized, uniform mode of representation which remains basically the same in all situations, irrespective of the differences in the child's functions.

Roughly speaking, the child performs two basic functions: those of victim and victimizer. Concerning the former one must admit that the child's "literary heritage," its age-old image as a symbol of innocence and vulnerability, establishes an immense advantage. In this pristine form the child makes the ideal victim in a genre that is absolutely dependent on masses of qualified victims. It by far surpasses the helpless female, even when she is at her very best; a screaming Fay Wray in the fist of King Kong or a terror-stricken Lucy on the run from Dracula can never be a match for a three-year-old that awaits its tormentor motionless, its huge blue eyes wide open, with nothing more than a pitiful whimper. The reader's or spectator's attitude towards the adult victim--male or female--is of course entirely different from his reaction to a child. This distinction is often, as in the above examples, at least partially based on the adult's sexuality, his or her being erotically connected with the victimizer (and the reader). Generally the child's gender is of no relevance at all, and, with very few exceptions, writers of horror fiction neglect and perhaps deliberately suppress the psychological discovery that the little ones might have a sexuality of their own. The child has to remain immaculate in order to attain the reader's full sympathy and concern--after all, it is not only the respective child he fears for, but his whole deep-rooted concept of purity, incarnate in this small human being, which is exposed to evil and danger.

Strangely enough, the child's traditional image as a pure, innocent creature also means an advantage in those cases when it acts as a monstrous killer. This latter function, which has grown so prevalent within the past three decades, is in a way typical of 20th-century fashions. In contrast to earlier periods, horror literature now more and more subsists on the subtle perverseness of its shocks. The new monsters can no longer be recognized by their outward appearance; the Gothic villain with black clothes and vicious glittering eyes and the gigantic roaring beast must tolerate the rise of a novel species that looks sweet, harmless, and, in a word, angelic. The possibility that such a creature could harbor the most hideous intentions, that it could turn on its own loving parents and kill them (which it frequently does), seems to be against the very laws of nature. The effect which the child produces within the reader is thus an exceptionally strong and enduring one.

Between these two extreme points, the victim and the victimizer, there has arisen a third type, the "evil innocent."[20] This category, which can be regarded as a literary product of the Twentieth Century as well, combines all the advantages of the other two in an ingenious way. Here the child is a perfectly amiable and tender creature which is driven to do evil things by forces beyond its control. It may either be possessed by demons and devils, or it has irrepressible, superhuman powers harmful to its surroundings. One may say that in these cases the child is both a victim and an aggressor and evokes controversial emotions accordingly. The child's freedom and true nature are violated (its supposed true nature is always the stereotyped "innocence"), which makes the reader feel pity--especially if there are intervals between its evil outbursts during which the child behaves "normally." It is a vessel for unnatural powers, and, while in their grip, is allowed to commit the vilest crimes without really arousing antipathy. The sense of perverseness discussed above works very well in this situation, but derives only partly from the child itself.

The child has to fulfill completely heterogeneous functions, but its representation remains basically the same. By which special means this is accomplished, how the child's rather uniform image can be successfully applied in the most different plots (without spoiling the originality of the whole work) will be one of the main points of interest in the following study.

According to a widespread popular opinion the way the child appears in horror fiction has its roots in the fairytale. The parallels between the genres, however, are superficial and must be dismissed after a thorough investigation. The most obvious similarity certainly consists in the child's frequent function as a victim, and in the utter brutality with which it is treated most of the time. It is endangered by man-eating ogres and witches and ruthlessly tortured by its own parents or step-parents. In the fairytale the child may also display a certain amount of activity--sometimes even killing its tormentors, as in "Hänsel und Gretel." Occasionally the child can be called a monster, but mainly with regard to its outward appearance. In most of these cases it is a changeling, a figure which enjoys great popularity in the fairytale, but is rarely made use of in horror fiction.

The way the child appears in the fairytale--as an active and a passive figure--may often appeal to the reader's emotions, arousing pity and compassion. This must be ascribed, however, to the fact that the most popular collections, though based on age-old oral traditions, were embellished and refined by such collectors as the Brothers Grimm. The romanticized presentation gives of course much greater depth to characters and action.[21] A more "primitive" collection, the Russian fairytales compiled by Afanasiev, provides one with clearer information as to the pure nature of the genre. In his treatise Das europäische Volksmärchen Max Lüthi gives his definition of the fairytale. Analogously with Vladimir Propp, who retraces every present form and variety to one ancient fundamental formula--which means that the Russian collection contains all the necessary clues to the basic traits of the European fairytale--Lüthi tries to find a unique basic form which is characteristic of all fairytales. He concentrates, above all, on the central "characters," which he rather defines as non-characters,[22] having neither physical nor psychic depth, but remaining one-dimensional in every respect. Lüthi, who regards them as mere linear figures which move like chessmen on a brightly illuminated surface (24), denies that they show deep emotions and motivations or enjoy lasting relationships to other figures. In the fairytale qualities and feelings are very seldom mentioned for their own sake or in order to create a certain atmosphere.

Whenever one of the figures is severely injured, even crippled or disfigured, only the simple fact is stated; the victim feels neither physical pain nor mental anguish. The reader is not invited to take these injuries seriously, for he sees no blood flowing, and even the victim's cut-off limbs may begin to grow again at a certain point of the narration (14). The figures of the fairytale always act in a basically cool and detached way; they may inflict the most barbarous punishments upon others, but not out of vindictiveness. They cannot go insane, simply because they do not have a real mind at all. All the atrocities of the fairytale are important to set and keep the action going; their extremeness is a reflection of the overall conception of this genre which does not tolerate nuances of any kind (28-30).

Considering all these basic traits, one will soon become aware of the enormous differences between fairytale and horror fiction. The latter genre depends on the deep emotions of its characters--fear, hatred, bloodthirstiness for its own sake--and on the reader's concern. Everything that seems strange and unnatural evokes uneasiness and alarm (and horror, of course), since, after all, the characters of horror fiction are infinitely closer to real life. When the hero of the fairytale comes across a giant, a witch, or an ogre, he does not show any astonishment, curiosity, let alone numinous fear. He calmly faces these "otherworldly" creatures, because for the hero there exists only one world where everything is possible.

Most of what has been said about the traditional fairytale cannot be applied to the Kunstmärchen. Unlike the Volksmärchen (to which it is usually opposed in order to attain at least a kind of "negative" specification), the Kunstmärchen still lacks a clear-cut definition.[23] Jens Tismar's statement that the Kunstmärchen is not based on any anonymous oral tradition but invented by an author as his individual creation[24] points out the crucial difference between the two genres; there are no unequivocal boundaries, however, between the Kunstmärchen and other forms of "literary" fiction, into which it frequently merges. The average reader who immediately comes to think of the literary productions of romanticism can nevertheless find several traits which can be applied to the overwhelming majority of these representatives. Here the author rather emphasizes the emotional capacity of his characters and tries to make his readers sympathize with the meek and the defenceless. It is here, too, that children are frequently employed for the very reasons which are important in horror literature (the connotation of innocence, purity, and delicacy), but they no longer appear in connection with cruelty and physical brutality. If, in the fairytales of Andersen, Hauff, Bechstein and others, the happiness of the central characters is disturbed, an atmosphere of sadness rather than dread prevails.[25] With the exception of E. T. A. Hoffmann, the great writers of fairytales tend to depict a reasonably humane world. Hoffmann's macabre and aggressive tales, such as "Klein Zaches, genannt Zinnober," show their immediate relationship to the author's "Nachtstücke;" the plot of one of his most famous Gothic tales, "Der Sandmann," is even based on a fairytale motif and the lasting impression it makes on a child's mind.

The above statements explain why fairytales (and the way children are presented in them) must not be taken into consideration as part of horror fiction, as a kind of popular "predecessor." On the other hand, it is highly interesting to examine how writers of horror fiction-- whether they presuppose a direct kinship between both genres or not-- make use of ancient fairytale motifs and thus give them new functions and meanings.

In spite of the basic differences there exists at least one important analogy. Vladimir Propp, another authority on popular fiction and the fairytale in particular, points out that numerous kinds of substitutions and sublimations have occurred during the development of the genre.[26] In the course of its history the fairytale has become a conglomeration of elements from popular customs, religion, superstition, and other sources. This means that "real life" entered it, but has been assimilated by draining the motifs of at least part of their original connotations. The fairytale reflects all that is essential to human existence (qualities, actions, relationships) in a specifically transformed manner.

Similar techniques of sublimating emotions and qualities can be observed in horror fiction--and to an exceptionally high degree with regard to the appearance of the child. There is much more to the fear and concern with which the child inspires its surroundings than the average reader might notice at first sight. The individual child represents an entire generation. Between its own generation and that of its parents there exists an insurmountable gap. Both groups regard each other as perfect strangers, and a true reconciliation is virtually impossible.

This problem has always existed in real life, but horror literature has found new channels to deal with it on another level--a primeval and much more straightforward one. What is "merely" considered a difficult question of general concern may literally become a matter of life and death in fiction. Whenever children play a central role, the generation conflict and the manifold ways of transforming and disguising it form the very basis of the respective literary work. The following analysis of the child's social environment includes no such chapter as "Children and Parents" for the simple reason that this immensely complex relationship affects all other themes of interest; its discussion cannot be confined to one single unit.

It has been pointed out that a desideratum like the complete critical analysis of horror fiction does not yet exist; although Stephen King's idiosyncratic Danse Macabre draws the reader's attention to numerous elucidating facts, figures, and features of the genre, these pieces of information are given in a spontaneous, associative conversational fashion. Neither a definition nor a consistent descrip-

tion which would cover the (admittedly vast) field of horror literature can be found here. On the other hand, King repeatedly discusses
works in which children play a dominant part (Ira Levin's Rosemary's
Baby, several stories by Ray Bradbury, The Doll Who Ate His Mother by
Ramsey Campbell, the novels Julia and Ghost Story by Peter Straub and
others), but these examples, interspersed between reflections of a
different nature, do not lead him to a more general excursion on the
role of the child. Shorter essays on horror fiction in "general" are
of no use here because these works usually do not even give the broad
survey their titles promise, let alone dwell on a single phenomenon.
Edmund Wilson's "A Treatise on Tales of Horror" is, in short, an
enumeration of individual literary representatives plus the critic's
respective applause or condemnation. Peter Penzoldt's "The Pure Tale
of Horror"[27] concentrates on five authors only and is based on the
premise that horror stories do not evoke "spiritual terror" within the
reader but inspire him with "physical repulsion" only. Works like Glen
St. John Barclay's Anatomy of Horror: The Masters of Occult Fiction
(London, 1978) or H. P. Lovecraft's pioneer study Supernatural Horror
in Literature (New York, 1945) indicate through their titles the re-
strictions in their fields of research. Marshall B. Tymm's semi-
encyclopedic work Horror Literature: A Core Collection and Reference
Guide (London, 1981) represents without doubt a major achievement, but
particular motifs are not considered here, either.
     Ironically enough, the only preparatory material this study can
rely on is provided by some of those critics who focus on science
fiction rather than horror literature. As the struggle between
children and adults is a social factor both in fiction and real life,
it is obvious that critics who pay attention to sociology and the
angles it offers are most likely to find out some of the basic laws
that are valid for the child, too. These critics do not explicitly
mention the child--after all, it is usually just an inconspicuous,
normal inhabitant of Earth--but their statements about the confrontation between two cultures, about adult man's being endangered by
aliens and monsters, can be applied to the child with almost no reservation.[28] Novels like John Wyndham's The Midwich Cuckoos (which deals
with the inhabitants of a small town who have to cope with their
extraterrestrial offspring) show that, in addition to the forms discussed earlier, another kind of sublimation takes place, for the
problems of the human race are "caused" by invaders or transferred to
outer space.
     In order to do justice to the child's sociological relevance in
horror fiction, the study will examine the basic social constellations
the child is involved in and simultaneously elucidate the nuances in
its figurative meaning which are brought about by the different varieties. In connection with the child as a solitary being all primary
connotations of its appearance can already be observed; brother and
sister represent the most frequent form of "doubling," whereas the
group of children brings in the aspect of the generation war. Apart
from these "internal" groupings, two elements which belong only indirectly to human society are worthy of being considered here, since
they serve as physical extensions of the child's mind and sphere of
influence: the beast and the doll. It will be shown in detail that
these factors (which also play independent roles in horror fiction)
are endowed with special meanings and functions whenever they go along

with the appearance of the child.

The second part of the analysis will concentrate on the child's functions as victim, "evil innocent," and monster, which were explained before. This section does not logically depend upon the preceding chapters, since social constellations and functions do not determine each other. As already indicated, the principal subject of this study is the examination of the child's overall representation, which remains uniform regardless of its different functions. As a "pictorial" complement, an appendix dealing with the horror film will demonstrate how well this uniformity is transferable to a visual medium.

ALIENS IN THE HOME

1. THE CHILD'S OUTWARD APPEARANCE

> She was a pretty thing, eleven years old, the cornflower
> blue of her dress matching her eyes, and the blond hair that
> only children possess cascading down her back and over her
> shoulders...
>
> John Saul, <u>Suffer the Children</u>[1]

The uniformity in the child's representation which was hinted at above finds clearest expression in its outward appearance. One is astonished to observe how little each single child differs from the rest of its "mates;" the reader might even be led to believe that all of them are brothers and sisters.

One can distinguish between two basic types--the blond child with blue eyes and the brown-haired, brown-eyed child. Unexpectedly, perhaps, boys and girls with black or red hair seldom appear, whereas children with green eyes can be found now and then. The recurrent combinations are not employed without a purpose; both "standard models" incarnate a special principle. The blond one represents the angelic type, the child-prodigy. Miles and Flora, the narrator's little charges in Henry James' <u>Turn of the Screw</u>, are brilliant examples of this connotation; as often as the colors of their hair and eyes are referred to, the narrator in her enthusiasm (or rather ecstasy) compares them with supernatural creatures. Throughout the whole narration she talks of them as "Raphael's holy infants,"[2] "cherubs" (36), a "pair of little grandees, of princes of the blood" (27), "divine creatures" and "angels" (122), and little Miles looks like a "fairy prince" (85). Eyes and hair are of course not simply mentioned as such; Flora has got "placid, heavenly eyes" and shining <u>golden</u> curls (76). The children's rosy complexion underlines the impression of unspoiled freshness, of uncorrupted purity and, one more time, of "innocence" (a word which is used hundreds of times in the book--one can really call it a <u>leitmotif</u>).

The deep effect which such radiant beauty produces on other people's minds becomes obvious through the narrator's reaction to her charges. In the same measure as her conviction is growing that the children are possessed by evil spirits, her attitude toward their physical charms gradually changes. Those features which aroused her devotion and adoration in the beginning slowly turn into objects of suspicion, mistrust, even aversion--<u>because of</u> their very perfection. A human being so beautiful and pleasing must never become an ally of dark powers; if it did its fall from grace would be ten times worse than that of Lucifer, since the hopes of mankind are based on the child's innate and unassailable goodness. In this religious context, which consists of nothing but extremes, an "angel" who commits the most trifling offence must instantly become a "devil." This fact is clearly expressed by the narrator, who at first reproaches herself for projecting her own knowledge of evil into the children ("To gaze into the depths of blue of the child's eyes and pronounce their loveliness a trick of premature cunning was to be guilty of a cynicism..."; 63). Later on, when she realizes that the word "divine" no longer suits the situation, she looks for a more appropriate expression--"Infernal, then!" (122)

One can observe that the blond, blue-eyed child is potentially more dangerous than the "brown one." Writers of horror fiction favor it as an aggressor, because the impression it produces in this function is basically different from that of the other type. In order to accentuate the basic traits one important addition is frequently made and thus another sub-variety, the child with china-blue eyes, arises. It is equally beautiful and attractive, but the very word "china" inspires the reader with a sense of uncertainty and awe. The child's character is, like its looks, cold and impenetrable; if it possesses a soul, its face can and will certainly never show it.

M. S. Waddell's story "The Pale Boy" contains an interesting example. The little boy in question is a mysterious, solitary creature ("He wasn't like the others though, for Paul was beautiful. His hair was flaxen, his eyes were large and solemn, china blue"[3]). Most people he meets recoil from him instinctively and are perfectly right in doing so. Only one quite insensitive lady, enchanted by his superficial beauty, insists on adopting him--only to discover that the object of her maternal feelings is a baby vampire.

Blue eyes can grow into an obsession for those who feel tormented by their look, as for instance the frightened parents of Ray Bradbury's "Small Assassin." They register every change of the baby's gaze that indicates its shifting moods, and are not calmed by the development they witness: "His blue eyes opened like fresh blue spring flowers;"[4] "the murderer looked up at David Leiber with a small, red-faced, blue-eyed calm" (8); "his eyes were a fiery blue" (12); "The baby lay wide-awake in its crib, staring straight at him, with deep, sharp blue eyes" (13). In D.H. Lawrence's frightening masterpiece "The Rocking-Horse Winner" the small boy's blue eyes are depicted with an intensity that makes the reader actually feel himself pierced by their maniac stare.

"Stare" is, in any event, a keyword in this context. The effect of the eyes--no matter what their color--is multiplied by the child's incessant unfathomable gaze and by the uncanny silence it maintains. The "silent watcher" is an archetype in horror literature; although a taciturn, ever-watching child appears more plausible and natural than, say, a dark fiend peeping from behind a curtain, the child leaves an equally strong feeling of unease. In numerous cases it has not yet reached the age of talking, and if it has, its behavior can be explained away as mere shyness or incomprehension. Deep inside, however, the reader wonders if the steady look of the child's huge eyes is not rather the sign of an unspeakable secret, an expression of evil experience; and if the little observer really conceals something dreadful, it is therefore infinitely superior to its adult environment. Knowledge of evil is doubly incongruous for someone who is hardly supposed to have any knowledge at all.

In Guy de Maupassant's story "L'Orphelin" action and suspense are actually based on a child's sinister gaze. An elderly lady, the orphan's foster mother, is nearly driven mad by the boy's behavior: "Si vous saviez comme il me regarde du matin au soir! Il ne me quitte pas des yeux! Par moments, j'ai envie de crier au secours, d'appeler les voisins, tant j'ai peur! Mais qu'est-ce que je leur dirais? Il ne me fait rien que de me regarder."[5] ("If you only knew how he is watching me from morning till night! His eyes do not leave me! For moments, I want to cry out for help, call for the neighbors, because I'm so afraid! But what would I tell them? He doesn't do anything to me but watch me.") She is perfectly sure that her charge is planning something evil--"C'était un être fermé, impénétrable, en qui semblait se faire sans cesse un travail mental, actif et dangereux" (76). ("He was a sealed, impenetrable being, within whom some mental work seemed to be going on that was active and dangerous.")

The child's eyes are by far its most important features. In addition to the presumption that eyes are "windows of the soul," they appear twice as remarkable in a tiny face that is completely dominated by them. The well-known principle which ethologists call Kindchen-schema is operating here.[6] In horror fiction most adults succumb to the strong stimulus at first; this automatic reaction often gives way to a superstition, the fear of the evil eye.

Brown eyes leave a strong impression as well as blue ones, but of a completely different kind. The brown-eyed child can be called the animal type. The striking connections writers tend to make between children and animals in almost every respect naturally refer to their outward appearance as well. An animal, savage or tame, is a creature as remote from adult understanding as an angel, fallen or not, but a child with animal qualities seems more "down-to-earth" and natural to the reader. Especially as a killer it acts in a simpler, much more immediate way, which is seldom determined by the cunning, cold intelligence a child with "sharp" blue eyes displays.

John Coyne's novel The Searing includes a perfect specimen. The center of the horror is a small girl who lives on her parents' farm. She belongs to the same level as cows and horses, for she is autistic and generally considered an imbecile. Her mother believes that God took away the child's mind, "leaving her as dumb as one of the farm animals."[7] The girl spends most of her days in the dark, damp, womb-like cellar, "curled up in a fetal position and rocking slowly to the beat of her heart"(16), her brown eyes staring into the void. When she roams about, she is attracted or repelled by her surroundings the way animals are, and she only kills when she feels attacked and cornered.

As a victim the brown-eyed child is greatly appreciated by writers of horror fiction. In these cases its eyes are usually compared to those of does or rabbits--harmless and defenceless creatures, of course. They are big and round and moist and shimmer like velvet. Such a child can be found in John Saul's Suffer the Children, an exemplary novel in more than one respect. There are two small sisters, a blond, blue-eyed killer and her pendant who represents the type mentioned above. And, once again, this latter child is mentally retarded and unable to speak. She can make herself understood, if at all, only with her pleading eyes and by retrieving objects like a dog. The crimes which her sister commits are blamed on her, because of her unfathomable, animal-like behavior. When she retrieves a bloody human limb one day, even her parents regard her as a beast of prey.[8]

The overwhelming majority of children in horror fiction are not just pretty, but endowed with a wonderful beauty. Even if several authors do not refer to single features, at least this overall quality is mentioned. Children never have ugly scars, wounds, or defects, either. They are frequently crippled, but their physical afflictions can only be seen in movement; their bodies do not show a trace. These deficiencies are to stir the reader's compassion, above all, and they also make a single child stand out from the community of its playmates. The child's skin, if it does not have the usual healthy color, is never depicted in a manner that could arouse repulsion or disgust. It rather reinforces other effects, as for instance the china-like eyes ("Her skin was clear and soft and as translucent as china"[9]); Bradbury's "Small Assassin" as a whole is compared to a porcelain figurine.[10]

Unnatural pallor is often hinted at as a sign of weakness and malnutrition. In the case of a little vampire or ghoul (as in "The Pale Boy," or Morag Greer's "Under the Flagstone"), whose "natural" color is thus revealed, this means of course a humorous (and often ironic) coincidence. It is but one example of the ambiguities which lie hidden in the so-called "typical" appearance of a child.

2. THE CHILD AND
ITS ENVIRONMENT

The Solitary Child

> The little body lay upon one side, with one soiled cheek
> upon one soiled hand, the other hand tucked away among the
> rags to make it warm, the other cheek washed clean and white
> at last, as for a kiss from one of God's great angels. It
> was observed--though nothing was thought of it at the time,
> the body being as yet unidentified--that the little fellow
> was lying upon the grave of Hetty Parlow. The grave, how-
> ever, had not opened to receive him.
> Ambrose Bierce, "A Baby Tramp"[1]

The solitary child is a recurrent figure in horror literature. A
solitary child need not necessarily be an only child; the important
fact is that it has no contact with anyone else, adult or child. It
may even belong to a family, surrounded by a loving father and a
tender mother, yet there exists no bond between them that is strong
enough to ward off evil and danger. Even physical nearness does not
help parents to protect their offspring from menacing powers; and, on
the other hand, their affectionate care does not protect parents from
their child's malevolence.

The child's being set apart from its coevals is much less a topic
of interest than one should assume--the distance between the child and
its parents being emphasized all the more. At closer view the reader
notices that this unilateral representation is due to the fact that
horror fiction must, above all, satisfy the needs (appeal to the
fears, that is) of an adult readership. In order to fulfill the basic
requirements authors must not depict a child the way it appears in
real life, as a complex human being with good and bad qualities; they
rather have to single out those traits of character which grown-up
readers love (or better: dread) to recognize. Most writers do not care
at all about child psychology and the discoveries it has brought
forth--and if they do, they pick out only those findings which suit
them best to give their gruesome accounts a scientific background.
This way of proceeding must by no means be considered primitive. The
most sophisticated authors make use of such oversimplification; Truman
Capote's brilliant story "Miriam" is as good an example in this
respect as Saki's "Sredni Vashtar" or even many of Ray Bradbury's
contributions. If handled so ingeniously, the technique (which is,
strictly speaking, an impoverishment) can enrich the effect a story
achieves.

In most cases the solitary child is, as indicated above, surrounded and at the same time separated from adults. The term "solitary" implies of course that there is no contact with other children,
either, but authors pay little attention to this point. Adults make up

the majority of victimizers as well. To the reader a big, strong assailant may seem more "appropriate" (after all, children are supposed to beware of a bogey man, an old witch and the like); emotionally he is certainly more deeply involved than he could be if children—who are unknown creatures, anyway—only kept to themselves, torturing and terrifying each other.

But fear is not the only emotion the child produces within the reader of horror fiction—and, quite astonishingly, it is by no means always the deepest feeling. To be sure, the reader identifies with a father who is mad with fear because he wants to protect his child and cannot reach it; or he feels with the parents whose lives are endangered by the attacks of their monstrous offspring. Deep inside, however, something else is stirred: the reader's profound sense of guilt. Although parents, foster-parents, tutors, and teachers—in short, all those in direct contact with children, and with direct responsibility—make up more than ninety per cent of the child's victims, it is obvious that the works under discussion are not written for these groups exclusively. Every grown-up reader responds to the subtle or sometimes not-so-subtle accusations that lie beneath the surface of what he considers just a thrilling story. His reaction to them can be called a subconscious one; astonishingly enough, many authors are also unaware that their works appeal to the reader's guilty conscience. If they were fully conscious of these implications, there would certainly arise something like a "didactic" element to accompany their narratives. (Very few authors actually do develop such a thing, and though tales with a moral may seem a bit unusual in genuine horror fiction, they belong to the ghastliest literary products in this field—like, for instance, Ludwig Hirsch's Schauerballade "Die gottverdammte Pleite"—"The Goddamned Failure.") Several writers who take interest in children at least point out the fact that a child who runs amuck must not always be held responsible for its behavior.

The "sins of the fathers" is a recurrent motif, the motto appearing either as a direct quotation (as in Suffer the Children[2]) or in a figurative sense. Rhoda, the little female killer in Maxwell Anderson's play Bad Seed, has inherited her murderous instincts from her grandmother, a notorious poisoner. Rhoda's mother, who was adopted and never knew about her own origin, unwittingly passes on her latent evil to her daughter. Happiness and love are nothing but a fragile façade in this family; evil breaks in on them from a dark, unknown side, and they must finally face the aftermath of the "original sin."

The reader's sense of guilt refers not only to the way adults treat children. On a more abstract level, the child represents much more—the future of Mankind. In this function it is a victim of all the great sins in history, including religious fanaticism and persecution, wars, the pollution of Man's natural environment, the misuse of science. Significantly, in horror literature there exist numerous examples in which children are involved in these violations, either as victims or as docile and talented emulators (on a rather small scale, but producing disastrous effects nonetheless). In the majority of stories, however, the child is largely made use of as a symbol. Whenever it is threatened or hurt, this means a punishment to its parents —not always a punishment for neglecting their offspring, but a penalty for any crime that has to do with the child's future. This fact is even more emphasized if the child turns on its parents. Though

the respective couple may have done nothing to provoke the catastrophe, the child retaliates for their share in the collective guilt
of adult mankind. The individual child need not be the immediate
object of its parents' sins, yet it starts running wild as a general
reaction. One is strongly reminded of Macbeth, where Duncan's horses,

                    the minions of their race,
     Turned wild in nature, broke their stalls, flung out,
     Contending 'gainst obedience, as they would make
     War with mankind (II, 4);

at the same time formerly harmless creatures kill beasts of prey and
devour them, because nature itself revolts against the crimes of Man.
The child fulfills this very same function in horror literature.
     The child's symbolic significance is not equally distinct in
every work under discussion. The reader has to examine a cross-section
of stories in order to find the underlying pattern, but after he has
found it he will be able to recognize at least part of it in each
single work. A novel like Stephen King's Firestarter certainly provides the reader with many important clues. Charlie, a seven-year-old
girl with pyrokinetic abilities, and her father are on the run from a
secret service department named "The Shop." At first sight everything
seems to contradict the thesis pointed out above; Charlie and her
father love each other sincerely and care for one another with devotion. When their antecedents are explained, however, it becomes clear
that Charlie's parents are perfectly responsible both for Charlie's
disastrous talent and for their being persecuted. They took part in a
secret experiment which resulted in changing their chromosomes. The
experiment was started by The Shop, and in this "shop" Charlie's
progenitors actually sold their bodies, prostituting themselves as
guinea-pigs. They are guilty and, as a side effect, perish through
their daughter's unnatural powers. Charlie cannot prevent that and is
inconsolable. The reader feels pity and deep concern, too, but somehow
he is aware that the parents cannot be saved from their destiny.
     When Charlie's father is dead, she shakes off all moral restric-
tions and deliberately starts destroying everyone in her way. Once
again the word "war" appears and significantly, the most savage of
modern wars are mentioned. Charlie, "small and deadly in her denim
jumper and dark-blue knee socks,"[3] fights all alone against a horde of
experienced killers, veterans of the Vietnam war; when the battle is
over, it looks as if "the place had been hit by a large incendiary
bomb or a World War II V-rocket" (378).
     One cannot help taking sides with Charlie, the blameless product
of society's (and her parents') delusion and unscrupulousness, who
strikes back with the same violence she has had to witness in her
adult environment. At the same time one must deeply admire the terrible beauty of the child's single-handed warfare; she does not even
have to stir a finger to burn her enemies to ashes. Trenches of fire
radiate from her toward them, "like strands of some deadly spider's
web" (371). But it was they, not her, who wove this net they are
trapped in now.
     The reader's sympathy with the child and its reactions produces a
cathartic effect. He is a part of the grown-up world which is frequently endangered, attacked, or at least badly shaken by its off-

spring. The satisfaction he feels at the child's final revenge, the apocalypse it is responsible for, has little to do with the gratification one is filled with whenever innocence defeats evil forces. Charlie, for instance, has lost her innocence through the experience with her own power--simply called the "Bad Thing" by her parents--and she is even aware of it (378). (Generally Charlie is a great exception among her coevals in horror fiction: she is endowed with a real character, and even with a very complex one. Her main antagonist, an Indian Shop agent, is accustomed to cracking his respective victim's mental code like a safe; Charlie, however, is the "toughest crack" he has ever come across.) Her victory is of course the triumph of the usually defenceless over a relentless tormentor. The reader nevertheless relates to himself the punishment that awaits the adults in the novel. Whether he, too, wishes to be punished in his subconscious mind is a difficult question, but a certain masochistic element is surely involved.

Firestarter is without doubt an exceptionally plain and drastic example of the struggle between two incompatible worlds. The novel also shows the special impressiveness of the relationship between the solitary child, a single representative of one group, and the entire adult community. There are enough hints given in this work to leave no doubt that The Shop represents America, that America for her part represents every state, totalitarian or not--and a state is, after all, a superior form of parental authority.

Employing the above relationship as a means to create an atmosphere of horror is a two-edged affair. On the one hand, one normally expects a rather unequal distribution of power when a small child stands alone against an overwhelming majority. The surprise and horror are all the greater if it is able to overcome its opponents. As a victim, too, the solitary child makes the greatest possible impression, since it has no one to cling to or share its fear. On the other hand, the deep gap and the latent hostility between adults and children are often much harder to recognize than in those cases where children form groups against the generation of their parents.

Moreover, the reader's standpoint depends to a great extent on the narrative technique employed in the respective story. Whenever a child's stream of consciousness is revealed (and this occurs ridiculously seldom, in any event) one can say for certain that the center of interest is a solitary child. This appears quite natural, since in horror fiction a group of children is practically never subdivided into "units" who think or act independently, and it would be problematic to demonstrate the train of thought of an entire--if unanimous--team. Now and then (as for example in Graham Greene's story "The Basement Room" or Barbara Benziger's "Dear Jeffy," which is a fictitious sample of a little girl's letters) a whole work is told from a child's point of view. Consequently, the reader is likely to identify with it rather than regard it as an incomprehensible stranger. One must note, however, that only the child-reader relationship undergoes a change. Particularly in the stories referred to above the distance between parents and child is tremendous; as a matter of fact, it is so great that the reader nearly begins to consider adults as alien, hostile creatures. As a victim the solitary child is, as already indicated, extremely effective. In one respect it can even be called unique. Because of its special nature, or rather its particular represen-

tation, the child is able to frighten both antagonists and reader to
the very core--even if it is the object of aggression. Alexander
Kielland takes full advantage of this astonishing possibility in his
novel Gift.

At first sight the incident in question seems totally commonplace
and trifling. A little schoolboy, Marius, is bad at Latin and forced
to take private lessons. These lessons are literally beaten into his
head by several teachers who all supposedly act with the best intentions. Marius continually fails to keep in mind the simplest con-
jugations. When one of his furious teachers accidentally hits him too
hard on his head the little boy seems to be severely injured. In fact
he is confined to bed and it soon becomes clear that this will be his
death-bed. The child's mother, unable to believe that, implores him to
talk to her, and Marius does answer her--in Latin. The boy has been
turned into an imbecile and is now able to repeat his Latin formulas
with clockwork precision. His mother, however, is a simple woman who
does not understand Latin at all, and who only intended to promote
Marius for his own benefit. The final "conversation" between the two
is really the height of sarcasm, and at the same time genuinely
frightening. On the one side we have a lonely, guilty mother who cannot reach her child any longer, though she keeps pleading with him in
a frenzy of despair. She confesses her sin, calling herself a
wretched, idle mother who destroyed her son with "that cursed erudi-
tion."[4] She only wants to hear something she can understand--the word
"mother." When she gladly believes that she has penetrated his clouded
mind (because Marius begins to smile serenely), her son, on the other
hand, shocks her one last time: he dies with the words "mensa rotunda"
on his lips.

The preceding episode is an ingenious example of both the separation of parents and children and the various forms of punishment a
child can inflict upon its tormentors. The reader learns almost
nothing about the child's feelings; Marius is, especially in the end,
a stranger to him. What he does learn is the fact that this child must
die because people treated him like an adult, forced him to do things
that were against his nature. Lack of communication means nothing
extraordinary in this context, and feeblemindedness is often its outer
expression. The peculiarity of the scene under discussion, however,
consists in the special manifestation of this imbecility. People have
tried to make an adult of the little boy, and his idiocy actually is
that of an adult, disguised behind a torrent of highflown vanities.

The omnipresent gap between the two groups need not exist from
the very beginning of a story; it may develop in the course of events.
Graham Greene's "Basement Room" includes a special variation on the
matter. Here a small boy, Philip, deliberately approaches the adult
world, and by this one and only glimpse his young life is nipped in
the bud, his vulnerable, trustful soul crushed irrecoverably. The
result is a complete withdrawal from all mankind that will determine
the rest of his life.[5] This fatal transformation is accomplished
within one single weekend. Significantly, Philip spends the first time
without his parents who, to begin with, only represent another sphere
to him; they live in rooms he has no access to as long as they are in
the house, and they use furniture and things which are hidden under
ugly coverings. Philip's parents shut out what he imagines must be

real life. When they have left Philip shivers with joy and fright. For
the first time he may leave the nursery all on his own--the realm he
has been confined to up to this point. It is obvious that the author
depicts an initiation ceremony, creating an atmosphere of great expectations and happy excitement.

Indications of place are immensely important in this story.
Philip's room and his parents' apartment, both upstairs, represent on
the one hand the twilight sleep of Philip's yet undisturbed mind, and
on the other hand the torpidness and dullness of his parents. It is
notable that both parties are locally separated from "real life"--
Philip has not yet entered it, his parents have already retired from
it. Accordingly, they all inhabit the "upper region." Life can only be
reached by going downstairs, by a descent. To Philip it seems that
life must be concentrated in the basement room, and the baseness of
life he is indeed about to discover. Yet, the true essence of life
cannot be found here, either. The only adult Philip regards as a
friend, even as an idol, is Baines, the butler. Ironically enough,
Baines is held in tutelage as well, living in constant fear of his
tyrannical wife. He only watches life, the life in the streets, from
behind the iron bars of his kitchen window (2), and he longs for freedom just as much as Philip does. The child and the grown-up man like
each other very much, but each completely misunderstands the other's
feelings and behavior. Baines, above all, overestimates the boy's
capacity to digest the novel impressions which assail him. He does not
realize that Philip, as a child, must take in "life" in tiny bits in
order not to become poisoned. Moreover, he considers the seven-year-
old an ally in his own revolt against authority and treats him like an
equal. This flatters Philip, of course, but the child feels uncomfort-
able; he wants to look up to the butler as a big, strong, respectable
man. Philip consequently adopts a pose to hide his puzzlement; he
imitates the sophisticated demeanor of lords and ladies who frequent
his parents' house.

Baines' misinterpretation of the child's nature leads him to con-
front Philip with an overdose of life--with adult passions. The boy
can understand emotions such as fear, envy, or greed, and he has experienced his share of small disappointments, but he does not know how
to react to other people's love, jealousy, and hatred. Baines, who has
smuggled in his mistress while his wife is away, forces secrets upon
Philip which weigh heavily on him. In the basement the two adults make
love to each other before his eyes, and Baines is obviously proud to
start with Philip's sexual instruction as well. In fact, the whole
situation only seems real to Baines because he has a witness; the
adult is not free at all, he merely acts the part of a man. He is a
voyeur of his own love ("Baines wasn't really happy; he was only
watching happiness from close to instead of from far away," 19). At
this point of the narration the author makes use of a strong sexual
imagery. When Baines' mistress wants her lover to restrain himself in
front of the child he tells her that "he's got to learn like the rest
of us" (18), while putting three sausages on Philip's plate ("This is
better than milk and biscuits, eh?"). This display of virility is
Baines' pose--in connection with his sexuality the very word "innocence" appears repeatedly. He prepares his own initiation as well; the
basic difference consists in the fact that the adult knows what he is
going to do. The presence of a child, of a pure being he wants to be

congenial to, appeases his guilty conscience. As long as a little boy
witnesses his actions, they cannot be all condemnable.

Philip is abused by yet another adult. Mrs. Baines, who represents the extreme opposite to her husband, forces her own secrets on
the boy. She is a figure that seems to have sprung from a fairytale--
to Philip, who sees everything in black and white and who distributes
his sympathies and antipathies accordingly, she is the embodiment of a
witch. Her black clothes, the grey strands of her hair, her wooden,
lifeless movements and her musty smell must surely evoke this impression in a child; he who reads between the lines learns that the
woman is a prisoner, too--only she is condemned to solitary confinement. She watches other people's supposed happiness and begrudges them
their togetherness. It is clear that these extreme poles of adult life
must clash; but they first tear little Philip to pieces with their
various forms of adult bribery, then crush him between them in their
final battle. When Baines' wife flutters down the staircase like some
ominous black bird and remains there motionless as a sack of coal
(23), it is not really important that she is dead. Philip does not
recognize this fact, anyway; deep in his heart he knows that the black
bundle has more power than ever. It has destroyed them all. Baines'
future life is ruined, but Philip's life has ended before it has even
begun.

Horror literature abounds with examples in which children have no
contact to adults at all or are eventually destroyed by such a
contact. This traditional literary motif can already be found in eery
ballads like Goethe's "Erlkönig." Here the father cannot protect his
son either, although he is physically very close: "er faßt ihn sicher,
er hält ihn warm" ("he holds him securely, he keeps him warm").[6] This
security is deceptive; the adult's strength can keep off any danger
except that which is produced within the child's own feverish mind.
Against an enemy visible only to his son, he is completely defenceless. Of course the "Erlkönig" is nothing but the outward projection
of the boy's fatal disease, which leaves the father helpless, too.
Nothing, however, can illustrate more clearly the complete separation
of adult and child than the fact that the boy imagines a male superior
being that tries to lure him away from his own father.

Ray Bradbury's story "The Night" concentrates on a child's being
exposed to primeval danger while in the presence of its mother. This
story does not really have a plot (a little boy and his mother are
waiting for the elder son and the father, become anxious, and go to
meet them); it is rather the highly sensitive description of an atmosphere of inescapable evil. The danger lurking in the "dark dark
dark"[7] of the summer night cannot be grasped by a child's understanding. It is all that has ever been frightening for a human being,
vaguely summarized under one term--death. "The Night" is one of the
rare stories based on a child's point of view, and this child is not
just any child. The reader is directly invited to identify with the
little boy, to become him: "You are a child in a small town. You are,
to be exact, eight years old...You and your mother are all alone at
home in the warm darkness of summer" (154). The reader is sent back to
a time when one is still inspired by an ultimate trust in the superior
power of every grown-up person ("you follow obediently behind brave,
fine, tall Mother who is defender of all the universe," 158). The boy
in question does not yet realize that his mother is nearly consumed

with fear. The author obviously does not choose a woman simply because
a big, bold man never fears the dark. This woman is not afraid of her
own death; she rather represents the type of a mother that would fight
like a lioness for her offspring. It is precisely her strong motherly
love which causes her dread. She fears for her elder son, who has
stayed out late playing kick-the-can and who might possibly never
return. There is no concrete reason for such a strong anxiety, except
the adult knowledge that death is always lying in ambush, striking
most violently, for instance, during a snug warm evening in a small
town. Going to meet her son means a possibility of doing at least
something, of keeping up the illusion that she is not entirely
helpless. At the edge of a ravine ("that pit of jungled blackness,"
158) she must admit to herself that her returning son will have to
make his way all alone--or not at all. The ravine is, literally and
symbolically, the gulf between mother and son. The mother is separated
from her younger son as well. She has taken him along to get a feeling
of security herself, but both realize that they are single units in
the universe, each forever alone with his fears and sorrows. Through
the little boy--who is still "you," the reader--one is confronted with
the first really shocking mental experience in life: "You realize you
are alone. You and your mother. Her hand trembles. Her hand
trembles....Mother is alone, too" (159). In "The Night" Bradbury makes
ingenious use of effects of every kind. He frequently appeals to one's
five senses, above all to vision, hearing, and smell. This technique
has several functions. First of all, it corresponds to the fact that
at night all impressions, though fewer in number, are infinitely
stronger than in the daytime, and people's senses become much more
acute. Secondly, the whole story is tuned in to the world of a little
boy, and a child--again like an animal--greatly depends on the
immediate physical stimuli it receives.

The rendering of sensory perception has still another function in
this story. It becomes clearest in the end, when the elder brother
returns safe and sound to his family, much against the reader's expectations. The atmosphere of dread has meanwhile got hold of the
reader's entire being; he can no longer imagine the boy's "escape,"
although no hint has been given that he has truly been endangered. One
has realized how one by one the lights blink out, and even the
crickets stop chirping, as if the dark is about to rush upon its
victims. All of a sudden the elder son answers his mother, and
instantly the darkness "pulls back, startled, shocked, angry," "pulls
back, losing its appetite at being so rudely interrupted as it
prepared to feed" (161). The arrival is running and giggling as if
nothing has happened--and for him, of course, nothing has. He is the
embodiment of life that has come back to his "moribund" relatives, and
indeed the boy radiates all the untamed vigor of his twelve-year-old
body. It is only sheer primitive animal life which brings consolation
in a situation like this, and in this context the most intimate and
primeval of the reader's senses is "employed": he is to smell the boy
("It smells like Skipper all right. Sweat and grass and his oiled
leather baseball glove," 161; "You smell the sweat of Skip beside you.
It is magic. You stop trembling," 162). Finally the boys are lying in
bed, where they belong, and the house is peaceful again. When the
father arrives, this means merely an additional reassurance. The
"real" danger has already been overcome--for the time being.

The separation motif finds equally strong expression in Guy de Maupassant's story "Madame Hermet." Among the author's numerous contributions to the theme in question, which are determined by the innate cruelty of the human soul rather than by any danger from "outside," this story deserves special attention, since it contains quite an extreme example of motherly love. Mme. Hermet, a beautiful widow, adores her little son with all her heart, but concentrates even more on her beauty and its preservation. Her growing son is the living reminder of her own unpreventable physical decline; for her, whose psychic balance absolutely depends on her attraction for men, the daily routine of scrutinizing her face in the mirror becomes a tormenting obsession. Of course there must come a crucial moment when she has to choose between the love for her son and the love for her body; her son's disease, smallpox, puts her to the ultimate test.

Mad with fear, the woman barricades herself in to shut out the germs which are supposedly pursuing her; she burns all kinds of disinfecting substances as if they were incense for a heathen god; she stays in bed and has a special diet as if she herself were the patient. Of course she never visits her son, the center of danger. When the boy begs her to come to him, for he feels his approaching death, she desperately refuses his urgent wish. Neither her son's entreaty nor the doctor's violent attempt to drag her along with him can overcome her fear: she simply starts screaming and clinging to a doorframe.

Once again, the child's reaction is almost more frightening than the mother's frenzy. His rather uncanny behavior is in a way ambiguous, since it can be explained by his increasing weakness. First of all, he keeps perfectly calm all the time, not showing his deep despair to the adults around him. Secondly, and this is even worse, he appears to be omniscient. The narrator calls it "cette espèce de pressentiment qu'ont parfois les moribonds" ("this capacity of presentiment which moribund people sometimes have").[8] In any event, the boy knows all, is aware of all, understands all, especially the frailties of grown-up people. Since he realizes that direct contact is impossible, he suggests that his mother could look at him through the window without any danger of contagion. He is denied even this restricted form of contact, because now his mother feels too ashamed to face him. The act of dying is mentioned laconically--"Il attendit longtemps, et la nuit vint. Alors il se retourna vers le mur et ne prononça plus une parole. Quand le jour parut, il était mort" ("He waited for a long time, and the night came. Thus, he turned toward the wall again and did not utter another word. When the day broke, he was dead," 104)-- but this only underlines its impact. The reader is shown the boy's façade and nothing more; from the child's former adoration for his mother one must deduce the unspeakable agony of his last hours.

Maupassant's story has something special in store for the embittered reader--a combined punishment/compensation/happy ending, which may, admittedly, seem a bit cynical. Mme. Hermet, for her part, cannot stand the absolute lack of contact either and goes insane. She is confined in an asylum, where, in her opinion, she is in treatment because of another disease--smallpox. Here she is able to make up for the physical communication she denied her dying son: she imagines herself suffering from the effects of her devoted nursing, which "rescued" her son but left her body marred, her face disfigured. Her madness not only gives her the chance to ignore her son's death and her own guilt, but also the opportunity of developing "visible" proofs of her supposed contact with her boy. Indeed, their intimacy must have been such a perfect one that it could engrave its marks into her very flesh. Her "smallpox scars" are stigmata, the signs of a mother's sacrifice. "Contact" has been achieved late, but all the more intense; the scars reappear each day, and each day the communion is renewed.

The most extreme variety of the solitary child is of course the orphan. In horror fiction particularly the orphan has always been the victim par excellence. Significantly, in the earliest (and many later) Gothic novels this does not so much refer to the orphan child, but rather to the young parentless girl frequently endangered by lascivious old villains who are after her dowry and/or her virginity. Young men may be welcome victims, too--especially impressionable dreamers like Aubrey in John William Polidori's "The Vampyre," whose "high romantic feeling of honour and candour"[3] and "propensity to extravagant ideas" predestine him to be abused by fiends like Lord Ruthven.

One should assume that the condition of being an orphan naturally implies a total separation of parents and child, that death creates a distance which cannot be imagined greater. The relationship between the orphaned child and its parents, however, is much more complicated than it may seem at first glance. Basically, one can distinguish two methods authors employ to deal with this situation. The first possibility is indeed relatively simple: the little orphan's former family relations are not referred to at all; the child's abandonment must appear perfectly "natural" to the reader, since he is to receive the impression that the child has always lived this way. Possible questions as to its origin and antecedents are both unwanted and superfluous. Parents represent, mathematically speaking, a kind of zero factor--the only thing that counts is the obvious want of a surrogate guardian. The child's mere solitary condition, reinforced by its outward appearance, appeals at least to the reader's instinct for protection of the weak. After all, a small orphan seems to be more exposed to danger and hardships than any other human being. A fragile creature like this is always supposed to be looking for a big and strong one, but whether the adult is needed as a defender, or as the defenseless host of a baby parasite, cannot be foretold by the child's status or demeanor alone.

The second possibility of relating the orphan with its adult environment actually depends on the bond between the child and its parents. It is exceedingly interesting to observe that dead parents often "enjoy" a much closer contact with their offspring than living parents do. At close view one can also notice that usually only one parent (the mother in most cases) is advanced to the center of interest, whereas the other one is neglected by the author. When a father or mother dies, he or she enters another sphere and no longer has anything to do with the wickedness and guilt of this world. Through this transition the dead parent is accordingly purged of all the sins he has so far shared with other adults. The orphan who remains alive (and in this world) feels strongly attracted by the dead parent and the realm of the dead in general. The "interaction" between child and parent(s) does not necessarily imply supernatural incidents and phenomena, but both the morbid imagery and characterization tend to evoke a ghostly atmosphere. Almost every attempt at a post-mortem reunion comes from the child, though there are of course nuances in the activity it displays. One can observe a wide range of possibilities, from a "simple" physical attraction (including death-bed cannibalism, as in Christine Trollope's story "Oysters") to a spiritual "parent worship," the creation of a real religion.

Ambrose Bierce's story "A Baby Tramp" is the account of such a "reunion" of mother and child. Although it is quite a typical example in this respect, one has to bear in mind that it also represents a typical group of Bierce's "civilian" tales. The fact that a person is drawn like a magnet to the grave of his beloved occurs in several of his stories ("The Death of Halpin Frayser" from his collection Can Such Things Be? being the most famous one), and works like these, in particular, have been blamed for the author's exaggerated reliance on "coincidence."[10] If a young man, as in the above tale, "aimlessly" wanders through half the American continent only to lie down and die exactly on the grave of his mother (whom he loved as one should not love one's mother, and of whose whereabouts he has no clue at all), this means indeed a strain on the reader's credulity. "A Baby Tramp," however, contains several basic differences which make the story stand out from the rest of its kind.

To be sure, the tale is a genuine horror story, but it is interspersed with countless ironic remarks which suggest that there is more to it than meets the eye. Taken at its face value, the story tells about a little orphan boy who is "a doin' home"[11] and, after long peregrinations, dies on his mother's grave. The narrator also gives some ironic hints to certain rumors which say that the dead mother has risen from her grave to call the child. Of course the action makes sense on this level, but leaves a rather poor impression. The real horror is hidden beneath the surface; it is a perfect illustration of all that has been said with regard to the fact that the child is a symbolic victim of the great sins of mankind. In this particular case the author gives numerous hints at the cruel excesses of religious persecution in America.

It is known that bigotry was one of Bierce's favorite targets, and he more than once praised America as the "Land where my father fried/Young witches and applied/Whips to the Quaker's hide/And made him spring."[12] Whether he has Quakers or witches in mind when he refers to the mysterious events in the city of Blackburg cannot be said with certainty--it does not really matter anyway. The imagery, however, is plain enough to tell the reader that the "disease" which extinguished half the population of Blackburg (including little Jo's parents) must have been of a religious kind. The catastrophe was announced by local versions of the biblical plagues--a "shower of small frogs," "crimson snow" with "the color of blood" (185-86) and other noteworthy phenomena. Incidents like these afforded, as recorded in the Blackburgian chronicles, "good growing-weather" for the (Catholic) Frenchmen. Furthermore, the nature of the fatal disease is not specified, but it is described as "epidemic, endemic, or the Lord knows what" (186).

Only little Jo, who is all alone in the world, "hardly old enough to be either just or unjust," and who does not come "under the law of impartial distribution," is spared from the fate of his elders. It is not certain at all if the boy really misses his parents; as usual, the reader is confronted with his outward appearance only. The orphan's clothes look miserable enough, and he is "sinfully dirty" (190); the astonishing fact is that he deliberately escapes all the people who react to his supposed want and try to take care of him (reminding the reader of Huckleberry Finn, who resists being "adopted," too): some distant relatives, a family of Piute Indians, a woman on one of the east-bound trains, a certain Mrs. Darnell, and an Infants' Sheltering Home. One could of course argue that the influence of Jo's dead mother prevents him from getting attached to any other _living_ person, but this idea seems ridiculous as soon as one learns that Jo was orphaned at the tender age of one year.

The fact that Jo, who has a promising start in "getting a long way from the condition of orphanage" (190), prefers to throw off the "multitude of parents between himself and that woeful state," can rather be ascribed to his aversion to all the forms of paternal "care" and "kindness" he has become acquainted with. He "returns" to his dead mother, not because he thinks that a graveyard is a cosy place for taking a nap, but because he is actually expelled from the bright and warm houses of the living—by their dogs ("brutes without meant brutality within," 192). As a matter of fact, the little boy is not aware at all that he enters a cemetery. Significantly, he is only looking for a place where there is no dog. This single metaphor expresses the whole meaning of the story; by "placing" the orphan child on the very grave of his mother (which is an ironic device in this case) the author additionally emphasizes the idea that a dead parent is ten times better than any living adult who tries to take this parent's place.

The narrator finally refers to the fact that the grave has not opened to receive little Jo, which is to his mind "a circumstance which...one may wish had been ordered otherwise" (193). This seemingly spoiled finale, however, can only disconcert those who have believed right until this point that the whole tale is a mere ghost story. The boy's supposed homecoming is just a means to point out that a child, having been born into a world of cruelty and hatred, may as well go back to the womb at once to spare himself further trouble.

"A Baby Tramp" is by no means the first American story in which a small boy is orphaned by the effects of religious persecution. Sixty years earlier, in 1832, Nathaniel Hawthorne anonymously published his eerie tale "The Gentle Boy." This "extremely severe indictment of Puritanical bigotry and viciousness," as Thomas E. Connolly calls it,[13] is not so subtle and ambiguous as Bierce's story. Hawthorne's profound hostility reveals itself here, and it is especially pointed at several of the author's own ancestors, who participated in the persecution of the Quakers. In "The Gentle Boy" Hawthorne takes sides neither with the Puritan majority nor with the cruelly tortured sectarians (who, as real martyrs, seem to enjoy being whipped and thrown into dungeons—after each chastisement they redouble their efforts to be imprisoned again). The only character who seems to deserve the reader's full sympathy and compassion is the gentle orphan boy.

One may argue about the question as to whether this tale (which is, particularly in connection with the child's appearance, gloomy and uncanny enough) can be called a genuine horror story.[14] Certain essential passages at least—among them the initial scene on the Quakers' place of execution and grave site—nourish the reader's expectations

of a ghost story. The gentle boy's very introduction suggests that he
might be a ghost himself. He is sitting upon his father's grave,
directly under the gallows (which is significantly called an "unhappy
tree"[15]); his mournful wailing, his pale, spiritual face, his sweet,
airy voice, and his eyes which seem to "mingle with the moonlight,"
make the observer believe that "the boy was in truth a being which had
sprung up out of the grave on which he sat" (335).

The boy's characterization is as "superficial" as it is the case
in all comparable stories in which nothing but the child's function as
a universal victim is to be pointed out in detail. If at all, the
child's feelings can only be guessed at through his outward appearance. The few definite facts given underline the little boy's strange-
ness--as, for instance, in the contrast between his infantile countenance and his refined, almost stilted mode of expression. He is
presented as a miniature adult in order to show that he possesses a
reasoning, understanding mind (which means he knows what is being done
to him), and he is depicted as a highly strung child to accentuate his
pure, immaculate soul. This mixture serves its purpose very well, but
little room is left, or intended, for psychological insights.[16]

Little Ilbrahim, the gentle boy, has followed his captured
father, witnessed his execution, and sought out the grave as his
future dwelling. He does not want to budge an inch, because to his
mind he belongs to this spot ("'I knew that my father was sleeping
here, and I said, this shall be my home,'" 335). He clings to the heap
of earth "as if the cold heart beneath it were warmer to him than any
in a living breast" (336). Curiously enough, in the course of the
story it becomes clear that Ilbrahim is not an orphan at all; his
mother, whom everybody considers dead and "disposed of," is still
alive. Her body, at least, still belongs to the world of the living,
whereas her mind already concentrates on another life. Convinced that
her husband and son are dead, she tries with all her might to become a
real martyr. Roaming about the land as a preacher, she intends to
provoke the Puritan community to put her to death. Incidentally she
preaches in the very same church where Ilbrahim has been taken by his
new Puritan foster-parents. This is the preparation for a scene of
highest dramatic irony.

The mother's ghastly appearance in the pulpit matches the introduction of the son. She is clad in "a shapeless robe of sackcloth"
(342), the blackness of her raven hair is "defiled by pale streaks of
ashes" strewn upon her head, and her deathly white countenance is
"wild with enthusiasm." When she curses her audience as murderers who
"cast forth the child, the tender infant, to wander homeless, and
hungry, and cold, till he die," she is not aware that in her
fanaticism she has just made her own child an orphan. She, as the
living parent, is responsible for the final, irrevocable separation--
which demonstrates once again that dead parents are more reliable than
living relatives.[17]

The preceding examples demonstrate more or less drastically that
parents are highly unreliable partners for the solitary child. Thus it
has to look for someone else to form an alliance with--not other
children, however, since this would mean a contradiction in itself.
Authors of horror fiction like to make use of a phenomenon which, in
real life, has long attracted general attention: the imaginary
playmate. Parents often "catch" their offspring talking to a friend

they have made up as a companion and confidant(e). This need not be a
serious affair at all. In horror literature, however, this invention
is naturally a welcome means to underline the effect of strangeness
and remoteness which surrounds the child and its world. No adult can
enter its private sphere, let alone understand it, and the worst thing
of all is the fact that the child's "ally" cannot be seen, but lives
in its own brain only.

There exist several possibilities to "explain" this mysterious
being in the child's mind. It can, for instance, be an extraterrestrial intruder who is looking for a host. John Wyndham's novel Chocky
contains a harmless specimen, but is, on the whole, a fascinating
account of the parents' perplexity and awe, and the author considers
all the subtle implications of the subject matter. The invisible playmate may be quite an ambiguous factor; the special charm in John
Saul's novels Suffer the Children and Comes the Blind Fury lies in the
reader's doubts as to whether the companion is a ghost or originates
in the child's deranged mind. All these latter examples, however, can
also be put under the term "obsession."

The stories which are most relevant in this respect are of course
those which contain a veritable "brain-child." A particular form that
is certainly extraordinarily impressive is schizophrenia, but since
the relationship between the child (or rather its body with the two
beings it harbors) and its surroundings is at least as interesting as
the struggle within its brain, authors do not have to rely on this
extreme manifestation alone. Katherine McLean's story "The Other"
deals with a basically normal though hypersensitive and vulnerable
boy, who has created a permanent other self, absolutely superior to
him in intellect and sophistication--an adult figure. This construct
(who recognizes himself as such: "I am a construct. You made me"[18]) is
the child's shield against the hostile outer world, his guardian and
advisor. Before Joey makes contact with adults he carries on conversa-
tions with the Other, who warns him whenever the careless grown-ups
are about to stumble into his mental sanctuary, "blunder and destroy
among the fragile things" (99). Being asked what exactly he is, the
Other defines his function to Joey: "I am part your mother and your
father and little parts and feelings of anyone who ever worried about
you and wanted you to stop doing things so that you would be all right
and strangers would not be angry at you" (98).

Ironically enough, Joey's wise, sensible protector gets him into
trouble, because adults want to face a simple, ingenuous, and ignorant
child only. For breaking this convention the boy is put into a
hospital for "observation." Both he and his companion know that they
must hide away the Other. When Joey once trusts a young doctor and
makes the Other talk to him ("'Talk for me. Tell them you're a doctor.
Use their words,'" 99), he meets with the alienist's (an ambiguous
expression in this context) refusal; through this single penetration
into his exposed interior he breaks down and withdraws completely from
the outside, adult world.

Deeply shocked by his disastrous failure, the young psychiatrist
also withdraws, though only into his private office, and only for a
moment. There he allows himself to cry--or rather, he allows his other
self to take over. An adult and a scientist must never weep, but the
"childish feeling" in him, the "ungrownup one" who must be concealed
from the world and who can be wounded by emotions (most of all,

however, by "being alone," 100), is entitled to weep--secretly.

At close consideration, this is but one more example of the disaster that is always lurking when the spheres of adults and children interfere with each other. Basically it does not matter at all if this clash takes place inside or outside a person. A child cannot rely on an adult--real or constructed--to protect it from the adult world, since neither is ever able to ignore the unseverable ties which keep them to their own age groups, and which are even stronger than family relations.

Brother and Sister

> Only three generations ago the Indian reigned where now
> Barnaby and Christie played. Two children, innocent of man-
> kind, past or present, children who delighted in finding
> agates and tiny pink shells and purple starfish and clam
> holes which spurted like naughty subterranean fairies.
> Two children who wandered, happy, brown and busily plotting
> murder with an insouciance that would have appalled the
> former savage tenants.
>
>   Rohan O'Grady, Let's Kill Uncle[1]

The combination of a little boy and a little girl (if possible,
of precisely the same age) is a very effective means to reinforce and
vary the basic mechanisms which have already been discussed with
regard to the solitary child. It is this special relationship, too,
which frequently represents a conscious continuation of the old
fairytale pattern. In fact, nearly all the horror stories that include
a fairytale plot, imagery, or fairytale figures depend on this small
couple as their central characters. Witnessing their nasty experiences
and dangerous adventures in the world of adults (usually with parents
and guardians) one is indeed strongly reminded of the children who are
exposed to die in the dark wood, who are hunted by wizards and ogres,
and similar unpleasant motifs long known to the reader of folklore.
These remarkable parallels refer to the surface only, but they are by
no means incidental. Whenever authors of horror fiction employ the
fairytale as a literary source they pursue very specific intentions.
    In this respect several interesting observations of a general
kind can be made. First of all, the figures who personify evil in horror literature (a role which, in the fairytale, is usually allotted to
supernatural creatures such as giants, witches and the like--but also
to parents) are, with almost no exception, human beings. The reasons
for hunting children also differ considerably in both genres. Hunger
for delicate human flesh, for instance, has been largely replaced by a
much more profane motivation: financial greed. Although this latter
impulse seems to be better suited for our "civilized" world, the
coursing itself is unparalleled in cruelty and sadism.
    A second peculiarity is the fact that the "mixed double" some-
times has to become the equivalent of a single well-known fairytale
figure. This is the case in Rohan O'Grady's (alias June Skinner's) un-
equalled masterpiece Let's Kill Uncle, whose main characters are
modern and, despite the fairytale symbolism, frighteningly realistic
versions of Little Red Riding Hood. The novel must be seen in another
tradition still: the complex development of the "island adventure."
One can retrace many steps from Robinson Crusoe (1719) over the rather
idyllic way of life in Ballantyne's Coral Island (1857) and Ransome's
Swallows and Amazons, and the flourishing youth of Stevenson's Trea-
sure Island (1883), to the viciousness and cynicism in Richard Hughes'
A High Wind in Jamaica (1929), Golding's Lord of the Flies (1954), and
the novel under discussion, which was written in 1963. With the exception of Defoe's novel all these works have several important features

in common--the romantic, paradisiac setting, the fact that children or
adolescents play a leading part, and the sharp contrast between "civilization" and "savagery." At the beginning of the Twentieth Century,
however, an obvious shift took place.[2] The author's entirely positive
basic attitude, the comparatively plain distinction between good and
evil, and the euphoric praise of the British Empire and its steadfast
representatives were replaced by an all-embracing bitterness. This
attitude has its roots in the knowledge of the corrupting influence of
the adult world on the sensibilities of the young. In each of the
three modern novels the constituents of their predecessors are taken
up again and shown in an entirely different light. In A High Wind in
Jamaica one has, on the one hand, the "evil" pirates Jonson and Otto,
on the other hand several "innocent" children who are kidnapped by
them. These popular clichés are completely destroyed in the course of
the novel, but even in the very beginning they by no means convince
the reader. Little Emily, the main character, inhabits a very sinister
world of her own. When, after being exposed to cruelty and violence,
she and the other children are finally released by the pirates, who
thus yield to their kindlier impulses, the "little ones" betray them.
Jonson and Otto are brought to the gallows for a murder committed by
Emily; moreover, the men are convicted solely on the testimony of the
child. In the end victims and victimizers can hardly be distinguished
from each other any more.
    Although the children in Golding's Lord of the Flies are locally
isolated from the world of grown-ups and seem to gradually develop
into savages on their own, it is made perfectly clear that their lonely island is surrounded by the brutality and barbarity of adult warfare. An atomic bomb is the reason why the children cannot be picked
up again in time (which means before the first unlicensed murder); a
battleship takes them back to "humanity" when it is all but too late.
The warrior symbolism is hinted at so often in the book and has been
so thoroughly discussed that there is neither room nor sense in
dealing with it in great detail here. One must keep in mind, above
all, that the children's running wild does not simply mean a regression to chaos because of the adults' absence. When in the end the
dashing officer asks the surviving boys why they have not continued
the British tradition like good English boys, he is not aware how well
they have succeeded in doing so. To be sure, the children, like all
human beings, bear the roots of evil in themselves when they enter the
island, but they have already witnessed a great deal of the pride and
glory in all parts of the British Empire (thus they can compare their
sojourns in "Gib.," "Addis," and many other cities[3]). They bring along
with them an amount of military knowledge which must not be under-
estimated: for instance, the fact that it is the uniform which makes
the man. The choir boys with their black, raven-like garments have a
discipline that could fill any officer with envy. Moreover, before
they have identified Ralph's conch they ask where the boy with the
trumpet is (27). The adults in the novel do of course not comprehend
these connections. They mistake warfare, an "adult affair," for
child's play. The soldiers' complete misinterpretation of the boys'
war-paint and the destruction around them is the preparation for the
absolute climax of the novel--the officer's jesting question as to
whether there are any dead bodies, and Ralph's laconic answer, "Only
two. And they've gone" (247). The clash between the two worlds can

neither be presented in a simpler nor in a more shocking manner.

Rohan O'Grady's island novel shows many parallels to the above example, but it is much more differentiated than its predecessor with regard to both plot and language. Concerning the latter one cannot help admiring the author for employing comic devices in order to create a genuine horror novel. In contrast to <u>Lord of the Flies</u> her work can be clearly classified as such, although it contains many features taken from various other genres, and her much too light and happy-go-lucky style contributes significantly to the overall gruesome impression. The atmosphere is so idyllic that it sends cold shivers down one's spine. Two "kiddies" who are happily planning to get rid of a wicked relative could indeed make up the stuff <u>Arsenic and Old Lace</u> is made of--but for the fact that the superficial fun does not merely cover grim humor. In reality it is abysmal cynicism.

In contrast to Golding's novel, but in correspondence with several of the other literary forerunners, the Canadian island in <u>Let's Kill Uncle</u> is inhabited. The two children do not have any peers; they are, apart from two exceptions, the only characters under forty, since all "island boys" were killed in World War II. One exception is Poor Desmond, the village idiot, whose intelligence does not exceed that of a four-year-old, and who is on excellent terms with the children. The second is Sergeant Coulter, a Mountie and the only survivor of the war, who has never really got over the shame of this latter flaw. Desmond is a "permanent child," whereas the Sergeant often indulges in his own childhood reminiscences (which, alas, does not help him in the slightest to understand the little couple).

The real monster in the novel--or one should say the most unequivocal one--is "Uncle." Although little Barnaby's uncle is not a character in the strict sense, but rather an allegorical figure, he shows a remarkable multifariousness of meanings and functions. He not only represents the Big Bad Wolf of the fairytale; he is one of the most convincing werewolves ever created in horror fiction. His greatest attraction is the fact that nearly all the werewolf's typical features might be explained away as those of an "ordinary" madman--his reaction to the lunar phases and the full moon in particular (which, after all, gave the lunatic his name), his cruel yellow eyes that are always hidden behind sunglasses, the mutual aversion to dogs, and his exceptionally fine physical condition. There is just one feature which seems out of the common: shaking Uncle's hand, Sergeant Coulter "could have sworn that the fellow had hair even on the palm of his hand."[4] But, as a rational thinker, he knows that this is utterly impossible.

Being an experienced werewolf, Uncle knows how to deceive people about his true nature. "People" means of course "adults," for the children are well aware of the danger they are in, and of the fact that they cannot expect help from grown-up people. Uncle is a respected member of society, with his carefully nurtured public school accent, his ascot tie and navy blazer, and his money which he freely spends on charities. Nobody comes to consider this cultivated gentleman a merciless killer.

But Uncle is still much more than a simple werewolf. He is, in the truest sense of the word, a warlock, the embodiment of bestial warfare as an end in itself. All forms of killing and all possible reasons for it are presented in the novel and make up its main topic. Uncle, however, is the only one who kills mainly for fun. He, too, keeps up the glorious tradition of the British Empire. In World War II he was one of the most brilliant soldiers, a clever and tough commando; the fact that his comrades called him "Silly Billy, or, sometimes jokingly, the Murdering Major, because of his mild disposition" (184) does not suggest a contradiction at all. Now, after he has erased Barnaby's family, he wants to kill his nephew for the money he is to inherit. The ruses he has learned during his military career must be adapted accordingly to times of peace.

Barnaby and Christie are Uncle's antagonists. Though they are not brother and sister by birth, they are united at least as firmly by several circumstances. First of all, both of them are separated from their parents, either by death or by divorce, and have to cling to each other. Secondly, and more importantly, as soon as Uncle (who arrives on the island several weeks later than the children) has found out how close their friendship is, he decides that they make a nice couple and really ought to be killed together. Self-defence thus becomes a further motive for their intimate relationship; they understand each other as "partners in crime" (162).

Though both of them are rather complex personalities (a rare fact in horror fiction), Barnaby and Christie illustrate the basic features of the brother-and-sister relationship. They are in some respects "miniature adults" (158); that means for instance that the diminutive couple is to represent "typical" attributes of the adult married couple. As a rule, the sexual element is excluded, though now and then discreet hints at a possible incestuous love may occur. The distribution of roles--the "male" and "female" patterns of behavior--is much more important. Authors generally depict the girl as perfectly helpless and vulnerable (and not very bright), whereas the boy appears as a tiny knight in shining armor who protects his little sister with all his might. This cliché is not employed in Let's Kill Uncle, but here the children show other features people consider typically masculine/feminine.

Christie is really an honor to her sex, a prodigy of practical-mindedness. When she senses Barnaby's distress about his uncle's plans, it is the most natural and self-evident thing in the world for her to suggest, "We'll just have to murder him first" (77). Christie represents the modern female; indeed she strongly reminds this reader of James Thurber's "Little Girl and the Wolf," whose protagonist simply takes an automatic out of her basket and shoots the wolf dead. The moral of this satire ("It is not so easy to fool little girls nowadays as it used to be"[5]) can be applied here, too. Christie is a cool, rational would-be killer; in the end, Uncle is not bagged by her, but by a "fellow"-beast--a cougar. When she is finally forced to kill (out of mercy, for the beloved cougar is mortally wounded), she does so following her sense of duty.

Barnaby, on the contrary, represents the passionate male hunter. Although, or because, he has been confronted with the vilest manifestations of "hunting," he feels irresistibly attracted by it. Having stolen a weapon, he is "too fascinated by the gun to be interested in food" (140). Lovingly, "almost gloatingly," he admires the instrument of death and is instantly able to handle it. Barnaby's behavior is determined by his uncontrolled emotions; sudden euphoria gives way to periods of Weltschmerz. Significantly, in the end the boy fails completely, literally glued to the spot when Uncle comes for him.

The greatest difficulty which lies in the characterization of the couple is the necessity to depict them not only as members of their respective sexes, but also as children. This refers of course to each of the literary examples presented here. It is quite clear that if the little ones appear as mere imitations of grown-up people, there is no basis given for the inevitable separation of children and adults which prevails in this context, too. Rohan O'Grady has found a good solution to this problem. Barnaby and Christie have no ally in the world of adults, though everybody is extremely fond of them--even Uncle, in his own nasty way. The island inhabitants excuse their numerous offences, which the children commit in order to draw people's attention to their dangerous situation, as harmless pranks. In their opinion children simply must behave that way; their long "abstinence" from having any children around has made them both more uncritical and more prejudiced than usual. This position is once again exemplary of the child's relationship to adults: it always enjoys their honest love, compassion, and adoration, but it must never hope for their real understanding or support. Even Sergeant Coulter with his "policeman's instinct" for "protection of the weak" (113) ignores Barnaby's and Christie's problem. Ironically enough, his subconscious, "ungrownup" mind senses the danger (he dreams of being a small boy in a medieval city, who hears the town crier's call "Beware, beware, there are wolves in the streets," 151); when he awakens, his rational adult mind dismisses the nightmare as nonsense.

To the islanders Barnaby and Christie appear to be typical children. The reader, too, is allowed to recognize part of the "typical" child he has become accustomed to. This is where the fairytale pattern comes in. The author employs abundant details to emphasize the parallels; the small protagonists are explicitly called "two little Red Ridinghoods" (158) who wander through the "silent, dead forest" that "fills them with awe." The wood is Uncle's "dark domain," the place where he wants to kill the children and bury them ("Uncle's real interest in horticulture lay deep in the gloomy heart of the forest. A pit, six feet deep, five feet long and three feet wide," 143). In his camouflage, a green suède jacket which makes him almost invisible, he even has the color of wood, and the children can only hear his "low chuckle from the bushes" (215). Just as in the fairytale, the Big Bad Wolf does not chase his victims openly, but tries to lure them with his soft, pleasant whispering voice ("Oh, Barnabeee...Uncle's here... Bar-na-beeeee--I've come for you," 218). The children, though watchful, spend most of their time picking mushrooms and berries; when the D-day of full moon has come they are sent on an errand with a basketful of cookies.

Of course the simple, two-dimensional structure of the fairytale has a special function within a novel as complex and profound as Let's Kill Uncle.[6] Here the pattern cannot fail to provide a grotesque element which underlines the author's general bitter attitude. If the reader feels that in connection with children like Barnaby and Christie the fairytale is quite out of place, this is exactly what the writer intended--wolves and monsters are nothing compared to the real world with its demons in human shape.

Very much like the boys in Lord of the Flies, the small couple shares Man's homicidal heritage. When they are looking at a gallery of great heroes of war, Christie, the descendant of "ragged, unforgiving Highland chieftains," feels that she can be a match for "any Sassenach soldier" (107). Barnaby, who looks like a toy soldier, is as stubborn and bullet-headed as his military predecessors were. Most significantly, the children's strategic headquarters is the war memorial, where (after having seen too much violence) they sit wearily, like "two old pensioners" (203). War itself is by no means presented as unnatural to human beings; people and animals will always kill and be killed for various reasons, and the author does not condemn this fact outright. Sergeant Coulter, for instance, is an embodiment of military virtues: he lives a Spartan life, he feels responsible for his island and the security of its inhabitants, and his feelings are straightforward and honest. When he is forced to kill, he does so in order to protect himself and others. Though he and Uncle are both ex-soldiers, the children are never tempted to draw a comparison between the two men. In contrast to Uncle, Sergeant Coulter is no "wily old pro" (136) and never will be. Barnaby rather sees a connection between One-ear, their beloved cougar, and Uncle, but Christie enlightens him: if One-ear enjoys killing, "that's the way cougars are supposed to act. Uncle's bad because he pretends to be a real person" (210). The children, who tried in vain to accustom the beast to a diet of candy and raspberry vinegar instead of blood, have long experienced the futility of their endeavor: "They had seen murder, and the forest was full of apples and serpents. It was the end of innocence, for they knew now that One-ear would never, never like cinnamon buns" (205).

Davis Grubb's ingenious novel The Night of the Hunter, written a decade before Let's Kill Uncle, contains many striking similarities to the later work. All the basic elements can be found here, too--the relationship between hunter and small couple, the adults around them who just watch in ignorance, bloodthirstiness and greed for money as the reasons for the persecution. The fairytale motif plays a significant role as well, though it serves a perfectly different, even contrary purpose. The children's "characters" exactly correspond to the popular cliché pointed out above. The nine-year-old John cares devotedly for his younger sister Pearl, who is not yet able to understand their situation (he "guards her with his life"[7]). John and Pearl are "classical" victims, vulnerable and defenseless; their only reaction is running away from their tormentor. Since both children and hunter must be called types rather than characters, the reader's attention is turned to the general effect of the novel, to all figures as a unity, and to the chilly, dreamlike atmosphere. These latter features happen to be the greatest merits of the work, vehicles for the author's message.

Preacher, the bogeyman of this novel, is almost identical with Uncle. Significantly, both men do have names, but are referred to exclusively by "generic terms"--a further hint at their being types or allegorical figures, not characters. Like Uncle, Preacher is a madman, consumed with greed, and an accomplished killer. Other prominent traits of his, hypocrisy and outward smoothness, underscore the most important and obvious points of resemblance. The direct equivalent to Uncle's "ecclesiastical manner," the way he "piously folds his hands over his paunchy, iron-muscled gut" (85) is Preacher's sweet high

clear tenor, his gospel tunes and flatteries. Unlike the Pied Piper of
Hamelin, however, the two only catch grown-up people; children are not
prone to their deception, but cannot keep their elders from succumbing
to the fiend's spell either. This fact creates a very special situation for the relationship between hunter and game: they seem to be
suspended in their very own sphere where nobody can reach them. The
three resemble a constellation in the night sky, untouchable and eternal. Thus, one must say that the children only have "contact" with one
adult person—not with their mother, but with their deadliest enemy.
Though it may sound perverse, Preacher in his infinite wickedness is
more reliable than the children's so-called friends. John at least
knows perfectly well what he and his sister have to expect from
Preacher; there are no doubts and no uncertainties since the hunter's
mercilessness is predictable.

The action of the novel is set in West Virginia, during the era
of Depression. Vices like greed for money and frailties like the worship of a false prophet can perhaps be more easily explained (and ex-
cused) in this particular situation than they could be at any other
time; they determine the life of every adult and are barely hidden
from view any longer. Preacher is the incarnation of a collective
evil, a collector of all the negative energies that fill the atmosphere. Yet the author does not present him as an inseparable part of
the epoch in which he appears. His lack of real attachment to his surroundings makes him a timeless figure who, together with the children,
never loses his topical importance. Apart from the mere indications of
place and time, there are not many clues given anyway; those informa-
tive details which do appear repeatedly have obtained a wider significance themselves—for instance, the hints at the Bryant campaign.

The plot of The Night of the Hunter is a suitable means of expressing the child's function as a universal victim. There are several
other points of interest which have been discussed before: the parents' direct guilt and responsibility for their children's fate, and
the close relationship between dead parents and their offspring. The
children's father, overcome by his greed, commits murder; still on the
run, he entrusts his booty to John and is later executed at the peni-
tentiary. Preacher shares his cell, and after his release he succeeds
in realizing his plan to marry the children's mother. He kills the
woman and pursues John and Pearl, until he is finally convicted of
several other murders in his career. At last the children find a
"shepherd," who guards her "small lambs against the night" (220)—old
Rachel, who picks up every lost child she comes across.

When John's father hands him the money he passes on a terrible
burden to his son ("that money had the curse of Cain on it," 65). The
secret which is connected with it establishes further grounds for the
alienation from his mother; John feels like a "solitary and stricken
Crusoe" in his own little island world (19). The children are hindered
from developing the way they should, even prevented from playing freely. Pearl's beloved doll Jenny becomes the hiding place for the money.
By ripping its belly open and removing the stuffing Pearl's father not
only transforms her doll, but her life as well. Child's play has become a deadly serious affair. There is even a stain of blood on the
toy ("That ain't doll's blood, Pearl honey. It's mine!" 105).

The secret of the money is the thread which holds father and
children together until the very end of the story. Their mother is

totally excluded to begin with; John's father does not trust her, and
subsequent events prove that he was right. Even her violent death does
not bring about a reunion, though it gives her absolution and peace
(129). The children are already entirely possessed by their father and
his evil heritage. It is clear that they can only live on quietly if
this bond is broken; thus, the novel has to end in a genuine exorcism.
John re-lives the exact situation of his father's capture when the
"blue men" come for his wicked stepfather. He mingles dream and reality, mistakes Preacher for his father, and must now face a fundamental
choice. He can either blindly follow his father's orders to keep the
money, or sacrifice it to save the father's life. He has waited for
this moment for a long time; in a frenzy, "his child's face twisted
and clenched like a fist," he gives back doll and responsibility:
"Here! Here! he screamed, flogging the man in the grass with the limp
doll until his arms ached. Here! Take it back! I can't stand it, Dad!
It's too much, Dad! I can't stand it! Here! I don't want it! I don't
want it! It's too much! I can't do it! Here! Here!" (201) Having got
rid of the curse, the little ones are no longer the "spawn of the
devil's own whore" Preacher has seen in them, but as pure again as
they were in the beginning. Autumn, the hunter's moon, has passed;
Christmas Day comes and with it "a brand-new brood" (214).

The idyllic ending of the novel has a very important function.
The final tableau in old Rachel's house is exactly the kind of scene
one would expect as the ideal framework for telling a fairytale--a
nice old lady with a flock of children around her, hanging on every
word she says, a warm kitchen, bright lights, and a starry night outside. From this safe harbor the story of the hunter seems more unreal
than ever, but for the fact that the protagonists share the very same
room, and that old Rachel could hardly tell them a story more ghastly
than the one they have just taken part in. Old Rachel's stream of consciousness reveals that she is not so happy as she appears to be in
front of the children; the reader is reminded that there are more
hunters in this world, and more children who must be protected in
order to spare them a similar nightmare. This is a rather simple message, to be sure, but it seems perfectly suitable for a novel whose
main attraction lies in its pristine simplicity.

Brother and sister appear very often in connection with fairytale
motifs, and not exclusively as modern equivalents of the old well-
known figures. Authors also invent their own figures, as Dorothy K.
Haines does in her story "The Bean-Nighe," in which a small girl has
to find out about her sick brother's fate by asking a mischievous and
dangerous old ghost, a washerwoman who prepares the shrouds for each
coming funeral. Again the fairytale motif is not employed for its own
sake, but as a device to unmask a family's cruelty and heartlessness.

The child, its relationship to parents and tutors, and especially
the couple who bid defiance to their adult environment are of special
importance in a field of American mainstream literature which critics
like Irving Malin and David Punter regard as contemporary Gothic
fiction.[8] Malin, for his part, presupposes a direct influence of the
"old Gothic" (represented by M. G. Lewis) and the "American followers
of the tradition" (Poe, Hawthorne, Melville, James) on Truman Capote,
Carson McCullers, J. D. Salinger and other modern authors. In the
critic's opinion this "new American Gothic" is primarily concerned

with the horrors of "disfiguring, narcissistic love" (6), a love which
causes parents to form (and deform) children in their own image: "They
'work' as does Frankenstein." Since the family is usually considered a
stable unit, new American Gothic tries to destroy it and, along with
this destruction, bring chaos into society. Unlike the old Gothic,
however, contemporary works do not offer any final possibility of re-
establishing the universal order. The "evil parents who thrust their
narcissistic designs upon innocent children" are recurrent types, as
well as their "crucified," ineffectual offspring who try to fight
them. Crippled and suppressed, children psychically return to the
womb, clinging to a brother or sister who shares their fate. In rather
harmless cases, as for instance those presented in Salinger's novels,
they merely try to remain eternal children; others emulate their
elders and form an "unholy family" of their own (65).

Irving Malin lists several features as essential to the genre and
the Gothic family in particular: characters who are flat, stylized and
almost inhuman because they are so obsessed with themselves; a basic
situation determined by the eternal conflict between parents and
children and their mutual hate-love, attraction and repulsion. Considering also Leslie Fiedler's remark that "the Gothic mode is essen-
tially a form of parody, a way of assailing clichés by exaggerating
them to the limit of grotesqueness,"[9] one feels strongly reminded of a
genre which, at least in its origin, shows remarkable correspondence
to horror fiction: the Absurd drama. Though Malin only refers to the
short story and novel in his discussion of Gothic elements, he repeatedly employs the term "poetry of disorder," which indicates that the
essence of the Gothic is not strictly limited to these literary forms.

Indeed, from its very beginning the Theatre of the Absurd has always made use of grotesque and shocking elements, and children play a
significant role. This is the more astonishing since they often do not
even appear on the stage, but are referred to in reminiscences or are
completely made up. The "symbolic family" of new American Gothic can
be found here, as well as the influence of "disastrous parents" (as
David Punter calls them) and the "insanity of social demands"[10] on the
psyche of the young. The methodical maiming which narcissistic parents
practice on their defenseless charges may even reach physical dimensions in the Absurd drama. Edward Albee, for instance, who has taken
great interest in the possibilities children offer since the start of
his writing career, provides the reader with several examples of this
more drastic version. In his comic nightmare The American Dream a conversation between Grandma and Mrs. Barker reveals to the appalled
audience that dear Mummy and Daddy have not always been so harmless
after all, that they crippled their first adopted child like experienced butchers: when the "bumble of joy" they have bought for
their precious money does not turn out the way they want it to--it
does not look like its parents, it cries its heart out, it only has
eyes for Daddy--they simply tear its eyes and tongue out and perform
other unpleasant operations ("But then, it began to develop an interest in its you-know-what.--In its you-know-what! Well! I hope they cut
its hands off at the wrists!--Well, yes, they did that eventually. But
first, they cut off its you-know-what.--A much better idea!"[11]). This
child is of course an emblem of America and the way the young nation
has been maltreated by its authorities, who additionally harmed a
fragile thing that had no guts and no spine to begin with, and whose

feet were made of clay. At closer view one will remark how much of
what has been said about the guilt of parents and the victimization of
children can be applied to this play.

In another of Albee's dramas an imaginary child is the latent
center of crisis and struggle. Not without reason the original title
(later reduced to a subtitle) of Who's Afraid of Virginia Woolf was
"The Exorcism."[12] When in the third, climactic act Martha's and
George's illusory son is sacrificed, the spectator realizes what the
couple's deadly battle was all about: their sterility, their physical
and psychic incapability of begetting and raising a child of their
own. The fact that this nonexistent son is spoken of as the American
dream[13] suggests the idea that George and Martha are tragic counter-
parts of Mummy and Daddy. While Martha indulges in fictitious details
of little Jimmy's childhood, dreams of teddy bears, banana boats and
the first cow in his life, George says the necessary prayers and gets
ready for the kill. He is aware that he and Martha can never settle
down with a phantom between them. Although George knows that he is not
a God (233), he is sure that he must sacrifice his only son to bring
peace to the "Earth Mother" (189), Martha.

One of the earliest representatives of the Absurd, on the other
hand, contains two very real and extremely active children. Roger
Vitrac's play Victor, ou Les enfants au pouvoir (1928) is dominated by
a nine-year-old boy and his little girlfriend, who spread chaos, death
and destruction among their elders. One can clearly perceive that
Victor is deeply rooted in the social comedy of the Nineteenth Century, which flourished especially in France. The first novel element
to strike spectators who are accustomed to this form of comedy is indeed the appearance of children, who were hardly ever allowed to appear, let alone dominate on the stage. One must, however, not forget
to mention that these children are (and have to be) played by adults--
because of their complicated lines and because of the fact that little
Victor has to be six feet tall. Nevertheless, the author takes full
advantage of the new characters he introduces. They are the ones who
carry all the great potentialities of a perfect Absurd drama.

Victor and the six-year-old Esther are, as usual in the Theatre
of the Absurd, symbols of the generation to come; they represent the
future of their whole country and expose the vices of society to worse
things than ridicule. Neither of the two can claim to be called an
authentic child-character--Victor is a premature genius, Esther is another "typical" little girl--and neither is meant to be. At any rate,
they show once more all essential ingredients of the relationship
between brother and sister and their parents. It is quite remarkable
that at the beginning of the play Victor and Esther are not presented
as brother and sister at all, but appear as the legitimate offspring
of two middle-aged couples who are on very friendly terms with each
other. In the course of the first few scenes the spectator grows more
attentive to all the furtive remarks concerning family likeness, and
he is not disappointed: Victor's father, M. Paumelle, is also the
father of Mme. Magneau's only daughter. Adultery and faithlessness are
the predominant topics of the drama and the mortal sins which finally
destroy three of the parents in a massacre. This bloodshed is carefully prepared by Victor and his devoted younger sister.

It is quite significant that the action begins on the evening of
Victor's ninth birthday. Victor has long decided to become a complete-

ly new person on this special occasion (this notion is underlined by a
pun on the word "neuf," which means both "nine" and "new": "J'ai neuf
ans...je suis décidé à être quelque chose...quelque chose de neuf, nom
de Dieu!"[14]). Under the mask of a model child he has been planning a
revolution, the assumption of power by the formerly disregarded and
abused ones who merely served as living furniture. In the short introductory scene, a preamble to the following war with his parents,
Victor carries on a conversation with their servant-girl Lili in which
he displays some of his basic ideas. In the presence of his elders,
however, he goes on playing the child (a synonym for "imbecile")--he
pretends to still believe in the "coco du dada," a horse that lays
eggs. This fertile "animal," a precious vase, is the first object he
deliberately destroys. His action bears great importance, since he expresses his contempt for sexual propagation, which adults embellish
and disguise, but which he has come to know as a source of betrayal
and deceit. Further symbolic meaning can be discovered in the fact
that Victor accuses Esther of having broken the vase (a lie which does
not offend her at all, despite the slaps in the face she receives from
her mother, but consolidates the bond between her and Victor). Though
little Esther does not really understand her brother, since she has
not yet reached the crucial age of nine, she supports Victor in everything he endeavors. Victor, on the other hand, separates and estranges
Esther, whom he considers a born victim like his mother, from the influence of her elders.
    Before all parents and a feeble-minded general of the glorious
French army have arrived, the children talk about the latest news, and
Esther repeats a compromising dialogue between Victor's father and her
mother. Though Esther mutilates and falsifies the expressions she does
not comprehend, Victor knows about their fatal impact. He only uses
them as a weapon, however, when the unwitting Mme. Paumelle makes a
terrible mistake. She thinks that the children make a nice couple who
ought to be married some day, and suggests that they play a married
couple for the delectation of the grown-up audience. It is not so much
the implication of incest which infuriates Victor, but the fact that
now he and Esther are supposed to continue the odious family tradition
of adultery and hypocrisy. The children take revenge by behaving "like
children": they play the identical scene they have heard from their
parents, including names and all. Of course they are not suspected of
acting consciously ("ils voient, ils répètent, ils nous imitent, les
singes!"--"they watch, they repeat, they imitate us, the monkeys!"
40). Nonetheless, the effect they produce is disastrous, though suicide and murder only begin in the last act of the play. Victor merely
has to complete his work of destruction by getting on the adults'
shattered nerves.
    Although children and adults are separated and unable to under-
stand each other (Victor can see through his parents, but not comprehend them), there exist mutual sympathies and likings. Victor is fond
of M. Magneau, the cuckold, who suffers from sudden fits of madness,
and of the general, who is an idiot. Both men represent the great
French military tradition--war and matrimony always have the same
meaning in the drama--and the final defeat. Magneau identifies himself
with Bazaine, a French marshal whose incapacity disgraced the whole
grande armée. A third person whom Victor loves at first sight is an
unexpected visitor, a mysterious farting lady. This woman cannot sup-

press her overwhelming impulse and is deeply ashamed, whereas Victor
regards her as a kind of saint--"Oh, catalyseuse! Qu'importent ces dé-
bordements sulfureux, quelques mauvaises passions peuvent en mourir"
("Oh, catalyst! How important are these sulfureous inundations, what
evil passions can die with them," 51)--who does not hide her filthi-
ness inside like the people he knows. Before she leaves he begs her to
fart one last time for him ("je voudrais que vous pétiez pour moi,"
55); unfortunately, the lady does not realize that the boy wants to
receive her benediction. He really means to say, "pray for me," and
before he continues his evil work he needs to make sure of her "péti-
tion." It is superfluous to say that the lady considers him a monster.

When the enervated parents retire to their respective bedrooms,
Victor goes on torturing his father and mother. His father, who has
already begun to treat the marriage bed with a plane, is nearly killed
when his wife attacks him with a hammer. Like civilized people, however, they apologize politely, and Victor has to resort to more drastic measures: he frankly suggests using the revolver that usually lies
beside the chamber-pot.

Having accomplished his task, Victor knows that he must die. He
is not allowed to grow one minute older than nine years exactly. With
him the family dies out; he would never have provided new offspring,
in any case, because his belly and his entrails are deranged. On the
one hand this is a physical reaction to the disgusting behavior of his
parents; on the other hand, his useless organs correspond to--and
contradict--his introductory mock praise of fecundity: "Et le fruit de
votre entaille est béni" ("And the fruit of your incision may be
blessed," 9).

One year after Roger Vitrac's drama, in 1929, another famous literary work dealing with an infernal couple appeared in France: Jean
Cocteau's Les Enfants terribles. Despite the proximity of time and the
fact that Victor and Esther are more than once called "enfants terribles," there exists little resemblance between the play and the narrative. In contradiction to the title, Cocteau's heroes Elisabeth and
Paul are much more "harmless" than their absurd predecessors. Though
their games end in death as well, there is no element of horror in
this final destruction. Elisabeth's suicide is rather worthy of a
Greek tragedy--the sacrifice of a "vierge sacrée"[15] in the temple of
her love, the room she shares with her brother. Critics have always
gladly focussed their attention on the couple's supposed incestuous
feelings,[16] but in this respect one must rather admit that they behave
more "child-like" than is usual for their age (the story covers several years, and in the end the "children" already have the age of
adults). The fact that they shut the world out from their private life
and hide in their bedroom is due to their fear of growing up; their
embrace is that of two children who cling together looking for protection, and who prefer death to "spoiling the game." If there is an
erotic element at all, it is even less emphasized than, say, in Poe's
"Fall of the House of Usher," a story which shows other striking parallels to Cocteau's work. The dreamy, narcotic atmosphere with which
Poe tends to surround his heroines can be found here, too, but it is
not the realm of adult passions--neither of the body nor the mind.
Paul and Elisabeth, who belong to one another like twins or members of
the same body, are made for childhood (90): the "drogue mystérieuse"
which these children of "cocainomanes" (102) and dipsomaniacs have in

their blood is a natural drug, the opium of childhood (74).

The title of Cocteau's narrative has meanwhile become a kind of household word. Although **Les Enfants terribles** represents only an indirect contribution to horror fiction, it has certainly helped to draw more attention to the possibility that children can be very effective as dark and sinister heroes in a work of art. Cocteau's protagonists do not take death seriously. On the contrary, Elisabeth regards her voluntary death as a means of perfecting the game between her and Paul; she tells him to join her in order to share her play forever. According to what has been said about the bond between brother and sister, it is clear that in horror literature death does not mean a definitive separation, either. Their relationship, though seemingly interrupted, always proves stronger than the connection to any living adult. Rosemary Timperley's story "Harry" is an extreme but appropriate example of this pattern. A little girl who was adopted through an agency when still a baby suddenly starts talking to a mysterious invisible boy. Her alarmed parents are calmed by a psychiatrist who explains to them "everything" about imaginary playmates. The girl's mother must realize, however, that the boy is a ghost (visible to children and madmen only), the materialization of the girl's brother who died while saving his sister's life from their real parents' violence. The brother claims her back now and cannot be prevented from taking her away: when the mother does not arrive at the schoolhouse in time to collect her daughter (which is the first trifling sign of neglect) she must learn that the boy has forestalled her.

Adults are cheated and outwitted whenever they want to take advantage of their apparently good and honest relationship to one of the two children. The wicked nanny in Dulcie Gray's "The Brindle Bull Terrier" must learn this in a drastic manner. The couple she has to take care of during the absence of their parents is "united" by a deadly mutual hatred. Each of the two wants to destroy the other completely. As hate is the direct reverse of love and an equally strong emotion, anyone who interferes with this explosive union must inevitably come to harm. The nanny, convinced that she enjoys the boy's affection, relies on his discretion and understanding when she maltreats the girl whom she deeply hates as well. Being forced to kill the escaping girl, she employs a fierce dog whom she sets upon her to tear her apart. When she "explains" the matter to the boy, she must admit to herself that she has been made use of the same way she has used the dog. The boy's complacency and cruel satisfaction appal even a woman like her, and his self-assured attempt at blackmail prepares her for many an unpleasant surprise in the future.

Ray Bradbury's vicious story "The Veld" also testifies that adults can never disturb their children's sphere without being brutally punished. Here this "sphere" can be located exactly: it lies inside the nursery and is even directly reflected by it. The parents and their little son and daughter inhabit a hyper-modern home where nothing has to be done by hand. The nursery is the most expensive and extravagant part of the house ("'But nothing's too good for our children'"[17]); it contains a mechanism which makes the children's innermost fantasies and wishes appear on its walls. The parents are frightened by the cruel world they see. Santa Claus, Aladdin, and the Wizard of Oz have recently been replaced by an oppressive African scene with hungry lions. The adults can only catch brief glimpses of the beasts' prey, but they often hear familiar voices screaming in agony. They only find out the truth when their fate is sealed; after they have announced that the nursery will be shut for good, they are lured into it by their offspring and devoured by the savage projections of the children's united minds.

Like all of Bradbury's stories, "The Veld" is much more than "just" a horror story, and it would also be misleading to call it pure science fiction. The setting is a means of creating a symbolical logical extension of reality. The underlying psychological state of affairs seems "realistic" and up-to-date enough: parents who surround their children with nothing but "creature comforts" to satisfy their animal needs must always fear encountering a roaring beast in return.

"The Veld" is certainly a fascinating story. Nonetheless, one must concede that it subsists to a considerable extent on its shock effects. It is absolutely possible to clothe the problem of the two clashing spheres in an inconspicuous, neat story and, because of the incongruity of action and result, gain an even stronger impression. A story by Celia Fremlin with the significant title "The Quiet Game" is such a contribution. This story needs neither monsters nor killers, but depicts a simple incident of daily life. The horror roots directly and exclusively in the unalterable separation of the worlds of adults and children. The children's realm is concentrated in one single feature generally considered the child's absolute privilege: the capability of total play, of becoming so absorbed in its fantasy that it becomes reality. Yet the children comply with certain basic rules they know by nature, not by convention. Hence adults can never learn these laws and must remain watching laymen.

The tragedy is close at hand when the mother of the four-year-old fraternal twins desperately wants to join their game. She and her children live in a modern skyscraper flat with very thin walls and very sharp-eared and quarrelsome neighbors. From morning till night the young woman is involved in a nervous war, because everybody complains of the "noise" the children produce with their most careful movements. When the mother buys a thick Persian carpet to soften the din, the children find an ingenious way of keeping themselves busy without a sound; on their "flying carpet" they travel to "Inkoo Land," the exotic land of fantasy. At first their mother is happy to "send them away" for a time, but she grows more and more envious when her own real surroundings become too bleak and desolate to suffer. Therefore, she cannot understand that her twins deliberately return to reality from time to time, and after a while even stop flying altogether. She wants to give a fresh impulse to their play and steps on the carpet, which of course does not move an inch. Growing frantic and frightening the couple away, she drags the limp carpet onto the window sill and "flies out."

Neither mother nor children can in any respect be called extraordinary. The young woman is by no means demented, as a superficial observer could deduce from her one and only outburst. As a rule, real madmen are the chosen few who--though grown-up--may occasionally have contact to children in horror fiction. They are the ones for whom, as Guy de Maupassant puts it, the old barriers to pure unrestrained imagination--logic, reason, common sense--break down and collapse completely. Obstacles of any kind no longer exist for them.[18] Thus they even go a step further than children, who "return" at tea-time. In the

story, however, important hints are given to the fact that the unnerved mother is merely dying to shake off reason in a tour de force.
If she had the fantasy of a child or a lunatic, she could fly to Inkoo
Land without the slightest physical or mental exertion. Whether she
likes it or not, she is still an adult who needs facts. For her the
carpet must really fly. Thus, she remains on the ground while the
children beside her are already traveling. Ironically enough, her
twins are able to distinguish between game and reality: they are
alarmed when their mother over and over again repeats her wish to get
the carpet going. After she has opened the window she is even implored
to play correctly, and when she moves the carpet towards it the little
ones begin to weep, cling to each other and recoil from her in horror.
They can perceive all too well the sense of alienation that fills the
familiar room. Grown-ups remain grown-ups and can never really join
children anymore. Ignoring reason to get rid of responsibility is no
way of reaching absolute liberty. A deficit of logic does not mean a
surplus of imagination.

"The Quiet Game" shows that a rather complex relationship and the
development of a nervous crisis can be unfolded within a few pages in
a very convincing manner. After all, the writer's intentions are basically directed at the surroundings of the family which drive them to
despair--life in a skyscraper, lack of space, intolerant fellow-
beings. The mother's estrangement from her offspring (which is of
course latent from the very beginning) becomes even clearer to the
reader because the whole account is given from the woman's deranged
perspective; and yet this estrangement is just another refined form of
the omnipresent demarcation.

Peer Groups

"You are another race entirely...You are not human. You
are--children."

Ray Bradbury, "Let's Play 'Poison'"[1]

The following section deals with a social constellation that has
always been by far the most popular and the most effective one in horror literature: a group of children who all act in perfect harmony
with the whole, like limbs of one monstrous body. It is this pattern
which provides the everlasting battle between adults and children with
a new, supreme variety--two great armies face each other and, though
not necessarily with evil intentions, they infallibly eradicate each
other. There are numerous inherent characteristics which must be discussed in connection with the peer group, including the children's
outward appearance, point of view, and the author's intentions. The
reader will recognize some of the characteristics as mere amplifica-
tions of qualities already explained in the previous sections (though
their effect is still worth while examining); other features are completely new and typical of the peer group only.

The first important peculiarity which catches the reader's attention is the en bloc presentation of the group. Adults are usually at
once confronted with the whole horde of children, who more or less all
look alike, and, even worse, who do not seem to need any internal com-
munication--at least none of the forms known to grown-up people. Adult
man is convinced that every civilized people depends on a common language, on a vehicle of verbal expression to adapt each single member
to new situations and necessities. Any species that does not require
such sources of information since it is "steered" by a superindividual
intelligence and will-power is easily classified as "primitive"--not
always because of man's innate arrogance, but because of his fear. It
is unthinkable for him that living units without "personal" motivation
may be superior to those connected insufficiently with and disunited
irrevocably from their fellow individuals by language. Facing a multitude of tiny creatures who appear to move by remote control is much
worse than being attacked by a giant individual (which is, by the way,
the reason why Saul Bass's film Phase IV surpasses even the celebrated
Formicula).

Children and ants have a great deal in common. Though small in
size and stature, they are strong as a mass, and capable of melting
into one entity. This special arrangement reinforces the conception of
children as an independent species with weapons of their own. In the
primeval battle between homo adultus and homo infans one can never
foretell the outcome.

The story "The Children" by W. Baker-Evans is a simple yet brilliant illustration of the way grown-ups may be confronted with this
alien kind. It is also a nasty travesty of the idyll that is normally
depicted--that is, outside horror fiction--when a good-natured, rather
puffy elderly gentleman (the uncle-type par excellence), while wandering through a peaceful wood, encounters a flock of beautiful, smiling

little darlings.

This British gentleman, who likes traveling abroad, has taken a taxi which breaks down at the edge of a forest. Having time in abundance, he decides to take a walk in the wood, though his driver desperately tries to hold him back. After a short while he sits down on a log and is soon surrounded by the children, who first watch him silently, then finger his thighs and start to "play" with him. Delighted, the man takes a little girl on his knee who supposedly wants to kiss him; this caress, however, turns out to be a kiss of death.

There is infinitely more to this short-short story than meets the reader's eye at first perusal. Though simple in structure, the story is so tricky that even the second perusal will lead him astray. Any reader who is versed in horror literature will instantly recognize the allusions to Bram Stoker's Dracula--the setting ("on a lonely by-road" somewhere around Yugoslavia and Rumania[2]), as well as the native's fruitless efforts to restrain the reckless English gentleman who, like Jonathan Harker, is not familiar with the surroundings. Of course, one is prepared to encounter a vampire in the course of the story. The little ones, however, are not vampires--they are cannibals who devour the intruder until nothing remains of him, and this is quite a significant difference. The symbolical implications of this feast are far more shocking than its physical dimension.

Mr. Gillespie's journey into the unknown forest is civilized man's return to the cruel, primitive world from which he stems, but which he has chosen to ignore and forget. The British gentleman only comes into this predicament because he did not rely on a travel agency--an institution which mercifully protects its clients from having to look at natural life too closely. The achievements of modern technology have deserted him, too, and he stands alone against a hostile environment.

Nevertheless, this situation is by no means the exclusive reason for the reader's growing anxiety. His feeling of unease is to a great extent due to the narrative technique the author employs in this story. The narrator reveals the protagonist's innermost thoughts and feelings to the reader, but simultaneously creates a distance by constantly referring to him as "Mr Gillespie;" in the final scene the contrast between this formal designation and the gruesome event is especially effective. Above all, it emphasizes the grotesque collision of civilization with the flesh-and-blood roots of violence.

Since the reader has a foreboding of disaster from the very beginning, he distinctly notices how insufficiently Mr. Gillespie is prepared for his adventure. Accustomed to absolute security, he finds everything very pleasant and agreeable. Ironically enough, he remembers having heard about all kinds of woods ("There are woods and woods. Some are mysterious, some threatening, some friendly, some aloof," 30), and at once considers the one in question as "benevolent." His senses and instincts have deteriorated like his flabby muscles, and his lack of suspicion is partly caused by his mental indolence.

Mr. Gillespie's encounter with the children is preluded in a fashion which is thoroughly characteristic of the story and the protagonist's attitude. Among other grave symptoms of decadence he exhibits, he is also an artist, a man who loves beauty and peace. He feels that there is something lacking in the lovely landscape he is sketching--"a small boy in a red jumper" who ought to give it "human interest" (30). Mr. Gillespie's attitude toward children is determined by the dubious clichés that prevail in civilized society, and which present children as sweet, delightful, and harmless, because this view neither troubles adult man nor disturbs his sense of security. After all, being embedded in a society which protects him, he need not worry since he and the other grown-ups form a majority.

Looking up from his work, Mr. Gillespie actually sees a boy. Immediately afterwards the entire group appears, "moving out from the shadow of the trees as silently as Red Indians" (31). The adult tries to apply the patterns of behavior he knows to these strange creatures, who can all perceive his ridiculous defencelessness ("they were all convulsed with laughter, open-mouthed and shrieking, tears in their eyes," 31). Mr. Gillespie is in every respect a "delicate" person. Verbal communication is utterly impossible, and the non-verbal forms of expression have totally different meanings for both sides. The children never intend to make any contact at all.

The sinister effect the children evoke within the reader is caused by their muteness and their identical outward appearance. Each of them is ten-years-old, wears a sack-like garment, has brown skin, flaxen hair, and green eyes. The children's age bears extreme importance, since it completely excludes the possibility that the little ones are merely the offspring of some mysterious anthropophageous forest tribe. The fact that they are all of the same age proves to the reader that he is confronted with a species of its own. Yet they are certainly genuine children with all the familiar gestures and movements. In their private hunting ground they show what their supposed "play" really means. Their laughter is in fact a sneer, their "tender" touch is a means of testing Mr. Gillespie for his nutritive value, the "gleeful" dance they involve their victim in has only one function; their "mad ring-o'-roses" (32) is to exhaust the man and keep him on the spot. To be sure, these children appear quite extraordinary to the reader, but when he again comes across the traits adults find so charming in "normal" children, he is likely to give them a second thought.

With his gripping tale "Children of the Corn" Stephen King demonstrates that his contributions in short fiction deserve the same attention his novels have already received for quite some time. The story under discussion shows several remarkable parallels to "The Children" and raises new points of interest as well; above all, it contains important additions concerning the factor of age. Like the child-tribe in the preceding example, the group of children in King's story inhabit a realm of their own which is geographically separated from the civilized world. Though the author does not employ some far-off Transylvanian forest for his setting but remains in the very heart of North America, his scenery is, and has to be, far more disquieting, because it is located in the middle of a huge area which cannot be imagined more artificial or man-made. This region, the cornland of Nebraska, has been shaped according to man's will and design--and somewhere in the center of this land a horde of children is re-shaping the fundamental structure in their own revolutionary fashion.

It seems significant that even one of the few writers who occasionally seek to explain part of the child's psyche in their works makes children appear as inscrutable strangers when they form a group.

Unlike The Shining or Carrie, however, the story does not focus on the
protagonist's (or antagonist's) psychic condition, his struggle with
an innate super-power, but makes use of the child's symbolic value.
Accordingly it is written from the point of view of two adults who
travel through the uniform, fertile, yet desolate landscape. Strangely
enough, even in the beginning the grown-up couple feels totally unnerved in an environment that has been arranged by their fellow-
beings, by plain, ordinary, commercially minded citizens. Physical
fertility and psychic sterility collide here in an obscene way which
is indeed hardly sufferable.

The story subsists on its atmosphere and suspense, above all, and
on its symbolic impact. Only few concrete facts are given—though
extremely drastic ones. Husband and wife are quarrelling as usual and
inattentive when their car hits a boy on the road. The adults find
that they are not responsible for his death, since his throat has been
cut. They load the corpse into the trunk to transport it to the
nearest village; on the way they open the boy's suitcase to find a
crucifix made of corn husks, and from the local radio station they
hear a holy mass celebrated in a rapturous manner by children. In the
village they notice that time has apparently stood still since a certain date twelve years ago; there are no adults to be seen, and the
buildings and machines adults usually need for their work and leisure
are rotten. Leaving his wife in the car, the husband enters the
church, which has been transformed into the place of worship of a
cruel "Old Testament Christ."[3] From the curious entries in the birth
and death registers he deduces that all adults were slaughtered by
their fanatic children to appease their malevolent corn god. Alarmed
by a blast of the automobile horn, he steps out in time to watch his
wife being murdered by a horde of children and receive a wound himself. He is able to escape into the corn and has come to feel safe,
when at sunset the god of the corn himself comes for him.

Children are the ones who give general significance to a tale
that abounds with clear, minute, even petty references to time and
place. The function these indications fulfill is evident: they strongly remind the reader of the fact that a bizarre, surrealistic landscape like the one in this story really exists, and that its eerie
effect is mainly due to "cultivation." Like the little ones in "The
Children," the offspring here represent a wild, hard, cruel form of
life that tolerates neither compromise nor weakness of any kind. This
does not mean, however, that their society may be considered primitive. They have killed their parents in a conspiracy to establish a
community of their own, an answer to the degenerate, domesticated
existence their fathers led. Despite the drastic way of abolishing
their customs, the children by no means invent anything novel. The god
they worship is basically the same god their parents prayed to, but
the children have erased the New Testament, which teaches frailties
such as meekness and loving one's enemies. They prefer the parts
dealing with human sacrifices, and injunctions to "let the iniquitous
be cut down so that the ground may be fertile again" (148). Just like
their parents, however, they do not really worship their supreme being
because they love him or expect spiritual welfare of him, but because
they want mundane repayment—a good harvest.

Though the corn belt of Nebraska, the "Bible belt," is full of
religious zealots, this area is more prone to paganism than any other

region. Everybody founds his own church; and hearing about the "nine thousand names of God only used in Nebraska" (145), nobody can be sure if there are not rather nine thousand gods people worship. Some of them, perhaps most, can be simply grouped under the "Golden Calf." By their straight, merciless interpretation of "Christian" religion the children unveil the real nature of a cult that is not only practiced in Nebraska. In this connection it is notable that the church they have converted was once a Baptist church, which implies that the children (regarded still as unworthy) were never baptized by their parents, but follow the Baptist tradition of religious separation.

In contrast to their parents, the children have become one with the land they work on. They are in fact children of the corn, because each of them has to undergo the Atonement and become a Christ of its own when its childhood reaches an end. Here the reader can notice an important variation on the age factor. The children are not all of the same age--they must not be, for their species has to propagate it- self--but childhood is strictly separated from adulthood by death. At the birth of each child the day of its death is already fixed, and also the procedure: every child must silently retire to a kind of Golgotha in the corn to be killed by its god.

In this respect one must also consider the fact that the "corn god" myth, the idea of a superior being living in the corn (and pro- viding for a good harvest), is a phenomenon which can be observed in all parts of the world and among the most different cultures. In his anthropological work The Golden Bough Sir James George Frazer points out the similarities between religious rites performed by peoples in all continents and all epochs of human history. From the sacrifices of red-haired men in ancient Egypt (who were "representatives of the corn-spirit himself, that is, of Osiris, and were slain for the ex- press purpose of making the corn turn red or golden"[4]) to the slaugh- ter of red-haired puppies in ancient Rome for the same purpose one can deduce that "the corn-spirit is represented sometimes in human, some- times in animal form, and that in both cases he is killed in the per- son of his representative and eaten sacramentally" (48). This happens almost always in the center of the harvest-field. The killing of human beings is reserved to the so-called savage races; other contemporary customs, which can be found in Sweden, France, and other European countries (among "civilized" people), consist in the eating of human replicas made of food. It is notable, however, that an advanced cul- ture like that of the Aztecs knew both the "direct" form of human sacrifices to the corn god (92-93) and a kind of transubstantiation which was at least as refined as the later Christian variation: human replicas made of dough (with the blood of children) were blessed in complicated ceremonies and given to the people in a communion. This procedure was called "killing the god Huitzilopochtli so that his body might be eaten" (90). It is also interesting that eyes and mouth of the dough-image were filled with grains of maize, since this is also done with the grinning Christ figure that hangs in the church of King's story, and with the human victims crucified in the corn.

The veneration of the corn god was exceedingly common among the Indian tribes of North America. The Creek Indians, the Yuchi tribe who called themselves Children of the Sun, the Seminoles and Natchez Indians all sacrificed to the corn god, though their modest attempts at agriculture can hardly be compared to the abundance of fruit in the

corn belt. During all their savage ceremonies children were excluded--
except if they served as human sacrifices.

Since Stephen King's story is mainly based on Christian religion,
the death of each child that reaches its age limit must be seen in yet
another tradition: "The Killing of the Divine King" and the "Sacrifice
of the King's Son."[5] Frazer also points out the universal custom of
the killing of kings at the end of a fixed term. The children of the
corn are sacrificed (or rather sacrifice themselves) in imitation of
Christ, who, after all, was God's Son, and whom death was predicted
from the beginning. The individual's silent retreat into the corn reminds one of another mythological source as well. The Greek myth of
Hylas, Amycus, and Phineus as presented by Robert Graves includes a
reference to Borimus, son of Upius, a youth of extraordinary beauty,
who once, at harvest time, went to a well to fetch water for the
reapers and never returned, caught by the nymphs in the water.[6]

The concept that children have to die as soon as their childhood
is over is very common in horror fiction. It is one more means of
emphasizing the gap between grown-ups and children, and it exempts the
reader from racking his brains over the question as to what will become of a child when it reaches a certain age. It is clear that there
would arise an intolerable confusion in the separation motif if a
child were allowed to live through infancy, adolescence, and adulthood
without any interruption. Such a violation of the great underlying
principle never occurs. Authors employ several methods in order to
avoid commingling fire and water. It is impossible to tell whether
they consciously conform to this unwritten law; in any event, the consistency which writers of horror fiction demonstrate is astonishing.

The first and simplest method to keep up the separation is of
course killing off a child when it has grown too old. Usually the
crucial age is puberty, which means that the sexual element is totally
excluded; the child may not live long enough to experience anything of
the kind. In this respect "Children of the Corn" is certainly an exception, but (apart from the fact that sexuality is reduced to an indispensable function and devoid of all eroticism) since one of the
main topics of the story is "fertility," this deviation is perfectly
justified. Nevertheless, the deaths in this tale are similar to "dying
from puberty;" each child has to disappear on its birthday and thus
dies a personal death. Within a group this lonely way of dying need
not always be the rule; the whole formation can perish at once like a
horde of lemmings, as is demonstrated in Marcel Schwob's "Croisade des
enfants." In any case, it entails other peculiar features. The preparation of the child's death is the only occasion on which it is ever
presented as an individual personality. The stage it is in would under
normal circumstances mean the initiation into adulthood; consequently,
in the same measure as the moribund child is estranged from its fel-
low-beings within the narration, it draws closer to the adult reader.

The ending of Stephen King's story serves as an excellent example
of this shift. Throughout the whole story, up to the death of the male
protagonist, the account is rendered from the point of view of the
adult couple. The majority of children--the aggressors--appear as the
usual unanimous mass. Basically there is no cogent reason why the
story should not stop at a point when there is no longer any adult
available whose train of thought reflects the strangeness of the
children. The very last paragraphs, however, reveal the point of view

of "those above the Age of Favor" (158), who only a short time ago
took part in the killing of "iniquitous" adults, and who now almost
belong to them. Significantly, through their perspective the reader
does not grow any fonder of the little ones. Especially the newly appointed prophet, a nine-year-old boy, represents a new breed **within**
the new generation, a group that is even more relentless, more cruel
and more fanatic. If growing older really means an increasing lack of
religious fervor, the little ones know a remedy: they simply lower the
Age of Favor.

   In order to heighten the perverse effect of the murderous
children, the group is endowed with the usual proper "childish" qualities. They may pray and preach in a deadly serious manner, they may
be dressed like Quaker parsons, but at bottom they are genuine
children--or at least they come up to the average adult's simplified
conception. From afar husband and wife already hear their "high and
joyous laughter" (143). They are indeed amusing themselves in their
own way; what appals the reader is the fact that the very same "innocent" laughter is mentioned when the children are crowding together
from all directions to slaughter the intruders. Filled with the most
inhuman intentions, they nudge each other, point and smile the "sweet
smiles of children" (151). Even during the kill their voices remain
"soft;" and while they are pursuing their second game they whoop and
shout with glee ("They're having more fun than a five-alarm fire, Burt
thought," 153).

   It is certainly no mere coincidence that the victims who encounter the wicked offspring are a grown-up married couple. They are the
ones who are entitled to be fruitful and multiply, but they cannot do
so, because their marriage is disrupted and their lives have become
sterile since there is nothing they can earnestly fight for or
against. Strangely enough, on his desperate run the husband realizes
that he feels physically better than he has felt in years: he is now
"grappling with a clear-cut problem" (154). Children and adults are at
war, and all trivialities must give way to bare self-defense. The
strength and energy he develops, however, come too late to save the
man. War imagery, by the way, can be found throughout the entire
story, as a reminder of one of the greatest sins in man's history.
Examining the wound of the dead boy on the road, the protagonist must
think of the "finer points of hand-to-hand assassination" (135) as
performed by an army sergeant; furthermore, he associates the pen-
etrating smell of fertilizer (which is the smell of blood) with the
stench he has come to know in Vietnam. Apart from the age-old unity of
death and fertility, the author might have thought of the fact that in
this war people used defoliants instead of fertilizers in order to
shape a landscape into neat, tidy rows.

   The story "Miri" by Adrian Spies is another apt illustration of
nearly all the basic aspects discussed above. Though originally written as a script for the "Star Trek" TV series, it may on no account be
discarded as pure science fiction. The action of this story is not
only embroidered with horror elements; it is, on the contrary, a
classic genuine horror plot which is transferred to another galaxy.
But for the shift in time and place and the intervention of the
"Enterprise" crew, one can well consider the whole story as another
interesting variation on the "mad scientist" motif.

   The perfectly "terrestrial" impression one gets of the conditions

on the "fourth planet in the solar system of 70 Ophiucus" is caused by
the fact that the population consists of human beings, descendants of
the first settlers who left this solar system. Very much like the
Pilgrim Fathers, these people left Earth to establish a society of
their own, which they defended blindly and stubbornly, and which
turned out all too human—even worse than on Earth.

Therefore, the surroundings the four members of the crew find on
the surface of the planet appear familiar to them, and even more to
the reader. "Familiar," however, does not mean "comfortable," for the
whole city they land in is deserted and seems to have been that way
throughout the centuries when no one has had contact to the inhabitants. The first person they meet is a decrepit old maniac who clasps a
child's tricycle with all his might. He dies shortly after, but the
officers can find someone else to interrogate—a little girl. From her
incoherent and naive comments the adults can deduce that there are
only children on the planet, whose parents started a "project for the
prolongation of human life" three hundred years ago. They created a
virus (note the moral connotation) which served their purposes in an
undesirable fashion: the thing remains benign in an infected person so
long as he or she is a child, and becomes malignant when puberty
begins. Of course, all of the adult scientists were instantly killed;
their offspring enjoy not an eternal, but at least an immensely pro-
longed childhood, to die a most unpleasant death before they can
grow up.

It goes without saying that the fearless and upright officers of
the "Enterprise" can handle this knotty problem and save the children
from their unnatural youth. The symbolic implications, ingenious in
their simplicity, cannot be spoiled by the requisite happy ending of
the story. One of the oldest taboos in human history, which has been
repeatedly employed in horror fiction, is the manipulation of the God-
given span of life (and of course man's unauthorized creation of life,
the direct consequences of which will be discussed later on). With
their offence against the inviolable mysteries of life the adult
scientists have cast a boomerang and are directly responsible for the
clear-cut separation of children and adults.

Though theoretically blameless in this matter, the adult visitors
from the ship of course become involved in the affair and soon show
symptoms of the disease. Adults and would-be adults are branded as
dangerous outcasts by blue spots on their skin. The original grown-ups
the children can remember and those who arise from their midst are
simply called the "grups;" each child loses its Christian name as soon
as it "changes sides." It is not only its imminent death that cuts off
the sick child from its kind, and not only the ugly sight of rapid
physical decay. Its mates have to withdraw because every adult human
being inevitably becomes a raving madman possessed by the urge to
destroy.

Logically it is a pubescent girl who must encounter the adult
officers. All of them are confined within one building, the Public
Health Administration, whereas the anonymous mass of children, unseen,
is playing outside. Once again a child's doom brings it closer to the
adult's point of view. It develops traits unknown to its cheerful companions of yore, who know nothing but incessant play. The girl falls
in love for the first time. Nevertheless, the reader is not invited to
really understand her, either; she still has too much of the child in

her. She shifts to and fro in unpredictable intervals, and the reader
is not allowed to follow her roamings outside. Yet her caprices are no
longer determined by mere childish playfulness, but also by the new,
adult emotion of jealousy.

Reluctantly, the girl cooperates with the officers as a mediator
between children and adults; she can finally convince the group to
enter the building. It is most remarkable that their grotesque procession is compared to a children's crusade, since this theme represents the expression of victimization par excellence and is frequently
dealt with in horror literature. The outward appearance of the little
ones is meant as an accusation in itself; they form a motley company
of all ages and colors (which underlines the universality of the
image) who are all ridiculously dressed in adults' clothing, which of
course does not fit them at all.

H. L. Lawrence's famous novel Children of Light points out another way in which adults may be punished for their sins. Here the
immediate reason for the separation from their offspring is the experimentation with atomic power which gets out of man's control. The
radioactive emission is not strong enough to kill people, but it
brings the universal sterility of the human race. The total extinction
of mankind is approaching. Only a group of children who were all born
during an atomic catastrophe cannot be harmed by radiation since they
are highly radioactive themselves.[7] They are the rescue and the hope
of humanity, but they are untouchable in two ways--no one beyond a
chosen few in high places may learn the truth, so that the children
are not endangered by a desperate mob; and no one may have physical
contact with them.

The protagonists of the novel, a grown-up couple on the run from
the police, accidentally enter the forbidden zone where the children
live. They are hidden away by the little ones in the private sanctuary
where none of their adult tutors ever goes. Confronted with the first
adults who do not wear protective clothing and helmets, the children
grow very fond of them and want to go on living with them; the couple,
however, have to leave the secret territory again because the authorities are on their track. Outside they soon begin to suffer from the
effects of the radiation they have been exposed to and die miserably.

It is perfectly natural that the grown-up "party" is represented
by a couple again. In addition to the symbolic guilt which all adults
share, neither of the two is faultless to begin with: the man has just
killed his faithless wife, the girl has been a member of a murderous
motor-cycle gang. Nonetheless, they have the reader's full sympathy,
because they, too, are victims of circumstances. As soon as they trespass upon the children's domain they lose their former identities:
they are declared dead for the outside world to prevent further in-
quiries and pursuit; anonymous bodies from the local morgue are blown
up in their place (an equivalent to being burned in effigy). Thus,
they have become as untouchable as the children. Of course they must
not enter the children's realm without punishment--after all, they are
strangers, if benevolent ones. Their very friendliness seals their
fate. Children and adults grow so fond of one another that a man and a
woman who have never before experienced such harmony and peace long to
become parents to the children. The radioactive offspring, who have
only had themselves up to this moment, feel so happy in their presence
that they are always around. In contrast to both groups the reader

knows about the danger and perceives the dramatic irony in this situation: the little ones literally love their new parents to death.

It is notable that the couple does not actually die inside the
children's territory--they "wait" until they are outside again. The
contaminated area may not simply be regarded as a center of death because human beings cannot stand radiation. On the contrary, the danger
zone is a fountain of new life on Earth. The outside world, however,
is doomed to die; its damnation is plainly visible through the countless facets of brutality and human inhumanity which are shown throughout the first and last thirds of the novel. The couple's instant death
is only due to their illicit contact with beings who have long outgrown the living conditions of their progenitors.

The children can easily be recognized as a new race by their outward appearance and their peculiar manners. All of them have silver
hair; in addition to the strong effect of uniformity, metallic colors
never fail to evoke associations with machines, non-human powers, and
coldness (this is also one of the functions of the children's golden
eyes in The Midwich Cuckoos). Indeed, the children are cold, and their
cold-bloodedness for its part is the physical equivalent of their mental structure. This does not mean that they are cold-hearted and without emotions, but their minds (which in any case are developed far
beyond human standards) function in an especially disciplined, pur-
poseful way. They are destined and trained to become a species that
acts as a whole, without rivalry or personal pride, to reach the aim
ordinary man has never been able to realize: peaceful progress. Their
"cold blood" is the price the children have to pay for such determination.

In this novel, too, the offspring are presented as a strange
though friendly group. The reader shares the adult couple's point of
view during their whole stay in the bunker. The children do master
verbal communication, since they have been educated through this medium, but their manner of speech gives the impression that they do not
really depend on language and only want to do their new acquaintances
a favor by using this old-fashioned vehicle of expression. As always,
these remarkable creatures show enough conventional traits to pass for
"typical" children. They are curious; they innocently touch their
visitors' warm skin; above all, they hide them from their stern
teachers, which is a most natural reaction for ten-year-olds.

A presentation like the one discussed above demonstrates (apart
from getting rid of the children altogether) a second possibility of
avoiding the problem of ageing. This method does not depend on action
(the act of dying), but most of all on the depiction of the children's
outward appearance and demeanor. Furthermore, it is not a rational explanation meant to satisfy the reader's intellect, but on the contrary
a means of lulling his possible curiosity concerning the children's
future. He must be so thoroughly convinced by the suggestion that
children form an independent species that any idea of their inevitable
physical and mental development is excluded from the start. In order
to achieve this effect the children's uniformity is employed as the
basic principle. Childhood in such an undifferentiated structure (no
gradations of age or physical shape, no idiosyncrasies) is likely to
be accepted without reservation as a fixed status, not as a phase.
Especially in Children of Light the success of this method is extremely important and therefore heightens the impact of the whole novel

considerably. Here it is even more difficult to veil the inherent contradiction between the fact that the children are prepared by a whole
secret organization to become responsible adults, and the necessity
that the offspring are presented as eternal children because of their
symbolic value.

Ronald Chetwynd-Hayes' story "The Brats" is in many respects an
interesting mixture of the preceding literary works. Again a new race
comes into being as the result of an atomic catastrophe (the use of
nuclear bombs); adults and children live in a permanent state of war
with each other, and the end of childhood is determined by a natural
death. A grown-up couple must face the children as an entire horde
("brats had the pack instinct"[8]); fertility has become the children's
affair, whereas the few remaining adults die out one by one. Of course
the children are described from the adult point of view. Through the
male protagonist, Peter Croft (adults have names, but children are
devoid both of names and clothing of any kind), the reader is provided
with scraps of information about the time before the "blow-up," the
present living conditions, and the nature of the children as Peter
"understands" it.

Though still in his early twenties, Peter is an "oldie," one of
those who were born before the complete devastation of the earth. The
reader learns that at this crucial point Peter was only two years old.
Any possible doubts concerning the guilt inherent in every grown-up
person, however, are removed by the fact that the brats have a very
clear-cut attitude towards this question: "Brats hated oldies. Oldies
lived on and on--brats died young. In some inexplicable way oldies
were responsible for the early death, the ruins that lay all around,
the never appeased hunger, the dog-packs, the stinking, never resting
rat hordes" (56). As a result of gamma rays and bacteria mutation
which infects the unborn foetus, brats die early, but are fully ma-
tured by ten and can reproduce their kind; oldies are not sterile, but
refrain from procreation, because every child becomes a brat ("'If
there is a child,' she whispered, 'you must kill it. Promise?'--'But
if we raised it--kept it away from the others...'--'I knew someone who
did that once. When it was six--it killed her,'" 69). A brat's natural
death is, just as in the story "Miri," accompanied by rapid outward
physical decay and a "madness sickness."

In the big city that forms the setting of the tale only two
buildings are left intact, the library (which, as an important symbol
of civilization, is a constant mockery) and the church, which has been
turned into the brats' headquarters, giving a "completely false impression of benign sanctuary" (57). Degeneration can be perceived in
every detail; the word "brat" itself suggests the children's proximity
to rats, and like the rodents they have nests in the sewer system.
Peter, however, has also chosen to live in cellars ("He must go underground. Become a human rat foraging in the bowels of a dead city,"
59). The two species are more similar to each other than they realize.
Brats are born with the instinct to kill grown-ups, whereas oldies
have returned to their formerly buried instincts, growling from between clenched teeth when they spot the "natural enemy."

The symbolic guilt Peter bears is additionally emphasized by his
hand-to-hand struggle with a brat that has entered his vault. The
creature, singled out from its group because it is on the brink of
death, attacks him with the common battle cry "Kill Dad." Significant-

ly, "Dad" is a derogatory term for oldie. When Peter has broken his enemy's apparently frail body, he is "still attached to that gruesome burden, that seemed like some obscene growth" (61). The brat is his personal charge and the monstrous deformation of the human race.

As usual, the homicidal, man-eating offspring have "childish" qualities which underline the perverseness of their activities. These traits become clearest in Peter's confrontation with a whole gang of brats that have caught a female oldie and prepare her for the feast: "Brats were rarely silent. The childish need to chatter, ejaculate those sinister giggles and squabble like a crowd of restless monkeys, could not for long be restrained. The only exception was if they were lying in wait for a likely victim, but even then the youngest--or the least mature--would more than likely give vent to a squeal of excitement" (63-64). Since children have always been "noted for a streak of unthinking cruelty" (which in the brats, however, has developed into a deliberate desire to inflict pain), the smallest of the horde torture the oldie girl, "emitting shrill yells of delight" when she screams.

The parallels to Robinson Crusoe can hardly be ignored: a human being, superior in intellect but physically inferior to the whole anthropophageous tribe, rescues the only other creature on his "desert island" who is qualified to become his mate. Nonetheless, the relation between male and female rather resembles that of Adam and Eve, who want to return to paradise. Peter and Lydia have attained knowledge; in contrast to the "innocent" brats Lydia is aware of her nakedness and shrinks back from Peter. Both dream of "dense green forests," though they hardly comprehend this obsolete expression, and the only apples they have ever seen (ironically wrapped in an old newspaper with the headline, "Noone Will Dare Use Nuclear Bombs Says Prime Minister," 60) are rotten to the core. Yet the two adults are the ones who are referred to as doomed children, or, after they have discovered a fresh leaf, as children who have found a new toy in a graveyard (70). Their rising hopes of finding a new Eden are finally baffled when the brats get in their way, and before he dies Peter realizes the true condition of mankind: "The brats--the inheritors--small, hideous, but for the first time Peter experienced a feeling of relationship. In a way they were his children; royal princes waiting with greedy hands to grab the imperial sceptre" (72).

The children of Lawrence's novel are all born on the same fatal day and form a new race by accident, through their first contact with the world they enter. John Wyndham's Midwich Cuckoos are "begotten" on the same day, implanted in their foster mothers' (incubators') wombs by an alien race. There they grow the usual nine months (the precision of time, however, is not so great that the children are all delivered on the very same day, since the bodies of the female human hosts are unreliable in this respect).

In The Midwich Cuckoos a third method of avoiding the age problem can be observed. The novel consists of two parts--the first one dealing with implantation, pregnancy, birth, and the first weeks after; the second one describing a rather short period within the children's ninth year up to their destruction. It is quite important (not only with regard to the narrative technique, but also symbolically) that the narrator of the whole account is absent from Midwich during the years which intervene, and that neither he nor his wife are directly involved in the affair. To him the children, who are such strange creatures by nature, must even appear a great deal stranger. In the first part of the book the impression of uniformity is created by a) the children's nearly simultaneous births, b) their golden eyes, and c) the fact that all new-born babies look alike, at least to a man who is not a father himself.

The lapse of time between the births and the narrator's return prevents the reader from witnessing any continual development of the mysterious offspring. Only through casual remarks dropped by some of the inhabitants does the reader catch short glimpses of the situation in the town at other points of time. The uniform presentation and the manipulation of time work hand in hand, heightening the impression of remoteness one gets of the children.

In the above novel the method of using intervals of time merely serves as a reinforcement and is not absolutely necessary. The second period which is pointed out in detail still lies in the children's childhood; moreover, the ending represents one of the possibilities already discussed: the little ones are done away with in a genuine holocaust. In other works, however, the method may be essential-- particularly in those stories and novels that deal with the childhood and adulthood of one and the same person. The impression of a straight linear development must be strictly avoided here, too. That means that the exact reverse of the Bildungsroman pattern is required. One has to be convinced that the two stages have nothing to do with each other; the character in question can often not even remember the child he once was, let alone the feelings and motivations which dominated his actions then. Child and adult are, as usual, strangers to each other, even within one person. As a rule, outward stimuli cause both parts to come together and clash more violently than two different people can do. Authors of horror fiction do not intend to demonstrate or even ex- plain how their protagonists have achieved the transition from one phase to the next--and they will certainly not object if the reader associates the available fragments with the genesis of an insect: the accomplished imago's shape seems to have nothing in common with the larva it stems from, although it sometimes takes parts of its chrysa- lis with it.

In John Wyndham's novel the children's uniformity is without doubt the prevailing feature. There are twenty-eight girls and thirty boys--though one must rather say "items,"[9] for the children are not only a unanimous group, but absolutely identical units of the whole. In The Midwich Cuckoos the depiction of the group reaches the purest and most unequivocal form possible: the combined brains of the indi- vidual children constitute a super-brain from which the unit receives instructions and powers, and to which it is to transmit "individual" experience and sensations. The whole formation is explicitly compared to an insect colony (123). Even the biological cause for such a phe- nomenon is the same for children and insects: "A number of forms that appear at first sight to be individuals turn out to be colonies--and many forms cannot survive at all unless they create colonies which operate as individuals....The laws of physics prevent them increasing in size, so they contrive greater efficiency by acting as a group."

Strictly speaking, the children of Midwich form two super spirits, a male and a female one (which can be deduced from the fact that the knowledge one boy gathers is at once available to all boys, not to the girls--and vice versa). This subdivision gives the narrative a future aspect similar to that in <u>Children of Light</u> (one of the leading characters terms both entities "Adam" and "Eve," 125); its possible effect, however, is more than counterbalanced by the children's overall appearance and their timely deaths.

The Midwich children appear to be much easier and clearer to recognize as "alien" than the offspring in Lawrence's novel; after all, their extraterrestrial, non-human origin seems to be indubitable. In reality John Wyndham, whom most critics and editors unfortunately label as a writer of pure science fiction,[10] has created a testing ground. It is not the kind of testing ground which an alien race may probe (93), but one where the author's complex philosophical conception is to be demonstrated, and one which is so full of clever traps that the reader must pay great attention not to be deceived by appearances. That the novel deals with serious problems which are only too human will be established in connection with the child-monster.

For the solitary child there exists a further method of avoiding the problem of ageing: the child simply refuses to grow older. In each case this is an act of exceptionally strong will-power, which may occasionally be reinforced by means of magical potions, secret sources of physical energy, and other aids. The boy or girl in question usually stops growing (physically and emotionally, but not always with regard to experience) at a certain point long before puberty. Very much like the hero of Günter Grass's novel <u>Die Blechtrommel</u>, the child does not want to have a share in the general corruption it can perceive in the adult world. Such an impertinent violation of the "rules" must of course offend grown-up people, and in horror fiction the consequences are disastrous. P. J. Plauger's story "Child of All Ages," for instance, deals with a small girl who has remained a child for hundreds of years, and who has therefore been dependent on a long series of foster-parents in the course of her lifetime. She has had to leave them all on her own account--not because they died, but because of the suspicions she has roused in each case by her extraordinary state. In the 1970's, however, living conditions seem to have become much more favorable to an "eternal" child, especially after she has met enlightened and unprejudiced people like the social worker and the chemist who adopt her. For the first time she dares to tell parents the whole truth about her nature and abilities. Her new family cannot quite understand why the girl deliberately renounces the "pleasures of adult life" (sex, above all); to their question as to how she can stand all the other "normal" children she is penned up with at school she explains that they behave like her, that all children are immortal--until they grow up.[11] The domestic harmony begins to crumble when the older members of the family become decrepit and do not believe the girl's affirmation that she cannot stop their process of ageing. Now the formerly "civilized" people behave worse than any medieval inquisitor and set modern hunters on her track: F.B.I. and C.I.A.

A writer who wants to arouse the reader's entire sympathy and compassion usually presents a group of children as a procession. This formation need not always have a religious connotation; beyond a feeling of uneasiness, at any rate, it evokes awe and reverence within the reader. The children in these cases are pure victims, innocent and immaculate. Because of these attributes people consider innate in small children every procession has something of a celebration about it.

In his story "The Happy Children" Arthur Machen takes full advantage of this effect in a very obtrusive and embarrassing manner. As in several of his other tales ("The Bowmen" serves as another bad example), Machen disguises political propaganda, sometimes even warmongering, beneath a supernatural, sensational plot. The fact that he makes his readers believe in an authentic account (some of his tales are the pseudo-comments of a reporter) introduces an additional aggravating factor. He gives, for instance, the assurance that all saints and angels—probably God himself—defend the holy cause of the British soldiers during World War I by sending them ghostly reinforcements against their wicked, godless enemies. The author superfluously hints at the ancient spirit of warfare and the fearless heroes of long ago; his whole method of incitement strikes the reader as utterly medieval.

The same might be said of the "Happy Children." Machen patches up a tedious frame for his one and only aim: he wants to shock his audience with the most innocent victims of warfare; but both victims and victimizers are simplistically defined. All of the brutal, relentless baby killers are German soldiers, whereas among the little ones not a single German child can be found. The narrator is on his way along the English coast on Christmas Day and has to spend the night in a sleepy harbor town. Having a stroll through the streets before supper, he comes across innumerable children who are merrily dancing and chanting in an apparently local dialect the narrator has never heard before. He asks the inn-keeper, who becomes frightened and tells him that, with their fathers at the front, the little ones are "running a bit wild."[12] Later, in the dead of night, he still sees the children, who are increasing in number and forming a gay procession that winds up a hill towards the abbey. Afterwards he remembers that this was the "Eve of the Holy Innocents," and is convinced that the children were the ghosts of innocent victims who wanted to celebrate their annual mass.

In contrast to the unimaginative framework, the description of the ghostly procession is very effective. The most impressive feature, which therefore appears in the title of the story, is the children's happiness, which seems to be totally incongruous with the cruelty of their deaths. First of all, their laughter and singing mean an acoustic contradiction to the deserted nocturnal town ("Hardly anyone was abroad in the streets; but all the courts and alleys seemed alive with children," 73). Furthermore, as indicated in the quotation, narrator and reader are initially confronted with the liveliest offspring ever seen, only to learn in the end that they are dead. This device, which is frequently made use of in ghost stories (the suspense in Rudyard Kipling's "They," Elizabeth Cleghorn Gaskell's "The Old Nurse's Story" or Sheridan LeFanu's "The Child Who Went With the Fairies" is nourished by it in similar ways), emphasizes another fact: through their deaths the children do not lose any of their "typical" traits; they remain the same cheerful, lighthearted creatures they were before. The crimes of other, adult people could not harm their souls, only their bodies. Their outward appearance forms a perfect contrast to their happiness as well—they all wear white robes, have scars on their throats, "dripping seaweed about their brows" (75); a tiny boy has a "dreadful wound above his heart," and (in obvious imitation of Jesus Christ) another child holds his hands wide apart, the palms "torn and bleeding, as if they had been pierced." The children's very happiness and the occasion on which they appear invite indignation and wrath. In former times these little boys and girls were cherished and celebrated as they deserved; now they are murdered, but the children bear their tormentors no grudge at all (they are too innocent for that), and thus it is up to the reader to condemn them.

As has been shown before, it is perfectly justifiable and conventional to present children as the victims of adult sins. In one basic respect Machen's story differs from other examples: the intended reader need not relate the accusation to himself, let alone feel remorse, unless he is German. Instead of giving his tale a universal meaning, the author deliberately picks out a certain group of guilty adults; it is clear that he thus deprives the story of any wider significance.[13]

Naturally, the children's crusade represents the most elaborate variety of the procession pattern. Apart from numerous realistic accounts about the historical crusade of 1212, there are several excellent variations on the theme in horror fiction. Marcel Schwob's adaptation of the original story deserves a special place in this context, since he expresses the children's victimization through symbolic vampirism.

"La Croisade des enfants" is a nightmarish symphony in red and white. It appeals to all the reader's senses, most of all to his vision, for the two dominant colors reappear throughout the whole story, suggesting the most different meanings. Visual effects occupy such a prominent position that one is inclined to call the work a painting rather than a literary product. The striking parallels to a musical opus must not be ignored, either. The story consists of eight "movements," rendered from eight different points of view; basically independent accounts in themselves, they are related to each other and the whole composition by the same recurrent imagery and, of course, the leitmotif. In addition, in both introduction and finale adult characters make their appearances ("solo" performances), whereas the very center is dedicated to a "choir" of three small children, to young pure voices.[14]

The famous case history of the seven thousand children who came together from all parts of Europe (on their way "versus Jherusalem, quaerere terram sanctam"[15]) and who perished by the hands of their adult Christian "brethren," died of hunger and disease, in shipwreck and slavery, is taken as the basis of Schwob's "Croisade." The author adheres closely to the historical facts and personages, but skillfully imparts new dimensions to them. He even succeeds in keeping the reader at a distance and simultaneously involving him in the events.

With the sole exceptions of the narrative of the three children and the "récit de la petite Allys," each of the component accounts presents the group of children as a strange formation whose feelings, motivations, origin and vocation no adult can fathom. This appears the more significant because the grown-up narrators (some of them are pseudo-correspondents) stem from heterogeneous social environments, differ remarkably in imaginative power and religious faith, and have contrasting attitudes toward the children. Most importantly, there are nuances in their physical contact with the procession. A mendicant friar watches them, and a leper even gets in touch with them, whereas two popes, Innocent III and Gregor IX, have only heard about them from their messengers.

To the author the story of the children's crusade provides an excellent basis for illustrating the rise and development of religious

aberration, as well the absurdity of seemingly "legitimate" beliefs.
For this purpose he makes use of "red" and "white." These simple
colors serve as examples since, like religion itself, they seem to
have the same unmistakable meaning for all human beings and to evoke
identical associations, but cause the most fatal misunderstandings instead. "White" in connection with the small children does in fact express purity, innocence, defencelessness and weakness (they are sucked
dry by a power beyond their comprehension); "red" mainly appears as a
synonym for blood. In order to take in the visual symbolism properly
one has to examine further objects connected with these colors and
trace their development.

    In the first part ("Récit du Goliard"), which is narrated by the
simple-minded, humble friar, the outward appearance of the "little
white children who bear the cross" (63) directly corresponds to Jesus,
who has "the color of lilies," but whose blood is crimson. To this
naive man the strange children are a miracle which deserves one's
deepest admiration; he does not ask their plans or their reasons and
simply accepts them. He believes that God will protect them and keep
them alive, as he makes the red and white flowers grow everywhere. But
even a simple soul like him has witnessed the cruelty of adult man,
who mutilates children and trains them to become beggars. It is significant that, however great his faith may be, he does not exclude the
possibility that God has not yet noticed these children, which implies
that not even the friar knows who has "sent" the mysterious nameless
creatures ("tous ces enfants m'ont paru n'avoir pas de noms," 62).

    The leper's story already brings radically novel aspects into the
red-and-white scheme. He identifies the little ones with Jesus, too
("Leurs corps étaient Son corps"--"Their bodies were His body," 65);
he even takes the biblical passage about the Lord's flesh and blood
too literally. Being an outcast who is forgotten by mankind and neglected by God till the day of Resurrection (64), he wants to drink
infant blood to purify his mortal body and re-enter the world of the
living. Despite the barbaric, "bloodthirsty" tone of his narrative,
this man is by no means a victimizer, and the vampirism he intends to
practice is by far not the worst form of exhausting a human being's
vital energy.

    On the contrary, the leper is a victim himself. He is the lone-
liest creature on earth, dreaded and loathed by others and tortured by
self-hate. Only his overwhelming desire for purity makes him attack
one of the white children, a boy with red hair. The leper himself is a
white being--clad in white, his head is covered by a white hood; with
his deformed white hands he does not dare to touch the red fruits he
lives on for fear of contaminating them. He considers his own whiteness a sign of punishment ("damnation pâle," 65), which corresponds to
the "paleness" of his sins. Only his teeth have retained their "natural whiteness." With these teeth the leper wants to bite the little
boy's throat, but his attempt is thwarted by the child's reaction: he
stays perfectly calm and placid and does not seem to notice the aggressor's disfigurement at all. Asked about his destination, he admits
that he does not know where Jerusalem is, but he knows for certain
that Jerusalem is the Lord and that the Lord is a white man, like the
leper. To the leper these naive words spoken by a pure being mean an
absolution from his sins ("Ma monstrueuse blancheur est semblable pour
lui à celle de son Seigneur"--"To him my monstrous whiteness resembles

that of his Lord," 66), and finally he, who bitterly laughed at the child's ignorance of his destination, protectively leads him through the dark forest.

In the secret prayer of Innocent III, which follows the leper's story, the author uses the etymological connection between the words "father" and "pope" as the basis of a play with names. Both Innocent and Gregor IX are historical persons, but within the narration the names conferred upon them have a deeper meaning. The priests are supposed to be the fathers and protectors of the faithful who are committed to their charge. Innocent, for one, does not live up to the obligation his name imposes upon him. In association with his person the color "white" means old age, which has drained him of both his physical strength and his enthusiasm and faith. His white vestments, his pale face and the bare white cell where he prays heighten the effect; to him even God's sun ("soleil" means "sun" and "monstrance") shines in a cold white. Neither the red sacramental wine, the blood of Jesus with which he tries to revive his exhausted body, nor the purple garments he wears outside the cell can regenerate him. Nonetheless he considers himself God's faithful and pure servant, even as innocent as a child ("mon coeur desseché est pur"--"my dried-up heart is pure," 71). He condemns the activities of the children as a devilish deception which disgraces the true religion. The Evil One, who likes to possess children, is obviously leading them to destruction like the Pied Piper of Hamelin (70). In reality, however, his "humble" prayer reveals that he is deeply envious of "those who do not know what they are doing" (71), of those who are pure without having to laboriously mortify their flesh and minds. He is also afraid that the children with their obviously foolish design could "shake the foundations of the Church," an institution which is as bloodless as its highest representative. Deep in his heart, however, he asks God (himself, that is) if the children have not possibly been given a sign which adult people cannot recognize; he even wonders if God wants his whiteness-- the whiteness of an old, experienced ruler--to become equal to that of an ignorant, weak child.

The "récit du Kalandar," the account of a Mohammedan beggar, shows the absurdity of religious fanaticism most clearly. Kalandar regards the little children as innocent, adorable superior beings as well, yet pities them because they are obviously "possessed by Satan" (80) and sent by the wicked infidels. They look like a herd of lambs (79), but Kalandar knows that they are not on their way to a butcher since the sultan, the ruler of all Faithful, has bought them to save their pure souls. Again the red-and-white imagery has a fundamental significance: the children are white, like the two white angels who once surrounded the sleeping prophet before he started his holy mission, and who opened his chest with a knife and drained all blood from his heart and intestines to purify him. The children have this superhuman purity, too.

The sinister nature of the children's vocation, however, becomes completely perceptible only in the children's own narrative. They were summoned in the dead of night by white voices which resembled the cries of dead birds in winter; at the same time they saw a multitude of dead little birds, whose throats were red, stretched on the snowy earth. The children are perfectly sure that the white voices will lead them safely through a territory full of red obstacles, ogres and werewolves; these are things only adults can fear, because they do not have the children's faith. The grown-ups, who either slander or pity them, are perfect strangers to the children. Among the little ones there is a blind boy who must be guided, but the others have to admit that they cannot see any more than he does. Nonetheless, they know that they are going to reach the Lord's tomb, and the white voices will rejoice in the night. They feel that Jerusalem, their white master, lies at the end of the water ("Et au bout de la mer se trouve Jérusalem," 74). They are quite right, but what they do not know, of course, is that for them the "end" will be the bottom of the sea.

The final part spoken by Gregor IX reveals his psychic reaction to the death of the majority of the children in the Mediterranean Sea. Having lost his faith, the Pope addresses the sea as a mediator between God and mankind, because he does not dare to blame everything on his God directly. He calls the "mer dévoratrice" an innocent-looking, treacherous nanny with many white mouths and a purple laugh (84-85). The sea has sucked in the children and betrayed God's confidence. Gregor feels, according to his name, like a member of the herd he is in charge of; he implores the sea to "give him back his children."

It is obvious that in Marcel Schwob's "Croisade des enfants" the vampiric influence that permeates the entire work implies a symbolic explanation for the religious mania which destroys the children. Among all the adults swept away by their ecstasy, no maniac is mad enough to go without a weapon and without the deepest mistrust of his fellow-Christians. Only the children take it for granted that the enthusiasm they experience everywhere must imply total confidence and trust in everyone and everything. They "do not know what they are doing"--and this is disastrous, because even the greatest zealots never totally ignore the evil world they live in.

The children in Bertolt Brecht's poem "Kinderkreuzzug 1939" are victims in quite a different regard. Genuine elements of horror in a piece by this author may seem astonishing,[16] but they serve his purpose admirably. The fifty-five children wandering through Poland form an uncanny lot, because they are so obviously not real children. The heroes of Schwob's narrative do not appear real, either, but in a different way: their group consists of identical units who act in accordance with the total movement. Brecht's children, on the other hand, are a motley company who--though it sounds absurd--seem to be individuals within their community because they are actually types, miniature representatives of all great adult associations naturally grown or founded on convention. Their respective "idiosyncrasies" are blended with the usual "childish" features to a degree which preserves the necessary homogeneity and prevents their falling apart. The children's relationship to adults invariably remains cold and detached, because the grown-ups are responsible for the chaos of war.

Poland is the starting-point of World War II and simultaneously that of the children's crusade. The author makes it clear that the fifty-five orphans and their fate are a direct projection of real wartime incidents; the reader already knows these events in detail, but is to look at them now from a totally different perspective. Children must play their parents' roles because the reader has become accustomed to the horrors of adult warfare; events that repeat themselves often enough seem to acquire the status of an institution, and only the perverse effect of children imitating their elders can stir his

dulled sense of indignation. Though the little ones are deeply involved in all the atrocities (as their victims), their presentation
leaves no doubt that they have a purely emblematic function. They are
removed in several ways: the narrator "retells" a legend he has heard
in the "eastern countries," which means that he has not personally
seen the mysterious children, but he can see other groups of children
in the sky, ghostly masses of infant victims who foreshadow other wars
and other sorrows to come.

In contrast to Schwob's crusaders, these children do not take up
their cross voluntarily; it is forced upon them by others. They are
not looking for great deeds to perform, either, all they want is a
land of peace. The adult part of each child bears a heavy guilt (the
"sins of the fathers"). There is, for instance, a taciturn little boy
who comes from a Nazi delegation and even holds himself somewhat apart
from his mates. The child part within each member of the group is the
redeeming factor which gives a playful, yet uniquely pathetic aura to
all their activities. By re-living their elders' crimes the children
at the same time accuse the adult offenders and alleviate their guilt,
for they take the edge off these acts in their particular manner. When
they bury a Jewish boy, the funeral procession significantly consists
of two little Germans and two Polish children; a Protestant, a Catholic, a Communist and the Nazi boy dig his grave together. Adult ceremonies are turned topsy-turvy: a trial is held at the end of which
the judge himself is found guilty. The little ones even begin a war
when they come across another group. They not only send their
"enemies" provisions, but soon stop fighting altogether for want of a
convincing reason.

The ending of the poem is pessimistic. The children have the best
intentions, but they do not know the way (the adults have turned round
all the signposts to mislead their enemies); depending on the grown-
ups at last, who have never been reliable, they must inevitably
perish. The dog they send out to bring help is the only being who
knows their whereabouts. He dies of starvation before he can make any
adult follow him.

A funeral procession of small children makes the final tableau of
Ida A. Wylie's "Witches' Sabbath," a story which shows important parallels to Brecht's poem. Though it does not explicitly describe a
crusade, it deals with a heavy cross the children have to bear. In a
small Bavarian town a very special kind of passion play unfolds itself, but the town is not Oberammergau, and the play ends in dead
earnest. The story includes a marvelous recapitulation of all the
social relationships that have been discussed so far. The protagonist,
a small Jewish boy, stands out from the rest of his coevals because of
his religion and descent. At first, however, he is by no means an out-
sider--just a special boy who is beloved by everybody. All his acquaintances think he is destined for an exceptional career, for he is
bright and gentle; the nature of his special mission only becomes
clear in the very end.

The action begins around Christmas time. Everything seems peaceful and idyllic, the social order is still intact and harmonious: all
inhabitants, the Jewish family and their Christian neighbors, even
children and adults, form one community. Beni, the little Jew, represents and defends the honor of his town in a school contest and is
celebrated like a hero. His parents, who sell Christmas tree decora-

tions in their shop, fulfill the boy's greatest wish and buy him a
tree, too. Everybody is convinced that this gesture smooths away all
differences.

The shadows which hover over the town and its inhabitants are already perceptible at this point of the narration. According to a
child's point of view, the dark powers that take possession of Vogel-
stadt are fairytale creatures, witches, ogres, and flocks of evil
black birds. Even on Christmas Eve, the "silent night," they are
lurking in the mountains around the town and waiting to rush upon
their unsuspecting prey. A good-natured boy like Beni who senses danger in the atmosphere must of course ascribe his foreboding to something "outside." After all, on the inside everything is so obviously
in good order. Therefore, the wicked fiends of his bedside stories
(the only evil he has ever learned of) become the projections of his
anguished mind. Black wings soon fill the air, and wherever the shadow
of the birds falls it seems to put a spell on people and transform
them mysteriously.

Beni has a faithful girlfriend with whom he frequently plays;
they always pretend to be a brother and sister in the dark wood[17] who
are hunted by the witch. Their play always ends well, because each
time there is a good fairy at hand. In reality, however, their relationship is put to a severe test. When the placatory, innocent snow of
Christmas has melted and the landscape is brown, bleak and desolate,
strange brown people arrive to introduce a new way of living. Their
emblem is a cross which is oddly bent out of shape (239). These men
have not come to congratulate Beni on his success, as he falsely pre-
sumes, but to inform the inhabitants that a pest like him is to be
shunned from now on. At once there occurs a total change in the social
order. The Jewish family has become non-existent (even to Beni his
parents appear like dead people who have not yet had time to fall,
230). Children and adults still form one group, because they are all
under the "spell of the birds;" only Beni has no one to cling to and
is exposed to a long series of humiliations and injuries. After his
final, climactic attempt to rejoin his former play-mates has ended in
a disaster, the others can sense a quiet determination within him
which makes them shrink back.

The children, whose voices resemble the flight of birds ("little
birds with sharp claws," 239), become afraid of his patience and meekness. Beni, who was celebrated and adored at Christmas and is now
heading for the meadow where the Easter lambs play, redeems the little
ones and takes the evil spell from them. When he is gone, the unity of
adults and children undergoes a complete reorganization. Two groups
are formed now—on the one hand the children, those who are free from
the spell, on the other hand the adults, whose guilt separates them
from their offspring.

Beni's girlfriend is the first child who is reunited with him.
She finds his body in the nearby river; her description suggests that
the boy's former "sister" has turned into a pietà. The rest of the
children carry the corpse back to town, through a wood where the birds
are silent now. They scrutinize their parents like strangers and dis-
miss them as "meaningless shadows" (247). They form a wall and do not
allow any adult person to touch Beni, whose body, though small, is in-
credibly heavy. When the procession is moving through the sunlight,
every grown-up can perceive that the children are untouchable (248).

"Witches' Sabbath" is a story which is determined by a constant change of attractions and repulsions; finally, however, the well-known two-group system prevails. The same applies to Julian Gloag's novel <u>Our Mother's House</u>, which is full of religious imagery as well. The principle that orphans prefer their dead parents to any living adult forms the basis of this work. Seven little brothers and sisters are the protagonists of this novel. In total contrast to the vast majority of horror stories and novels, each of the children has an exceedingly complex character. These idiosyncrasies are not static, either; within the single year that lies between their mother's death and their commitment to the orphanage they develop individually and form different overlapping sub-groups. The sociological aspect of the novel is interesting: the internal groupings largely depend on the children's contact with the adults they meet, and in the end it becomes clear that these are phases necessary for their finding out about their true selves and the identity of the whole group of children.

The gloomy story really begins when the little ones try to conceal the death of their bedridden mother from the outside world and from their own innermost understanding. Though her watch has stopped in the minute of her death,[18] the children want to go on living as if nothing has happened. The first steps they take are sending away their curious charwoman and building a tabernacle on the secret grave in the garden. Unconsciously trying to keep up the previous hierarchy, they cause their "mother" to give them instructions through one of their sisters, who functions as a medium. Everything which shows a connection with their mother receives a metaphysical meaning--"Mothersmell" and "Mothertime" are just two examples of their new religious vocabulary. Their unguided childish fervor makes them display a rigidity which by far surpasses the mother's, who, as a vicar's daughter, simply liked to read out passages from the Bible and interpret them. The little medium soon becomes a kind of high priestess, whereas one of the boys acts as a prophet and executor; both of them exert such intolerable pressure upon the others--all in the name of their mother--that the smallest boy is led to decide, "I hate Mother--she's cruel" (96). The musty tabernacle, filled with the mother's furniture and accessories, becomes the permanent center of life, and the medium soon ceases to "read about Jesus any more" (77), but prefers the <u>Old Testament</u> instead. The first death is the inevitable consequence of this development. The five-year-old Gerty is mercilessly punished for committing a sacrilege; she followed a man and allowed him to molest her after telling her to <u>pretend he was her daddy</u>. Gerty is apparently branded as a "harlot," but deep in their hearts the others mainly resent her wish to join another living adult. She eventually dies from the effects of the treatment, because "Mother" does not like doctors, and thus the first evil contact with a grown-up indirectly causes destruction.

Only the nine-year-old Hubert, from whose point of view the whole novel is narrated, never becomes infected by the others' excesses, but tries to follow his own line of conduct. He really becomes a sensible, responsible "little man;" this is foreshadowed by the fact that he has his first erection while he digs his mother's grave--when he thrusts his spade into Mother Earth ("gradually he and the spade seemed to become one moving thing drawing its power from the hard pulsating centre," 47). He has to do all the housework on his own for quite a

time, because his brothers and sisters neglect such mundane affairs
and grow more and more apathetic. Hubert instinctively knows that the
futile, dogged mother-worship drains the children's vital energy, and
begins to look out for surrogate parents--first unconsciously (he
thinks about asking in the neighbor, a policeman, even three ladies
lounging at the street corner, not knowing they are whores), then deliberately by sending his mother's husband a letter. This man's existence has always been hushed up; none of the children even knows him.
Meanwhile, the situation is changed through the arrival of a
small boy who has left his own parents on purpose to live with the
children. This flesh-and-blood boy gives them a real duty and at once
destroys the mystic bond to their mother; though he is formally
"adopted" by her in the tabernacle, the medium sadly admits to Hubert
that she has had to make up everything herself. The new brother has
much in common with the others. He possesses something dead and
beloved at his mother's place: an ammonite ("'How can it be stone, if
it's an animal?'--'That's what happens. It dies, then slowly it
becomes petrified,'" 148). The children do not allow anyone to take
him away again.
At this point the reader gets the unique opportunity to look at
the children's concentrated defence from their own point of view. When
their teacher comes for the new member of the group, they defy her as
one. Hubert's order to go away is repeated like an incantation ("'Go
away, go away, go away.' They made it into a chant of violence that
swept Miss Deke's words away," 155-56). The reader has long become
completely involved in the children's way of life; he can understand
the "murderous fury" of these "unnatural" (156) creatures, for whom
the adult is an unwanted intruder. On the other hand, he is also able
to comprehend the teacher's terror. He witnesses the woman's reaction
to the en masse presentation he is normally confronted with himself.
Since he is an "insider" in this particular case, he can collect new
"voyeuristic" insights here.
It is significant that the children's father enters the same
moment they try to expel their enemy. He at once assumes a role which
he continues to play till the very end; by seemingly protecting the
children from other adults--non-relatives--he strengthens his own
position from the start. The little ones can even be persuaded that
their "adoptive brother" has to be sent away for the family's sake.
Though they must never call him "Dad" ("'Dad' makes me feel like an
institution," 157), the children one by one succumb to his attraction,
whereas the remnants of their mother's spell are destroyed in the same
measure. Catching each other in the garden, the former high priestess
and the newcomer get closer than ever; the girl even surrenders physically to the man, while her smallest brother may commit a desecration
without punishment ("on the roof of Mother's tomb Willy danced in
time," 186). Even Hubert is captivated and excuses his father when he
has the tabernacle torn down in secret.
The children's abrupt disillusionment becomes the more violent.
They could put up with their father's drinking, smoking, gambling and
boasting, but he has infinitely more wicked surprises in store for
them. Together with another adult who should have friendlier intentions (Mrs. Stork, the "stork" who helped to bring the children into
the world as a midwife), he squanders their last pecuniary resources,
for which he has come in the first place, and then tries to sell their

house over their heads and put them in an orphanage.

By underestimating the children's combined strength and will-power he provokes his doom, and the last blow he strikes them is his own death-blow. Slowly stripping himself of all the qualities the children adored in their father is bad enough; when he unveils the true nature of their sacred mother (who conceived each of them from a different father), his most faithful idolator, Hubert, slays him with a poker. This murder is by no means determined by blind rage; it is a cold, deliberate act of resuming power ("The brass knob was cool as a golden pomegranate, and the sceptre was heavy," 257). Though the children have forfeited their independent existence, they have learned now that absolute solidarity is necessary to face the evil adult world, and they are confident: "'We've got each other. That's enough, isn't it?'"

FRIENDS, FOES, AND ALLIES

Children and Beasts

And one day, out of Heaven knows what material, he spun the
beast a wonderful name, and from that moment it grew into a
god and a religion. The Woman indulged in religion once a
week at a church near by, and took Conradin with her, but to
him the church service was an alien rite in the House of
Rimmon. Every Thursday, in the dim and musty silence of the
tool-shed, he worshipped with mystic and elaborate ceremo-
nial before the wooden hutch where dwelt Sredni Vashtar, the
great ferret.

Saki, "Sredni Vashtar"[1]

Children and animals are connected in manifold, complicated ways.
The basic reason for the popularity of all these combinations is an
extremely simple one, which has been hinted at before: adults like to
put children on the same primeval level as subhuman creatures, because
both are equally incomprehensible to their refined intellect. Roughly
speaking, adulthood is synonymous with "civilization" (or at least the
thin veneer of decency which mercifully covers man's savage nature),
whereas childhood means rich, untamed life based on instinct and unspoiled by the ballast of education. A child's close contact with a
wild animal does not always imply that they are on good terms (the
child may in fact be terribly afraid of the beast); such relations,
however, always signify that the child is familiar with the Beast in
human nature. Still at the very roots of humanity, the child is
directly exposed to a being that is quite insufficiently buried in its
parents and which they have chosen to ignore. There are many ways in
which the Beast may influence a child, and within the plot of a story
the interaction between beast and child functions as the simple but
impressive outward projection of the processes within the human being
at the dawn of its life. Of course evil can assume the most different
physical shapes, according to the particular animal "traits of
character" which are required in the respective story. Thus, a whole
menagerie of savage beasts and not-quite-domestic animals is provided
to keep the little ones company.
    Regardless of each animal's size, shape, and behavior, the rela-
tionship between child and brute always emphasizes the separation of
children and adults. Whether children try to make use of beasts to
kill their parents, or whether parents helplessly watch their offspring being brutalized by savage creatures, children and animals inhabit a sphere no grown-up can enter. In many cases this separation is
additionally expressed through a shift of place: the human offspring
prefer to live with their companions in a shed rather than stay in the
comfortable domain of their strange parents.
    The famous story "Sredni Vashtar" by Saki (alias Hector Hugh
Munro) introduces several basic peculiarities which recur frequently
in this sub-genre. As in most stories dealing with such relationships,

the protagonist is a solitary child. This can be explained by the simple fact that it is much more likely to depend on a non-human helper than a whole group are. In order to point out the complex nature of this special relationship--which, by the way, is a perfectly unilateral one--the author here employs the stream-of-consciousness technique; though this occurs repeatedly (especially whenever a child creates forms of religious and semi-religious worship), it is by no means a general rule to show the child's point of view. Saki himself, who wrote several other stories in which children intend to kill their enemies with the help of animals (using them as tools, however, instead of imploring them as deities), does not seem interested at all in the psyche of the rest of his child protagonists. Conradin, the hero in the story under discussion, is the outcome of his only attempt to create something like a child-character.

If the reader were not given the possibility to read Conradin's thoughts, he could never properly conceive the development of a religion for the weak and defeated, which is the main topic of the story. Conradin is a frail, sickly ten-year-old; the doctor has "pronounced his professional opinion that the boy would not live another five years,"[2] which implies that he will not survive childhood and thus never have a chance to take revenge on his tormentors with weapons other than those of a child--patience, hope against hope, and a considerable amount of cunning. The child in horror fiction must always make up for its physical disadvantages by trying means of its own; the beast sometimes functions as the physical executor of the child's mental design.

A being like the great ferret cannot simply be manipulated by punishment and reward. Though kept in a cage, Sredni Vashtar is a perfectly independent, unpredictable creature, representing precisely those traits of character Conradin desires for himself ("he was a God who laid some special stress on the fierce impatient side of things," 137). It is not difficult to recognize that Conradin's relations to the ferret imply an intercourse with the savage, bloodthirsty side of his own character. Before the "Woman," his cousin and guardian, maliciously destroys the other inhabitant of the tool-shed, a "ragged-plumaged" (137), sickly hen, Conradin is "dreadfully afraid of the lithe, sharp-fanged beast." When the weak hen, the vulnerable, defenceless pendant of the beast (and the Beast, of course) is killed, the secret inhabitant of Conradin's dwelling becomes the sole ruler. It is significant that the good side of the boy's nature has had to be protected by iron bars from its evil neighbor, who could easily have swallowed it in one bite. Any fundamental struggle between the two halves of Conradin's soul, like any shift of affection on the boy's side, is thwarted from outside. After the Woman has deliberately extinguished one component, she must take the consequences and face its liberated partner. Expecting an outburst of grief and sorrow because of the hen's death, she is both disappointed and, for the first time, frightened of her charge ("something perhaps in his white set face gave her a momentary qualm," 138). All tender emotions have been destroyed with the hen; now Conradin no longer feels fear of, but only for the embodiment of his darker side. Now he is no longer content with adoration, either; he wants his master to do something for him.

The Woman is Conradin's deadly enemy because she represents to him everything that is antagonistic to his own nature ("those three-

fifths of the world that are necessary and disagreeable and real,"
136)--the other two-fifths, he and his imagination, have to struggle
desperately not to succumb prematurely to the necessities of reality
which his approaching illness and death will bring along. The final
revenge, carried out by Sredni Vashtar, accordingly takes place on two
levels: in Conradin's imagination, and in reality. Within the story,
however, reality means the logical extension of the animal symbolism
rather than a plausible chain of events. While the Woman enters the
shed, rightly suspecting that there is still something going on in the
boy's domicile, the reader stays with Conradin in the main house. He
is confronted with the boy's fervent prayers and awaits the Woman's
death through the sheer concentration of Conradin's will-power. The
real facts rather seem to contradict the final result: the cage is
still shut when she enters, and one can hardly imagine how a creature
as small as a ferret can kill a grown-up woman. But, after all,
Conradin has opened the cage in his imagination and freed the Beast,
and this new energy, finally released, is deadly enough.

The ferret belongs to a group of animals which is exceedingly
popular in connection with children--rodents. They are endowed with
several striking attributes that clearly explain their preference;
they are small (like children), and generally considered cunning and
smart. Above all, most adults loathe ferrets, rats, bats and their
kind. It is evident that the gap between children and adults becomes
even greater (and the child appears stranger than ever) if the little
ones set their hearts on "ugly" creatures whose mere existence means
an offence to their elders.

The children's affection for their four-legged companions may
also be brought about by their parents' repulsion--and/or the perverse
attraction which lies in the repulsive features of an animal. Such a
feature, for instance, is the rodent's thirst for blood. Another ferret, the hero of Patricia Highsmith's "Harry: A Ferret" (from her
anthology The Animal-Lover's Book of Beastly Murder), points out a
frequent connotation of this characteristic--a conversation between
the boy who cares for Harry and a friend gives the most obvious clue:
"'I have a new friend,' Roland said, putting on a voice with a foreign
accent. 'He has claws and drinks blood. Guess what he is?'--'A--a vampire?'"[3] Indeed, children and beasts often enter into vampiric bonds.
In each of these cases the child feeds the animal with its own blood,
a deed which symbolizes the fact that the child mentally and emotionally succumbs to the spell of the beast. At the same time the child
expects its partner to take its own place and act as a vampire to destroy parents and other adult enemies. This "vampirism by proxy"
reaches its most elaborate form if the bestial friend is a bat, but in
Harry's case every detail fits in the pattern as well.

Harry's owner, Roland, is obsessed by his subconscious desire for
revolution, for shaking off all forms and representatives of parental
authority. His very first contact to the ferret reveals both to him
and the reader that the two are made for each other; when the animal
bites the boy with its needle-like teeth, Roland is so fascinated by
the sight of his own blood that he is ready to pay any price for the
ferret. He buys it in a cage and seems still to be satisfied to only
look at it; yet the initial bite has already triggered off an inevitable development. The beast even has the suitable shape for a miniature conspirator and assassin (it can "hunch itself into a very short

length as if its body were made like an accordion," 189). At first
there is no urgent reason for a war strategy. Roland is not allowed to
keep his pet in his private sanctuary in the house, but quite readily
transfers his headquarters to the wood that surrounds it, which is the
ferret's original domain. The boy is convinced that he is the master
of the beast; the mere shift of place, however, indicates the real
distribution of powers. Roland feels doubly attracted by blood: out of
his innate sadism, and because of his indistinct realization that
blood means life, freshness, and youth. The sheer "primitiveness" of a
ferret's life excites him, especially their "falling asleep, often
close to their victims for warmth, after they had drunk the blood of
their prey" (193). When the elderly factotum (who is "so aged as to be
a joke to Roland, something left over from another century and mysteriously still alive," 189) is bitten by the beast, Roland is deeply
astonished at the undreamt-of possibility of drawing blood from such
an "old creature."

    After several manifestations of its savage nature the beast
(which Roland meanwhile literally keeps close to his heart) is to be
disposed of. It is the factotum, the personification of everything
Roland is rebelling against, who opens the cage to let the beast loose
in the wood. The dark side of Roland's nature is set free at the same
moment, though the boy, who still regards the ferret as his tool, confuses cause and effect. During Harry's struggle with the servant,
which ends in the old man's death, Roland believes that he is manipu-
lating the movements of the beast. In reality he is a slave to the
wild thing, which falls instantly and peacefully asleep after it has
torn out the man's throat, since it can be sure that it will be attended to by the boy--now and in their common future. While the boy is
obediently burying the corpse, he thinks about new ways of "using" his
partner in crime. Brimful of blood, the beast feels "as heavy as a
pistol" (202) in Roland's hand--but Roland is unaware that he does not
have his finger on the trigger.

    "Hamsters vs Websters," from the same collection by Patricia
Highsmith, deals with another case of mental vampirism. It is highly
significant that although the overall topic of the book is the war between animals and men, children always "betray" their adult fellow-
humans and their own origin as soon as the battle starts. Furthermore,
it is quite important that the majority of stories are narrated from
the viewpoint of the respective animal protagonist. On the other hand,
precisely those stories that deal with a union of beasts and children
are told through the eyes of the child. Children and animals are thus
clearly marked as congenial creatures who have the same status, share
many physical attributes and often follow the same sinister instincts.

    The attack of the rodents in the tale under discussion symbolizes
once again the basic conflict between civilization and nature. The
father of ten-year-old Larry is the prototype of Civilized Man (a successful sales manager who has his first heart attack at thirty-seven);
when he moves to the countryside for "recreation," he is already planning to cultivate the landscape, too. Larry is meanwhile breeding hamsters in enormous quantities. To avoid his parents' suspicion he sets
several groups of them free in the garden. He wants to become the
great "protector of hamsters" (173) and create his own institution
called Hamster Heaven. By giving his animal friends a new home outside
he helps to undermine the domain of his parents, in every sense of the

word. Soon the ground is so honeycombed that one can hardly walk on it without sinking into one of the hidden holes. The boy assists nature to reclaim the territory which civilization has estranged from it, and his father blames him for that: "Larry, you take the cake for destroying property! Your own property!" (178)

Of course modern man cannot tolerate such a challenge, especially not if the only direct enemies he sees are tiny vermin. Larry's father does not know what he provokes when he decides to build a swimming-pool in the battlefield (which ironically is to have a "boomerang shape," 170). Though excavators and exterminators are involved in the affair, he feels personally insulted and fully responsible for a solution. Like a madman he hobbles from hole to hole to smoke out his enemies one by one. The hamsters of course grow more and more furious in the general confusion, while Larry tries to summon his "army" to defend themselves. Both he and the beasts concentrate their efforts on Larry's father. As soon as it gets dark, the man literally has to pay his debt to nature: the "nocturnal" (172) creatures emerge from the earth and attack him savagely. In the hospital no blood transfusion can save him--because his jugular vein has been pierced in two places.

The vampirism in David Grant's story "The Bats" is not restricted to subtle symbolic indications as in the above example; neither is the social criticism that lies beneath. Again the parents of eight-year-old Mervyn are the ones who must take the blame for the separation from their son--both for their physical distance and their emotional estrangement. When they let him have the old wooden hut in the garden where they usually keep their "junk," they explain this abandonment with their wish to make an independent, self-sufficient boy of him. In reality they want to get rid of him in a "pleasant" way to have time for their various amusements. At first the boy is indeed perfectly content in his own realm: he accordingly starts raising harmless little animals, which even please his indifferent parents. They are far more pleased with the convenient development of the situation and leave their home every night without telling their son.

An accident harshly confronts Mervyn with the true extent of his loneliness. This incident explains the revulsion of his feelings and his later vampiric tendency. Having severely injured himself during the work for his good-natured charges, he longs for his parents' help and finds the house "in darkness."[4] Since he is indeed a "self-suffi-cient" boy, he manages to apply a makeshift bandage to his injured hand before losing consciousness, but only after he has left a trail of his blood in his parents' empty world. Dressing his wound, he has watched his blood "dripping out of his life" (36), and from now on his hand hangs "clawlike" by his side. Of course he secretly vows revenge on his parents ("they had no idea then of the punishment their son had in store for them," 37).

The reader is right to expect a radical change in the composition of Mervyn's menagerie. Immediately after the shock of his life the boy hides some new and special guests in a corner of his hut. According to their different disposition, these creatures of the night, a flock of bats, inhabit the dark side of Mervyn's domain, which is separated from the rest by a curtain. Mervyn cares for his favorites with affection ("He could not feel them, but he knew that there were two tiny wounds there, wounds he was pleased to have. After all, his friends must feed," 39). Yet he still confines himself to nurture for its own sake, without having any plans for his beasts.

Feeling the boy's unwonted condescension and frostiness, Mervyn's parents think of getting their son back by destroying his hut and his animals, the outward sign of his independent mind. Though they realize how terrible the loss must be for him ("'They're his whole life now. If we took them away he'd have nothing left!'" 38), they intend to deliberately cripple him one more time in order to make him dependent again ("'Of course he'd have something left: us,'" 38). Their last scruples are put aside when they notice the marks on Mervyn's throat, his "luminous pallor" and growing listlessness. They cannot tolerate that their son willingly sacrifices the very same vital energy to his friends which they drained from him through their carelessness. When they finally do decide to demolish the boy's refuge, he must defend his personality and strike first, giving his bats two new hosts on which to feed.

Three years before the publication of his celebrated vampire novel I Am Legend (1954), Richard Matheson wrote an original little story entitled "Drink My Blood." Though the relationship between Jules, the small hero of the tale, and the vampire bat he comes across at the zoo has a rather drastic ending, the ironic undertones make it perfectly clear that the work is, above all, an excellent satire. Nevertheless, it contains most of the basic peculiarities that also mark the preceding examples.

In his early childhood Jules already differs considerably from his coevals. His blank stare, pale skin, frail body and his "unnatural," coarse guttural tongue make people recoil from him, and even his doctor assures his parents that there is indeed something special about him ("He told them that Jules, with his largehead might be a genius or an idiot. It turned out he was an idiot"[5]). The first word he utters at the age of five is "death," and from then on he invents his own catalogue of words ranging from "nighttouch" to "killove." Apart from that, however, he is never involved in any scandal; like other healthy children he merely practices vivisection on his pets or undresses little girls. His first contact to Count Dracula (on the screen and in the book) shows him the direction of his hitherto vague but violent longing. After he has read out a composition in class--"My Ambition, by Jules Dracula" ("'When I grow up I want to be a vampire,'" 166)--people start to remember that they have always guessed at his "true" nature.

The main topic of the story is Jules' search for his own personality and for a new parent. Although his peregrinations are somewhat ridiculously enwrapped in the vampiric plot, one can still perceive a touch of pathos beneath. The only fact Jules knows for sure is that his real, human parents are not quite the company he enjoys. Communication, either with them or with his teacher, is impossible, and thus he prefers the monster on the screen to his next of kin, since unlike his parents the Count does not appear to be a stranger to him. His encounter with the bat does not work out the way it usually does (at least in the stories mentioned before), for the bat is just an ordinary bat, not the Count in disguise, and Jules is just an ordinary, though overstrung boy. Correspondingly, the horror in this story is not so much based on the child's wish to devote his life to an evil power, but on the fatal misunderstanding which costs his life. The reader is continuously aware that the "superior" being Jules has found after his desperate search ("He looked in alleys. He looked in garbage cans. He looked in lots. He looked on the east side and the west side and in the middle," 167) is a very profane creature. The circumstances under which the feeding takes place do not seem appropriate to the solemn event, either. Jules, however, who has left his "snoring," unwitting parents for good and, after the first bite of the bat, happily believes that he is already transformed ("He couldn't go home. He had to have a place," 169), behaves as though in trance.

The clash between the real world as described by the narrator and the boy's feverish ecstasy is the main source of the gruesome impression the climactic scene evokes in the reader. There is not a vestige of the sinister romanticism that usually accompanies a vampiric initiation ceremony; Jules and his bat retire to a "little deserted shack" full of "rubble and tin cans and soggy cardboard and excrement" (169), and Jules must--all against the common rule--open his jugular vein himself with a penknife and force the beast to drink. In the same measure as his life-blood flows out of him, the veils of illusion are drawn from his mind; he realizes for a moment that he is merely "lying half-naked on garbage and letting a flying bat drink his blood" (171). In the end, however, his imagination, strengthened through the weakness of his approaching death, provides him with the object of his longing: the "real" father of "Jules Dracula," who gently lifts the child from the ground and accepts him as his son. In this unorthodox manner death unites him with the being he loves more than his parents.

Apart from the numerous boys who have contact to rodents, there exist all forms of unions with domestic animals, which basically fulfill the same function. One of Saki's favorites, for instance, is the pig. Though the ordinary pig may at first sight not show any spectacular traits, Saki and several other writers make ingenious use of this animal, taking advantage of the common notion that it is just fat, ugly, stupid, and made to be eaten. The way they present it is the more perverse because the very degeneration of the pig seems to account for other, more unpleasant sides of its nature, such as cannibalism. The influence of civilization has made this animal more bestial than its ancestors, and children like to employ it as a weapon whenever they fight against civilized adult man. After all, pigs and men have many things in common, including an omnivorous inclination.

One can observe that the presentation of a child greatly depends on the nature of its animal companion. Rodents, for example, are never depicted as stupid or slow-witted; in their presence children usually appear inferior and exposed to their friends' whims. They do not entirely control the evil powers they have raised. Pigs, on the other hand, are both an equivalent of civilized man and a tool with which to threaten him; in this function they can certainly be dominated by the children who make use of them. Saki's story "The Penance," for instance, deals with this possibility. It simultaneously presents several other creatures, whose mutual enmity and destruction form the basis of the action and a parallel to the relationships of the human beings involved. The adult protagonist, Octavian, is deep in his heart a very gentle person, but when he has to kill a cat in order to protect his own "poor helpless chickens"[6] from its raids, he has to endure the silent reproach of its three little owners. His own remorse ("It had been a distasteful and seemingly ruthless deed, but circumstances had demanded the doing of it," 422) is disproportionately aggravated by their behavior. The gap between him and the children is symbolized by the "long blank wall" that divides his property from theirs; indeed, Octavian comes up against a blank wall whenever he tries to reconcile with them. Immediately after he has committed the crime, the children's faces appear over the wall, only to demonstrate another perfect example of the way children are described when they form a group of hostile strangers: "Three white set faces were looking down at him, and if ever an artist wanted a threefold study of cold human hate, impotent yet unyielding, raging yet masked in stillness, he would have found it in the triple gaze that met Octavian's eye" (423). Most significantly in this context, the only word the children spit out at him is "Beast."

The offspring in their strangeness are really the ones who are presented as brutal creatures. Once again their "childish" features, which are completely misinterpreted by the unsuspecting Octavian, create this impression. Octavian tries to lure them with his own baby daughter, who becomes a helpless object in the hands of the children. The adult notes "with delight" the growing interest that dawns "in that hitherto sternly hostile quarter" (424); he gladly picks some flowers for his opponents ("Child-like, they had asked for what lay farthest from hand," 425)--and, returning, finds the blank wall "blanker and more deserted than ever" and his daughter gone. The children have taken her to the piggery to throw her to the pigs, and they are fully conscious of what they are doing: with their inexorable "child-logic" they declare, "We shall be very sorry when we've killed Olivia, but we can't be sorry till we've done it" (426). After long negotiations Octavian can save his daughter's life, but not before he has promised to spend a night by the grave of the cat and repeat the words, "I'm a miserable Beast."

In another of his stories, "Hyacinth," Saki also depicts a case of blackmail committed with the assistance of pigs. This incident is at least as impressive as the preceding one; it concerns a small boy who is to take part in an election campaign as a mere public attraction, but settles the outcome of this election on his own. Hyacinth, who seems to "serve as a model for any seraph-child" (519), outwardly initially represents his father's naval career ("the new sailor suit...is just in the right shade of blue for our election colours, and it will exactly match the blue of his eyes," 519). By his later demeanor he exaggerates and unveils the true machinery of adult policy, which means that he indeed represents his elders in an unexpected way. Under the grown-up spectators' "delighted eyes" he gives sweets to the children of his father's rival. When the election is in full swing he kidnaps them and threatens to throw the offspring to a huge sow whose rage he has already stirred for this purpose. Basically he follows the identical motives which determine the adult politicians' behavior (though, in this special situation, the father of the hostages desperately wishes not to have the majority); Hyacinth, however, acts out his primitive drives in actual warfare and does not cover them under the rites of civilization. Neither does he disguise himself any longer ("his angel smile exchanged for a look of demoniacal determination," 521). How well he has represented the true spirit of contest becomes clear in the end, when the boy's relatives, despite their embarrassment, declare him not altogether unfit for politics.

Apart from entering into alliances with beasts, children themselves can be identified with certain animals. The hero in Robert
Bloch's "The Funnel of God" suffers from a trauma because his last
name is Wolf. Both he and his playmates regard him as the personification of his name and treat him accordingly--especially after they have
all seen a cartoon about the Three Little Pigs: "his little American
playmates insisted on calling him 'The Big Bad Wolf' when they innocently ganged up on him at recess and tried to emulate the punishments
inflicted by the heroic little pigs in the film."[7] This picture does
more harm to him than The Wolf Man and all its sequels. His name makes
a welcome victim of him, although (at least in a psychiatrist's opinion) the other children's aggressions are basically aimed at someone
else: "a child unconsciously identified with the small animal who destroyed the larger tormentor; the bigger creature symbolized Daddy or
Mama or some authority-figure, and it was satisfying to witness their
defeat" (305).

Children can literally become animals, as in Brian Lumley's nasty
tale "David's Worm." Though it seems quite insignificant at first
sight--just a long chain of ghastly killings--the story has a high
symbolic value, which will be still easier to recognize if one recap-
itulates the essential elements pointed out so far. Little David's
father is a scientist who, above all, carries out experiments with
animals he has treated with atomic radiation (in other words, he tries
to manipulate the laws of nature). He is even a celebrated genius in
his field of research, a representative of the whole scientific world.
Just as (real) scientists like him are confident that the mutations
they bring about are perfectly harmless and under human control, the
tiny worm David takes with him seems to be dead already. David, the
worthy descendant of a family of scholars, has inherited a profound
fascination for biology, but his love for "Flatty," the worm, is not
the sterile interest of his father. David wants to revive the professor's creature and cannot foresee the consequences: in his new
"nutritive liquid," a nearby pond which has been filled by an adjacent
rivulet in the course of nine months, the seemingly dead worm is
restored to life and develops uncontrollably.

Through the effect of the radiation Flatty has gained new abilities; whenever it devours another creature it takes over the intelligence and instincts, even the personality of its victim. The incredible speed with which the worm grows, eating one organism after the
other on an ascending scale, must be understood in several ways: it
demonstrates that nature always strikes back with overwhelming force,
and it is an equivalent of the rapidity with which an embryo goes
through all the phases of its evolutionary history. Having repeated
the development of animal life, and having gained the necessary size
for taking action, the worm (which is actually, among many other
animals, a worm and a small carp and a large pike and a dog) attacks a
human being. The special assimilating nature of the creature also symbolizes two things: nature seems to be cruel because its basic principle is eating and being eaten; the voracious beast, however, is not
merely the winner of the struggle for survival, but a conglomeration
of the many varieties of animal life which face the last link in the
evolutionary chain, Man, as one single enemy. When David comes to the
pond and, trustingly extending his hands to Flatty, exhibits all the
weakness of humanity, he is devoured by the creature he has revived.

The grotesque climax of the story emphasizes once more the most important principle in the relationship between children and parents. David has "changed sides" by becoming a part of the beast; he and his parents can no longer reach each other. This does not mean that David tries to avoid contact; on the contrary, his attempt to approach his parents shows the real extent of their separation. He is now an animal (or the animal is him), but his memories and habits make the worm act the way David would behave. His unwitting parents loathe the creature that has entered their home and kill it by stuffing it into the kitchen stove. Its affectionate touch has caused them great damage, because David's new "skin" consists of acid. The greatest shock awaits them after they have found their son's bed deserted. Now David's mother remembers having heard the creature (which was sitting at the kitchen table) mumble a word that sounded like "Mummy."

Roger Dunkley's story "A Problem Called Albert" is based on the very interchangeability of children and beasts. A wife who has long buried her deep yearning for a baby and adopted a tomcat instead (reminding one in a way of Hemingway's "Cat in the Rain") does everything to keep up her illusions and protect her "offspring." In this tale, too, the main theme is nature and its influence on apparently civilized human beings. A real baby comes in as well at a crucial point of the action; the cat kills it and brings it home as a trophy after the beast has been "adjusted"[8] by a veterinarian--in other words, after its true nature has been violated. Though Albert's "mother" is somewhat appalled, she dutifully covers up all traces of the slaughter. The perverseness of her maternal feelings causes the reader's growing uneasiness; immediately before the unpleasant incident she has read in her horoscope about "a young arrival in the house." This cue stirs for a moment all her former hopes and desires. When the young arrival has come in an unforeseen shape one can notice how deep her natural wish for offspring is buried in favor of the feline "child": for "Mummy's naughty, furry baby" (120) she is able to remove the infant's mutilated corpse and put it in a dustbin as the physical remnants of her shattered dreams.

Another reason for mixing up children with animals is given in Forbes Bramble's story "Holiday." Strangely enough, the direct cause for the separation of the parents and their daughter is the parents' fear of such a separation. When the three of them pitch camp at a lonely Scotch loch, Sheila's father hears a tale about ghostly seals which bring mischief to human beings. His anxiety about the animals is really a sublimation of his sorrows concerning his broken marriage and his daughter's future. The idea that his wife tries to estrange his daughter from him is covered by the seemingly more important and acute danger of losing Sheila to the "uncanny" seals. The creatures which slowly begin to crowd round the rock Sheila is sitting on are ordinary seals, whose arrival at this time of the year has nothing unusual about it. Yet Sheila's father is convinced that these animals, whose heads look like "blackened skulls,"[9] which come ashore like "grey corpses," and which wail like small children, have gathered to lure his daughter away from him. A confrontation with these visible enemies, onto which he projects the hostility he perceives, does not leave him as helpless as the struggle with his domestic problems. The word "domestic" must be understood on two levels, for it also expresses the fact that Sheila's father "prefers" fighting against a

primitive, beastly opponent to coping with the obscure difficulties
his civilized social life brings about.

Sheila, who conspicuously has many features in common with animals (the hard heels of her brown sandals "drum" and clatter "like
horses' hoofs," which shows her untamed vitality and joy of life, 3),
seems to carry on an intimate communication with the seals. In reality
she only gives free play to her fancy and curiosity, as her father has
always taught her. Now he believes in a kind of mystic bond between
child and beasts. His growing anxiety is communicated to Sheila, who
has not been so insensitive to the imminent disruption of the family
as her parents (and the reader) were led to believe. By and by the
seals assume a new meaning for her; she starts to think that they know
and share her sorrows. The more her father loathes the animals and
tries to keep her away from them, the more she feels their attraction.
It is obvious that a crisis is inevitable; it is finally caused by a
violent outburst of the father, who throws rocks down on the seals to
smash their heads. He is aware that he behaves "like a madman" (13),
but his blind reaction seems "immensely important" to him. Sheila witnesses his insane behavior and feels personally attacked. Gripping her
father's legs with the strength of a man, she threatens to kill herself, since her friends "have suffered enough" (13). At night Sheila
realizes her threat and tries to drown herself, but this is by no
means the ultimate manifestation of separation. Sheila's father,
roused by a slobbery sound, discovers her in her tent with one of the
seals beside her; with a club he cracks the skull of the "cold and
nauseous" (15) creature that seems to embrace his daughter, who begins
to wail softly. Together with Sheila's mother, who has meanwhile become as frantic as her husband, he dresses their "white and cold"
daughter and leaves the place in a headlong flight. Panic-stricken, he
steers their car over a precipice into a river.

Of course Sheila's father has not rescued his daughter from the
influence of the beast. The reader, who has up to this point of the
story been manipulated by the father's point of view—and by the
assumption that the tale is a genuine ghost story—is finally able to
reconstruct the whole event. From the conclusion of the story he can
deduce that Sheila's suicide attempt has failed, that she has returned
from the sea to rejoin her parents, and that her father has mistaken
her for a seal. The creature in the arms of Sheila's mother is a seal,
and the policemen who salvage the car cannot quite understand why the
beast wears a child's clothing.

Lisa Tuttle's story "The Horse Lord" contains several striking
parallels to the previous example. This tale, too, seems to be a real
ghost story, but is actually based on the projections of the protagonist's anguished mind. This woman has to face children who seem
strange in a twofold way: they resemble animals, and they form an apparently hostile group. The children are more or less imposed upon her
(she has agreed to adopt her husband's orphaned nephews and nieces),
and though all five are friendly at the beginning, their new mother
nearly despairs of the unwonted responsibility. Furthermore, she is a
writer of suspense novels, who had to change her New York City apartment for a desolate abode ("The old house and the eerily empty countryside formed a setting very much like one Marilyn...had once created
for a story"[10]); both her character and her surroundings account for
her heightened sensitivity. Thus, her overall reaction to the children

does not astonish the reader: she explicitly calls them a "herd" (81),
who have intruded into her life in disregard of the "typical fashion,"
which is "one at a time, with a proper interval between."

When she finds out about an ancient local superstition that deals
with ghostly horses which kill and devour their human masters, she
begins to fear for her charges, who are longing to keep horses in the
"cursed barn," the center of the supposed evil spell. She already
feels that children have a special contact with the supernatural, with
animals, and consequently with ghostly creatures in particular. Even
her husband, as a child, felt deeply affected by the legend, which
leads the wife to the simple but momentous remark, "We become
different people when we grow up" (83). Along with the physical shift
(the children have chosen the barn as their own new domicile) the
psychic separation is growing: the mother regards their strictly
organized work in the barn as the drill of a "small but diligent army"
(87), because she cannot comprehend the pattern beneath their
behavior. Children who act with such self-imposed discipline seem
unnatural to her; unaccustomed to children she does not know how
efficiently they can work if they are enthusiastic about a project. To
their adopted mother the children appear to "live in another world"
(90). A casual statement uttered by one of her charges unbalances her
for good: learning about the violent death of one of her ancestors,
the child believes that the horses must have been perfectly right to
kill him, for "horses will put up with almost anything" (88).

The protagonist falsely interprets this as a reproach and a
threat; she accuses herself of having failed ("How did people cope
with the tremendous responsibility of other lives under their protection? It was an impossible task," 87). The last, predictable step in
the development of her monomania is the total identification of
children and animals. The children have finished preparing the barn
and are now waiting for the first horse they see--obviously for a new,
beastly master who will tell them to destroy their former rulers,
their parents. It is interesting how explicitly the children's mother
expresses the key notion which determines each of the stories presented in this chapter: "'Children are a bit like animals, don't you
think? At least, people treat them as if they were--adults, I mean'"
(93). When the children cannot find a horse, they start playing horses
themselves. The very last details their mother perceives before losing
her senses are the children's prancing feet, tossing heads, wild
cries, and their strong, square teeth (93).

Children can enter into relationships with all kinds of animals,
savage or tame. In Noel Langley's "Serenade For Baboons" a white physician comes across two dark-skinned, animal-like children ("There was
something more than imbecility in the eyes gazing into his. His mind
flew back to animals again, and he remembered a sick Gibbon monkey he
had once tried to save from dying. It had cried like a human
being"[11]); in fact, the creatures are able to summon a horde of
baboons and make them lacerate the children's human master. In another
of Saki's contributions, "The Lumber Room," a boy regards a hunting
scene on an old piece of tapestry as a parallel to the relationship
between himself, his aunt, and his small cousins, who are always in
alliance with him against the omnipotent adult. For the human hunter
in the picture it is no difficulty to hit the cornered stag "at a
ridiculously short range,"[12] but he is not aware of the pack of wolves

that are silently gathering round him.

The symbolic connection between the flesh-and-blood beast and the wild, dark side of human nature (the Beast as a synonym of the Evil One) becomes clearest in those stories which contain a canine representative. On the other hand, canines may as well personify the extreme opposite: sainthood, even angelic qualities. This apparent contradiction dissolves at once if one takes into consideration how the relationship between canine and man has changed throughout human history. One of man's deadliest enemies, the wolf, has been turned into his very best friend, as a result of domestication and through the influence of civilization.[13] Generally the classification concerning benevolent and malevolent creatures is relatively simple; savage beasts such as wolves, foxes, hyenas and others are usually incarnations of evil, whereas the ordinary housedog displays its friendly disposition. The most obvious example of the former category can be found in David Seltzer's novel The Omen. Damien, the new-born Antichrist, is brought forth by the Beast—as the son of a bitch jackal.

Ray Bradbury's "Emissary," a dog, is a miraculous creature while alive and a literally transcendental being after death. For Martin, the bedridden boy, Dog is a walking cross-section of all the life he encounters on his excursions ("this incredible beast was October!"[14]); along with the voluptuous scents of nature (which Martin takes in through every pore, like an animal) the dog carries the very mysteries of life: "Through the loomings of the universe Dog shuttled; the design was hid in his pelt" (77). Once he brings a visitor to his master who can "read and interpret" Dog as well as Martin can. The boy's parents, however, have no contact with the dog nor with their son; Martin's insensitive mother even tries to keep Dog in the house ("Martin looked at this woman as if she were a stranger," 78).

Death cannot change Dog's most prominent qualities, his love for people and his worst habit, "digging where he shouldn't." His decease is significantly caused by the "wild throngings of civilization" (81). According to his new sphere of existence, the guest he now brings to the sick boy is Death, and the last sign Martin deciphers is cemetery earth. Dog has never dug so deep during his lifetime; he is the mediator of a different power. The fact that an animal determines the life and even more the death of a child underlines their homogeneity. Dog is a pantheistic equivalent of Jesus Christ, the Shepherd who brings adult Christians home (besides the fact that his very name is an anagram of "God"). The very same term is used in connection with the guests Dog takes along: "Dog brought...any friend or near-friend, encountered, cornered, begged, worried, and at last shepherded home."

It has been shown in detail that civilization, the achievement and domain of adult man, is a fragile and often deceptive construct. The same goes for the effect civilization has on a domesticated animal: the thin cover of "good nature," which man has come to regard as the sole nature his four-legged friend possesses, can be torn off on the most trifling occasions and give way to the primeval ferocity beneath. Stephen King's novel Cujo is an ingenious synthesis of all major points of interest which concern the beast: the parallel between the physical entity and the evil powers in human nature, the savageness which can be all too easily roused from its hibernation, and the fact that children have the closest contact with the B(b)east and are helplessly exposed to it.

Ignoring the immensely complicated symbolic structure of the novel, one could object to the main plot as rather dull and unimaginative: a dog becomes rabid and kills several people in various ways. The novel contains a considerable number of subplots, which at first glance have nothing to do with each other, but which are all subtly linked through the Beast. Each of these subplots amounts to the same basic idea--the comforts of civilization are nothing more than useless talismans against the untamed, cruel power of nature, which is infinitely stronger than mankind. A most trivial incident, for instance, nearly stops the promising career of a young advertising manager, the child protagonist's father. A new cereal with a dark orange color has conquered the market; some children with a gastric disorder throw up their breakfast, giving their horrified mothers the impression that they are bleeding to death from an internal wound, as the liquid is streaming down all over their bodies. The "blood" is only undigested food dye, perfectly harmless (for the body), but consumers cannot forgive the producer for the disillusioning effect of the whole affair. After all, death could one fine day really destroy the delusive peace of an average American breakfast table. The awakening is all the more brutal since the Sharp Cereal Professor, a popular authority figure in commercial spots, has lulled his audience all along with the very words that make the motto of the novel: "Nope, nothing wrong here."[15]

The image of sleeping evil becomes most explicit in the main plot dealing with Cujo, a dog that lives on a farm somewhere in rural Maine. At first Cujo is by no means a monster, rather the opposite--a holy creature, a Saint Bernard. Displaying all the virtues ascribed to his kind, Cujo pulls his weight ("two hundred pounds of Saint Bernard," 111) for his human masters and never disappoints them. A year before the crucial change in the animal's life the boy Tad, who is to become Cujo's victim, meets him for the first time; three-year-old Tad falls in love with the dog at once, whereas his parents consider the mere size of the dog and cannot suppress their anxiety about the possibility of danger: "Tad had now put one of his small hands into Cujo's mouth and was peering in like the world's smallest dentist. That gave Vic another uneasy moment, but then Tad was running back to them again. 'Doggy's got teeth,' he told Vic. 'Yes,' Vic said. 'Lots of teeth'" (15).

The way Cujo meets his fate is significant in more than one respect: the dog literally sticks his nose too deep in a hidden underground cave and stirs the creatures of the night which have been sleeping there. Though the bats do not have a strictly "vampiric function" in this case, they change the dog's nature entirely by scratching the muzzle he has dug too pertly into the darkness. Cujo does not understand the secret he has stumbled upon (as an outward sign of this fact he has received a long, curving wound in the shape of a question mark, 20). The rabies which the bats pass on to him is of course more than a simple disease; it represents the madness and rage which are the primary force in the natural struggle. Yet the actual symptoms of "ordinary" rabies also illustrate the image of vampirism. Shortly after the contagion Cujo avoids all those elements which were essential to his original life--sunlight, water, and food (which are the things a vampire must shun, too). Like a vampire he returns to his beloved ones, but is still restrained by a fading echo of his former affection. His ten-year-old master is appalled by the change: "The dog he had grown up with...bore only the slightest resemblance to the muddy, matted apparition slowly materializing from the morning mist. The Saint Bernard's big, sad eyes were now reddish and stupid and lowering: more pig's eyes than dog's eyes....His muzzle was wrinkled back in a terrible mock grin that froze Brett with horror." The very first impression the boy gets, however, comes closest to the point: "His first panicky thought, like a child who has suddenly tumbled into a fairy tale, was wolf..." (98)

The author emphasizes the universal meaning of the Beast by giving it another extremely important "manifestation." When the boy Tad has almost fallen asleep in his room, he sees the door of his closet swing open and reveal the face of a terrible monster, half man, half wolf, whose amber-colored eyes glow fiercely in the dark and whose entire position indicates that it is ready to rush upon its small victim. Tad's parents, awakened by his scream, try to calm him, his mother with "reasonable" arguments (ironically enough she addresses her husband, "I told you three hot dogs was too many, Vic!"), his father by opening the closet, which now looks perfectly reassuring: it is filled with innocent things like clean sheets, and instead of the beast Tad's teddy bear appears. In spite of all the good totems and good magic in his room and despite his father's solemn affirmation that nothing in their good house can harm him Tad does not feel convinced at all, for no adult can really understand his situation. Immediately after the grown-ups have left his doubts are confirmed by the monster itself: "'I told you they'd go away, Tad,' it whispered. 'They always do, in the end. And then I can come back. I like to come back. I like you, Tad....one night...I'll pounce, and then I'll eat you and you'll be in me'" (7).

The occasions on which the monster in the closet reappears indicate that it is at least half human—it is, for instance, the embodiment of a notorious killer who haunted the town years ago and has become a modern bogeyman. The monster is part of Tad's parents, too; the door slides open whenever Tad senses the insufferable tension between them. Their struggle, which they try in vain to conceal from their son, is caused by the affair Tad's mother maintains with an educated "brute": a creature from the jungle with academic degrees, who appeals to the woman's animal needs only ("It occurred to her suddenly that although she had seen his penis close up—had had it in her mouth—she had never really seen what his face looked like," 40). When he is driven away by his mistress (whom he calls the Bitch Goddess, 196), he devastates the married couple's home during their absence and leaves his sperm on the marriage bed he has never had access to—like a dog that urinates on the territory it claims.

The climax of the novel, Tad's and his mother's encounter with the rabid Cujo, is another, utterly unsurpassable demonstration of the omnipresent separation motif. Without advance notice both drive out to the combined farm and repair shop where Cujo's masters live. On this particular afternoon, however, the dog has torn his adult master to pieces, and the two human beings must face the beast all alone in the deserted countryside. They have arrived in one of the favorite products of civilization, which breaks down right in front of the dog. Mother and child are completely surprised by the dog's violent attack. The sudden appearance of the beast's mad face and its very closeness have the same effect on them a screen monster would cause by entering

reality against all laws of common sense. Though they are in a car,
their adventure has nothing to do with the safe pleasures of a drive-
in cinema. Tad's frightened mother believes that the beast regards
their car as quite a different sort of technical achievement; the
monster seems to say: "Just as soon as I find a way to get into this
tin can, I'll eat you alive..." (152) In fact the dog only needs to
wait for his victims; they are nearly fried alive in their car, which
is fully exposed to a merciless summer sun (ironically enough, Tad's
mother remembers having read an SPCA handout which said that because
of this "greenhouse effect" humans should never shut their dogs up in
a car, 185).

Tad's father, who is far away on a business trip, has left him a
piece of paper with a written incantation against the beast in the
closet. Although the boy cannot read the "Monster Words" he has taken
them with him. Of course they offer no protection against the real
danger, the monster that, as Tad believes, has "got out of the
closet." With his mother close by his side, he rather concentrates on
the tiny piece he has left of his father and on his fantasy world, for
"it was better there than with Mommy, because the monster was where
Mommy was" (212). Tad's mother cannot cope with the situation; she is
unable to make quick, apt decisions, gets lost in idle intellectual
games and waits for help from outside. Only when Tad is about to die
of dehydration does she leave the car, and in her despair she is even
able to struggle with the beast. Once she has smashed the dog's skull
she loses all human traits: she goes on wildly beating the corpse and
is deeply pleased every time she hears a bone crack ("She was the
harpies, the Weird Sisters, she was all vengeance--not for herself,
but for what had been done to her boy," 287). For all her superhuman,
or rather subhuman exertions, she does not save her son's life. The
Beast has finally come for Tad; his mother must realize that his life
"slid away" the same moment the dog's life ended (291). All her
belated attempts to keep the boy's body ("She would not let Vic near
the boy. When he came near, she bared her teeth and growled soundless-
ly at him," 292) cannot alter the fact that Tad's mother has lost her
child to a beast.

Children and Dolls

Monica, sound asleep, was playing with her beloved doll, but
in her sleep. She was indubitably in deep slumber. Her fingers, however, were roughing the doll this way and that, as
though some dream perplexed her. The child was mumbling in
her sleep, though no words were distinguishable. Muffled
sighs and groans issued from her lips. Yet another sound
there certainly was, though it could not have issued from
the child's mouth. Whence, then, did it come?

Algernon Blackwood, "The Doll"[1]

Relationships between children and animals or children and dolls
have many features and functions in common. The reader will notice
that the vast majority of works dealing with children and beasts center upon a male protagonist, particularly if the beast in question is
generally considered dangerous and repulsive. The reason for this male
predominance cannot be only explained by the author's possible assumption that boys love beasts more than girls do, or that boys have
closer contact with animals in real life. In horror fiction the association with subhuman creatures is chiefly a male affair, because boys
also represent the archetype of the male hunter, who is curious and
bold and who must be "primitive" enough himself to perceive the
beast's presence, master it or be destroyed in the struggle with his
adversary.
    Like the beast, the doll can help the solitary child in its per-
manent conflict with its parents; the doll is able to carry out its
master's commands, but frequently haunts the child it belongs to as
well. The reader is right to presume a female majority in this field,
though the girls' preponderance is not quite so overwhelming as might
be expected. The distribution of roles, the functions and characteristics both sexes display through the contact with beasts/dolls, are not
totally predictable either. Neither boys nor girls simply comply with
the traditional notion that males have to face jungle warfare whereas
females, caring for their offspring only, may enjoy domestic security.
Since this conception usually implies a certain value system (namely
the superiority of primitive strength to apparent passivity and defencelessness), it cannot be applied in this context at all. A girl's
"maternal instinct," expressed in the child's contact to her doll, is
the very first association which comes to the reader's mind; certainly
this pattern of behavior plays a major role in the relationship. Apart
from the fact, however, that along with the distorted meanings motherhood can have in horror fiction, a quality like "motherliness" may accordingly acquire novel, sinister connotations, the girl's connection
to her doll includes other, much more universal aspects.
    In his tale "The Doll" Algernon Blackwood drops a hint at the
most important feature in the relationship between child and doll when
he makes the adult protagonist, the girl's governess, ponder over the
nature of this particular toy:

> The child fondles and caresses her doll with passionate
> love, cares for it, seeks its welfare, yet stuffs it down
> into the perambulator, its head and neck twisted, its limbs
> broken and contorted, leaving it atrociously upside down so
> that blood and breathing cannot possibly function, while she
> runs to the window to see if the rain has stopped or the sun
> has come out....The maternity instinct defies, even denies
> death. The doll, whether left upside down on the floor with
> broken teeth and ruined eyes, or lovingly arranged to be
> overlaid in the night, squashed, tortured, mutilated, sur-
> vives all cruelties and disasters, and asserts finally its
> immortal qualities. It is unkillable. It is beyond death.[2]

The governess, "influenced perhaps by her bitter subconscious griev-
ance against nature for depriving her of a child of her own" (15),
only sees the maternal suggestion in a girl's relationship to that
"horrible plaything;" and although she has hit the mark with her
thoughts about the doll's immortality, she completely misunderstands
the true source of this condition. It is the girl, not her toy, who
owns and exercises the power over life, "non-life," and sometimes even
death. Her imagination enables her to animate and resuscitate her possession whenever she likes and transform it into everything and everybody she wants. The desired result of her creative efforts is by no
means always a "baby" of her own, as most adults superficially
suppose.

Boys and girls alike have contact with nonhuman life; through the
basic differences in these relationships the sexes can be distinguished from each other. At close consideration girls no longer appear
inferior because they prefer to deal with manifestations of life in
the comparative security of their nurseries. In contrast to boys, who
must handle those beings they meet by chance--beasts which are already
existent--and cope with them for better or worse, girls themselves
decide which objects they bring to life and in which direction they
steer their creatures. Girls, far from having to bother with unpleasant things like blood and gore, thus show their refinement: they are
not tamers, but sorceresses. Occasionally, of course, a girl falls
victim to her own skills--an occupational hazard for all those engaged
in black magic. As a rule, adult people seldom perceive anything
extraordinary in the way children manipulate their playthings, and if
they do, they certainly misinterpret the actual distribution of power
and the true source of evil. For most parents and tutors, however, a
doll is only a doll, one of the most harmless things in the world; unlike the disquieted reader, they are perfectly unaware that its use
(and abuse) is often the direct preparation for their own destruction.

One of the crucial episodes in James Herbert's novel The Dark is
a rather crude demonstration of the development of evil. Though the
incident in question reveals some of the basic principles in the immensely complex relationship between girl and doll, the reader only
catches an insignificant glimpse at its groundwork and is not "sensi-
tized" at all to the delicate nuances other writers cleverly employ.
The murderous conflict between eleven-year-old Susie, her doll, and
her parents is described in the same purely sensational manner that
determines the entire novel. Susie has already undergone psychiatric
treatment because of her pyromaniacal tendency, a disorder which roots

in her parents' broken marriage. The "play" with her doll serves as
the direct prelude to the "real thing," burning down the house with
the couple upstairs. First the girl projects her own personality into
the toy ("'You mustn't stare when you're at the dinner table! Mummy
doesn't like it!'"³) and assumes her mother's role. She is not simply
mimicking her mother's language and gestures; her atrocities are grotesque exaggerations of the supposedly milder forms of punishment her
mother inflicts upon her. The girl takes great delight in pulling out
her doll's hair and twisting its limbs, which eventually come off one
by one. Her sadism is veiled by a "pedagogical" justification ("'Now
you can't run away and you can't get into mischief,'" 16)--a mockery
of the peculiar explanations that sometimes accompany adult forms of
"correction." Obviously Susie punishes herself, at the same time realizing the injustice of this punishment, and instead of relieving her
aggressions she thus builds up additional tension, which must, at
least for a deranged child, cause disaster. Nonetheless, the writer's
clumsy attempt at a psychological elucidation does not convince the
reader at all, the more because the consequent arson is done away with
in a single sentence two chapters later: only the smiling girl in
front of the blazing house is mentioned.

Saki's story "Morlvera" is a far more impressive contribution to
the main point of interest, the conflict between children and adults.
The author does not make use of fire or blood, but relies entirely on
the imaginative powers of his small protagonists. The "battle" takes
place in their minds only, which accounts for the admirable (and horrifying) subtlety of the tale. Ten-year-old Emmeline and her small
companion are standing in front of the "Olympic Toy Emporium," making
up a "biography" for the star among the dolls in the window, an el-
egant lady in peach-colored velvet with leopard-skin accessories. This
particular doll is a typical representative of the whole commercial
institution, which, though it should be designed and decorated according to the needs and delights of children, is much more an attraction
for adults. The emporium with its cold splendor does not deserve the
"pulse-quickening name of toyshop;"⁴ only "exclamatory parents and
bored, silent children" can be found here.

The two children who are interpreting the doll subconsciously
take it for granted that the toy belongs to the cruel world of grown-
ups, not into a cozy nursery. For them the lady seems to have character, but a bad character, cold and hostile, expressed by the "sinister
lowering of one eyebrow and a merciless hardness about the corners of
the mouth" (337). Inspired by the doll's outward appearance, Emmeline
and her friend create their own picture of adult vices:

"She's a bad lot, that one is," declared Emmeline, after a
long unfriendly stare; "'er usbind 'ates 'er."--"'E knocks
'er abart."--"No, 'e don't, cos 'e's dead; she poisoned 'im
slow and gradual, so that nobody didn't know. Now she wants
to marry a lord, with 'eaps and 'eaps of money. 'E's got a
wife already, but she's going to poison 'er, too....if
there's fish going, she eats 'er own share and 'er little
girl's as well, though the little girl is dellikit."--"She
'ad a little boy once...but she pushed 'im into the water
when nobody wasn't looking."--"No, she didn't, she sent 'im
away to be kep' by poor people, so 'er 'usbind wouldn't know

where 'e was. They ill-treat 'im somethink cruel." (338)

The name "Morlvera" immediately comes to Emmeline's mind, because it seems as cold and pretentious as the toy lady, who nevertheless fascinates her.

The children's reflections are interrupted by the arrival of a lady and a boy with a "very black scowl on his face and a very white sailor suit over the rest of him" (338-39). The boy's sulky temper is caused by the fact that he is to buy a birthday present for a girl-cousin he detests. His mother, one of the "exclamatory parents" who form the clientele of the emporium, picks out Morlvera at once; this doll infallibly appeals to every grown-up person because of their similarities in character. The children outside watch Morlvera's departure with mixed feelings, bereavement and excitement. Seeing the "look of sinister triumph" that seems to glow in Morlvera's "hard, inquisitorial face" (339), Emmeline predicts, "She's up to no good." The boy Victor, however, whom they have been "inclined to side with" from the very beginning, and who has behaved conspicuously well after the purchase, thwarts Morlvera's wicked plans ("Very stealthily, very gently, very mercilessly Victor sent Morlvera flying over his shoulder"); under the carriage wheels the doll is reduced to a mess of sawdust and leopard skin. From the children's fancy Victor emerges as the hero in a tragedy of childish revenge: "I've bin finking. Do you know oo 'e was? 'E was 'er little boy wot she'd sent away to live wiv poor folks. 'E come back and done that" (341).

One of the most elaborate and certainly one of the ghastliest narratives dealing with a girl and her toy is Michael Kernan's "The Doll Named Silvio." This complex story can be understood on several very different levels; though it was originally published in an anthology of ghost stories, the supernatural plays the least significant part. The author mainly concentrates on the symbolic value which the doll Silvio displays, the various dimensions of meaning that are all based on a child's peculiar attachment to her favorite doll. Kathy, the sinister heroine of the tale, rules over an immense collection of two hundred and thirty-one dolls, minutely categorized into groups, families, even entire dynasties. Only Silvio stands out from the rest; he is not Kathy's powerless subject, but a kind of wooden equivalent of her own self, the outward sign of her despotic government. On a symbolic level, Kathy and Silvio are perfectly identical in nature and descent, and their concerted relentless exertion of authority over dolls and human beings roots in their homogeneity.

The plot of the story vividly and originally combines authentic details of Venetian history with the apparently less momentous background of Kathy's personal problems and private affairs. The girl, an only child, is the last descendant of an eccentric millionaire who tried to create a "Gran Venetia" in the swamps of Florida. The estate has quickly deteriorated in the hot, damp climate; canals, bridges, gondolas and other replicas have rotted away or disappeared altogether, and only the main building, the "nightmare"⁵ of any connoisseur, has maintained its original, threatening splendor. Kathy is the "grande-dame" of this palace; apart from two servants she lives there all alone. Though her father loves her, he shuns her company and prefers traveling to Europe, because Kathy is a personification of the decay of the family domain: her birth killed her mother, and Kathy's

club foot is the cause for her physical and emotional retardation.
Kathy's father wants to get rid of the whole estate and make it a
museum on her nineteenth birthday, which would imply the girl's "expulsion" from her personal empire.

Silvio, the only genuine Venetian piece of art in "Cay Doge,"
symbolizes a similar deprivation of power. Actually Silvio is a wooden
statue, about two feet tall, which lacks feet (Kathy's new governess
supposes that a thief inexpertly removed it from a portal), whose out-
stretched hands have lost the object they once held, and whose black
eyes, gleaming with malevolence, seem to hypnotize every adult onlooker. Despite its colorful and somewhat ridiculous outward appearance the statue by no means represents a figure of the Commedia dell'
Arte; it wears a doge's cap, the sign of highest authority. Like
Kathy, and like the doges of Venice, Silvio has been deprived of his
original position. The doges, absolute rulers in their empire, endowed
with power in all branches of their government (especially judica-
ture), gradually lost most of their influence after an attempt by the
Orseolo family to make the doge's position a hereditary one, an endeavor which was thwarted by the fierce opposition of the nobility.[6]
The doges no longer managed financial affairs, and the only undisputed
right finally left to them was the power of sending out Venetian
troops against enemies. Basically the doge was reduced to the president and executive of the Signoria, since 1310 of the "Dieci Inquisi-
tori dello Stato," a council that rigorously supervised all his
actions in public and private life and finally even exerted juridical
power over one of the doges (the execution of Marino Falieri in 1355).
The doges of Venice, the doll Silvio, and the girl Kathy have all one
common enemy: a superior authority.

The action sets in with the arrival of Kathy's governess, the
narrator of the story (a figure strongly reminiscent of the Jamesian
governess in The Turn of the Screw; this woman, however, is rather too
cautious in her sinister speculations). The term "governess," by the
way, is introduced by her employer, with whom she has previously had a
short conversation. It is interesting that Kathy's father prefers this
expression, which signifies control and supervision, whereas the woman
considers herself a "companion." Kathy's father wants her to be a sub-
stitute who acts out his parental authority; in the end she thus becomes a scapegoat. When she meets Kathy for the first time, she is
disconcerted to discover that her charge is crippled, and in a way
glad that the girl seems to have found some consolation in her dolls.
The woman eagerly participates in Kathy's play with her numerous toys,
or rather, she watches Kathy's brilliant solo performances: the girl
inspires each doll with a voice, behavior, an entire personality of
its own. Still unsuspecting, the governess is convinced that only on
occasions like these can she catch a glimpse at Kathy's "real self"--
on the contrary, by playing such a variety of roles the girl hides her
real nature completely from any grown-up person.

There are two kinds of "family meetings" Kathy celebrates in the
course of the month. She has worked out a detailed timetable for each
gathering and each group of dolls. During the normal parties she
"imitates" a family life she herself has always been denied. Perfect
harmony and untroubled fun determine the atmosphere then. On the nineteenth of each month, however, Kathy dines strictly in private with a
chosen few and Silvio. The number nineteen must be seen in connection

with the doom that awaits Kathy on her nineteenth birthday, the day of her transition to adult life. The girl anticipates the revenge for her coming dispossession in a cruel monthly ritual. One of the dolls, her formerly beloved playmate, must undergo the initiation ceremony that will be Kathy's destruction and join a very special group, the "Boones." These dolls have changed sides, have become grown-ups on a symbolic level. One of the oldest symbols of superior power--especially of divine or parental supervision--is employed in this context: Kathy ties each new candidate for the "Boones" to a board and tears its eyes out. Then it takes a place in the semicircle of the "adult," yet impotent human replicas.

The governess misunderstands her first encounter with the Boones, explaining the ghastly sight away with the more child-like idea of a "doll hospital." She senses Kathy's fanatic hatred, however, and begins to feel personally accused (80) while looking at the dolls' empty eyesockets. Silvio, on the other hand, repels her at once and completely; she imagines that the object that was taken from the statue's hands must have been a sacrificial bowl for some evil Inca idol. She does not yet know the ceremony, and she is not aware that she is responsible for the choice of the next victim--any doll that "witnesses" Kathy's being rebuked or treated as inferior must suffer the ordeal. Only after finding out the true facts does the governess try to have the playroom barred, and she is astonished at the servants' indifference. Her attempt to interfere with the girl's mode of existence stirs Kathy's wrath. The narrator becomes the first human victim, a fact that, ironically enough, is only "subtly" hinted at: the governess is lured to the girl's room, sees an "amphitheatre" (87) of hundreds of dolls with Silvio in the center (the doge in the midst of the Signoria), carrying a silver hook in his hands. She awakes in darkness, which she cannot interpret at first. She cannot understand, either, why Kathy's father seems to be more upset by her own destiny than by Kathy's madness. The reader knows, of course, that the man fears for his own life, aware that his daughter's development has merely reached a new phase.

The relationship between the doll Silvio and its owner, as already hinted at, contains no strictly supernatural elements. To the narrator Silvio seems to have a character of his own and an evil influence on Kathy, but even in her final state of fright and terror she never relates any real manifestations of her speculations concerning the doll. Without doubt all activity originates from the child alone, and Silvio's "life" has its exclusive source in Kathy's imagination. Nevertheless, the doll is her assistant; its repulsive features and cunning facial expression certainly have a suggestive effect on Kathy as well, which has caused her to make him her alter ego. Forms of schizophrenia can be quite frequently observed whenever a girl enters a bond with her doll. In most cases the mental disease is carefully veiled; authors tend to give its symptoms pointedly different explanations on the surface level of narration. The ambiguities which thus arise can heighten the attraction of a story considerably; in John Saul's novels Suffer the Children and Comes the Blind Fury, which lack profundity in every other respect, equivocations form the only interesting aspect. All plots invented by this writer are based on a single cruel incident in the remote past which is revenged in the present and which usually seems to imply supernatural interference.

Initially Elizabeth, the murderess in <u>Suffer the Children</u>, appears to be possessed by the spirit of a girl who was raped and killed by her father a century before. She claims to have made contact with the victim by means of her ouija board. The facts that Elizabeth systematically kills her cat and a girl and a boy of her own age, and that she suffers from blackouts after these occurrences can as well be interpreted as the direct results of the effects her disrupted family life has upon the girl's psyche. By killing these special victims she takes symbolic revenge on her own family as well, because the three represent "Mummy," "Daddy," and "Baby." Elizabeth has to care for her imbecile sister (which she does with great devotion during her sane phases); both her parents are fully occupied by their work and glad to have a daughter like Elizabeth who willingly accepts a burden which should be theirs. In her subconsciousness the girl has developed a murderous hatred because she has no one who talks to her.

Therefore it is quite remarkable that she replaces each "mute" next of kin by a plaything--her individual kind of "doll." For this reason she celebrates four so-called parties at regular intervals. During the first she dresses the dead cat in a doll's dress, socks, shoes and bonnet, giving the feline child the place of honor it deserves and retains on all further occasions. The cat replaces Elizabeth's sister; the "doll" does not talk to her either, but this way it exactly answers Elizabeth's purpose: the naughty "sister" may now be tortured without punishment ("She suddenly leapt at the cat, grabbing the corpse and yanking it across the table. She flipped it over, held it on her knee, and began spanking it. The slapping of her hand against the cat's haunches echoed back at her, and she put all her strength into the beating she was administering. Then she set the cat back on the rock and smiled at it"[7]). During the second and third imaginary tea-parties the human victims are introduced to their "Baby" and have to punish it for remaining silent. By the end of the fourth party Elizabeth has killed the children and symbolically reduced her parents to mere playthings, too. She makes sure to leave the two corpses tidily propped up beside the cat, so that, while decaying, they still form a happy family. Having accomplished her revenge, Elizabeth again behaves in a perfectly normal manner and is able to live on contentedly with her parents.

The doll symbolism plays an exceedingly important role in this novel, since the complex distribution of power between children and parents is reflected by it. The presentation of facts that are basically plausible and elucidating, however, must be regarded as a complete failure. The author indulges in the most primitive perversions (which he considers genuine elements of "horror") to an extent that the sense of the macabre gives way to sheer crudity and obscenity. The small boy's forced copulation with the dead cat, for instance, is hardly a means of inviting the reader's refined interpretation; nor are the descriptions of the various tortures the captured and starving children must suffer.

Apart from the promising but spoiled imagery there is one other positive aspect worth mentioning: the dramatic irony which lies in the conclusion of the plot. After people have found the children's corpses Elizabeth's imbecile sister is charged with the crimes and taken to an asylum. Now a mental disease as the possible cause for the murders is indeed hinted at, though only in connection with the innocent sister, who has been suspicious to her surroundings from the very start: "Sarah might do anything. Schizophrenia, they said, was unpredictable" (45). Furthermore, in this unforeseen way Elizabeth has been able to fulfill her most ardent desire--she has always wanted to be an "only child" (282).

The female killer of Comes the Blind Fury is comparable to her predecessor in many respects. She murders other children as well, but again her parents ought to take the blame; she suffers from spells of amnesia, afterwards telling her parents about some mysterious fog that surrounded her during the killings. The most significant similarity consists in the fact that she commits her crimes for the sake of her doll, which she regards as the embodiment of a real girl killed a century before. Being a lonely child, exposed to ridicule because of her lameness, she confuses the legend of the dead blind girl with her own destiny. On the whole, the novel does not appear as sensational as Suffer the Children, but the presentation of a possible case of schizophrenia lacks the ingenuity of the preceding example.

The interaction between the girl and her clown-doll in Brenda Brown Canary's The Voice of the Clown can hardly be surpassed in complexity and profundity; although the novel shows considerable flaws in style and composition, it is still worth examining in detail. The simple plot appears rather far-fetched, but it offers great possibilities for the central relationship between child and doll. The present action has its roots in the past, too: a white man who has grown up with an Indian girl and, engaged to her, made her pregnant, leaves her for a rich white girl he marries soon after. The Indian, still in love, vows revenge to the white woman only and commits a ritual suicide to be reborn as her rival's daughter. In this shape she intends to destroy her enemy and win her lover back.

The reincarnation motif, which determines both action and imagery of this novel, is--certainly against all expectations--employed extremely rarely in connection with the child in horror fiction. The reader may well be prepared to assume that this motif in particular could provide one of the child's uncontested "domains;" after all, according to traditional beliefs concerning metempsychosis a soul normally leaves the corpse of a fully grown person to enter the body of a child at the moment of its birth, because it is still a tabula rasa then.[6] Since the origins of Gothic literature, however, the reincarnation motif has not undergone any noticeable alteration, let alone a development. The human soul, its entanglement with good and evil forces, and its eventual redemption or damnation were always major points of interest; the child, on the other hand, was excluded from attention because its nature hardly seemed to qualify it as a personality in which spiritual struggles like the ones "required" may take place. Consequently, souls preferred to transmigrate into the bodies of adults instead (or even into those of animals, as in Poe's "Metzengerstein"). Nevertheless, one of the rare Gothic tales that deal with children (the only one in Poe's entire literary work), "Morella," centers upon metempsychosis. At once the reader can perceive that the child in question, Morella's offspring, could not correspond less to the image of a flesh-and-blood girl. She appears even more ethereal than her mother; strictly avoiding all erotic allusions, as usual, Poe makes his narrator conceal the fact of Morella's pregnancy up to the very moment of death/birth. The daughter's first ten years are covered by one remark about the miraculous speed with which she is growing; as she is meant to be an exact copy of the original Morella, the description of her features is merely a detailed repetition of what has been remarked about Morella's outward appearance and behavior. Without any doubt the child is an adult from the first moment of her life; Morella's "restoration" rather resembles the rebirth of a phoenix than the beginning of a new kind of karma.

Considering such a "characterization" of a child, which was--and has remained--totally commonplace in horror fiction, one must say that The Voice of the Clown deserves additional attention, because in this case the reincarnation motif surprisingly accounts for an enrichment of the child's personality. Strictly speaking, it causes another (this time explicit) case of schizophrenia: the protagonist is born with a dominant "childish" half and an "inner voice" she cannot quite grasp or define in her simple terms of thinking, but which the reader recognizes as the adult Indian sorceress. During the first part of the novel, however, the girl Laura connects the voice she hears with the doll she has possessed since the day of her birth. She is convinced that the toy, whose origin no one can explain, and which she always keeps close to her body like an extra limb, constantly speaks to her. This internal dialogue is the only form of verbal communication Laura ever pursues; in the course of the action she never utters a word to anyone (except her mother), because she intuitively knows that talking includes the risk of giving oneself away.

Laura's double personality imparts a fascinating quality of ambiguity to all her emotions and activities. Like any normal six-year-old girl Laura wants to marry her father some day;[9] she likes his masculine smell, and his kiss makes her shiver with delight. The oedipal connotation is originally combined with the signs of adult passion; only in such a peculiar arrangement are erotic, even sexual allusions allowed in connection with small children. (The further possibility of sexual acts being performed by a possessed child will be discussed in detail as well.) Laura's deadly aversion to her mother can be explained in a twofold way accordingly. Both parts of her psyche claim the father and want to destroy the mother; the "child's" methods may be simpler in design, but they evidence a cruelty which is at least as relentless as that of an adult, for it is due to "natural" egotism instead of passionate hatred. The differentiated emotional background of Laura's struggle against her mother is counterbalanced by an equally complex motivation on her "enemy's" side: the woman loves her child, though she has always felt Laura's absolute rejection of her maternal feelings, and she talks in earnest when she announces that she will fight against her daughter with all the weapons she has, for Laura's own sake (35). She is overjoyed when the girl speaks to her for the first time, because this proves that Laura is not imbecilic after all. She cannot imagine that Laura only intends to make her mother look like a madwoman in front of the family, and her appearance is rather pathetic when, tears of joy streaming down her face, she asks Laura in vain to repeat her wonderful first sentence: "She said it. She did! Tell her, Laura. Say 'Kate, you are a fat pig'" (48).

Even without the influence of the clown's voice Laura is a murderous creature. Excited by the mere sight of blood, she does not shrink from trying to stab her new-born sister with a syringe, after her mother has refused her the breast, though she has fed the odious baby (again two ambivalent actions). It is significant that Laura regards the baby as an inconvenient, loathsome object, whereas her beloved doll is a living person, her most intimate friend. When the clown "tells" her to tear him apart (so that her mother and brother will be charged with this offense), this means to Laura the greatest sacrifice of which she is capable: she believes that she has killed her sole advisor and assistant and is later on astonished to hear the clown's voice inside her head. The baby is "as wilful as her clown" (199), but much uglier, and "sacrificing the mud-baby...would be easy compared to that" (201). After Laura has killed the baby, she cannot comprehend why its death upsets her family, whereas they have only shrugged their shoulders after the clown's destruction.

In the end the clown's body and its voice are strictly separated entities. An Indian sorcerer, who knows about the reincarnation and tries to put an end to Laura's crimes, talks only to the "clown" inside her, while the child remains a passive witness of their spiritual conflict. The fact that the man feels pity for the child in Laura's body helps the adult half escape from his spell. The remains of the clown's body finally acquire a new function: Laura sews its head to a key ring, meaning to give her father her most precious possession, whereas her other half has chosen this object as a means of enchantment ("'It is the perfect charm for him,'" 266). Only in the very last moment of her life does the child realize that it has never been the clown's intention to let Laura grow to adulthood (278). In a wild dance she and her father stumble over the precipice where the Indian girl committed suicide in the beginning, and their deaths are interpreted as the result of reckless childish play. In this very peculiar manner the child (or at least the child half) becomes the victim of adult passion.

A direct physical relationship between a child and its doll is by no means an exception in horror fiction. F. Terry Newman's story "Marius, the Doll" shows the simplest (though not least remarkable) form of such bodily interaction. "Marius" is the name of both a small orphan boy and the doll he possesses. An artist has created the toy as an exact copy of the boy's features, and whatever happens to it (trifling injuries or a serious damage) is transmitted to the child's body.[10] When the color of his doll is scraped off, Marius has a scar on the respective part of his body the next day, whereas the toy no longer shows any trace of the abrasion. Marius is an extremely introverted boy, who only seems to communicate with his doll, which he caresses and fondles all day, never letting it go for a single moment.

Marius' close connection to his companion can again be explained on several levels. Witchcraft is certainly the first possibility that comes to the reader's mind (after all, the story must basically be considered a ghost story); the narrator himself adds another aspect, some "mysterious and inexplicable psycho-physiological" influence[11] which may be caused by Marius' and the doll's common antecedents: the boy's family was killed in an accident, and only he and his small sister's toy "survived." In the deaths of Marius' relatives the "boomerang effect" of adult sins becomes evident once more. The narrator is told that, decades after World War II, the family was destroyed by the war; an old mine that was floating down a river brought about the end of their peaceful holiday ("for some, the war has never ended," 8). When the doll is severely damaged and Marius on the verge of death, only another artist whose crippled leg is a reminder of the war as well can rescue the boy by restoring the toy. This man, who has specialized in expressionism (the possibility of making a person's inner life visible on the canvas, 10) seems to feel how the doll's "heart" starts beating again under his hands, and he is convinced that during his exertions someone is watching him from behind.

Some of the "symptoms" revealed in the preceding relationship are reminiscent of the magical powers voodoo masters are supposed to exert on their victims. Black slaves brought the voodoo cult, a form of fetishistic devil worship, to America and the Caribbean islands, where it has been kept up to the present day, enriched by a number of elements borrowed from Christianity. It is significant that initially the central part of the voodoo ritual consisted in the sacrifice of the "ram without horns," a girl.[12] Later the female human victim was replaced by an animal, preferably a dog, bull, or cock; this more "civilized" version must mainly be ascribed to the influence of missionaries and civil authorities. Through self-hypnosis and drugs the participants in the nocturnal rituals are able to fall into a trance-like condition.

In reality, dolls as a medium of "remote control" are exclusively instruments of adult sorcerers. In horror fiction, on the contrary, authors greatly favor small girls (who would otherwise serve as perfect victims) as voodoo sorceresses who can manipulate and command their adult victims. The girl's "playthings" thus deserve their name in a double sense. The protagonist of Virginia Kester Smiley's novel High Country Nurse, for instance, has to care for a twelve-year-old girl who wants to destroy her adult brother by means of witchcraft. Confined to a wheel-chair, the child concentrates all her mental powers on her brother, whom she accuses of having caused her invalidism. She is fascinated by literature about sorcery; through this self-instruction she tries to accomplish her aim to become a witch. Among crystal balls and a painting of the witch-house in Salem her dearest possession is a simple rag doll without a face, which she pierces with pins during her spare time, and which of course represents her brother. In her case, however, the supernatural exists solely in her own mind, and all her efforts must remain fruitless.

The small girl in Arthur Machen's story "The White People" seems to be destined for a much more promising career. She is the protagonist of a tale within a tale and the elucidating example of an introductory definition of true sinners and pure evil, which demands the absence of any carnal-mindedness and sensuality in a human being and, above all, an unconscious striving and longing for forbidden spheres.[13] This theory, brought forward in a precise, apparently simple kind of lecture, is the more fascinating as it clashes completely with the common opinion that evil depends on knowledge and consciousness of vice. The child, an ideal representative of the thesis developed by the "lunatic sage" (67), presumably Machen's mouthpiece, appears of course more unfamiliar than ever, considered as a person capable of superior and refined (yet not sophisticated) wickedness.

From her earliest infancy the girl is sensitive to the presence of dark powers, able to speak unknown languages and perform unknown rites she does not understand herself. She discovers a mysterious country nobody else has ever entered. Her nurse has always secretly acted as her teacher of witchcraft, but even she is appalled at the extent of the girl's innate capacity, which surpasses her own. With regard to the "premises" of the tale it is significant that the nurse teaches her eight-year-old apprentice the basic elements of voodoo without revealing the evil meaning to her:

> ...she sat down again, and took the clay in her hands and began to shape it into a doll, but not like the dolls I have at home, and she made the queerest doll I had ever seen, all out of the wet clay, and hid it under a bush to get dry and hard, and all the time she was making it she was singing these rhymes to herself, and her face got redder and redder...she said we must "pay our respects," and she would show me what to do, and I must watch her all the time. So she did all sorts of queer things with the little clay man, and I noticed she was all streaming with perspiration, though we had walked so slowly, and then told me to "pay my respects," and I did everything she did because I liked her, and it was such an odd game. And she said that if one loved very much, the clay man was very good, if one did certain things with it, and if one hated very much, it was just as good, only one had to do different things, and we played with it a long time, and pretended all sorts of things. (90)

In such an "innocent" way the child is confronted with evil, and, still unaware, she will far exceed her nurse's humble experiments.

The most ruthless killer of all can be found in Robert Bloch's story "Sweets to the Sweet." The small protagonist, whose late mother was a genuine witch (as the widowed father suspects), wants to commit patricide. Though the father is aware of her latent wish to kill him, he cannot prevent his doom: through the very doll he has given her as a present the girl is able to destroy him; after some preparatory needle tortures the father perishes, while the doll is burning to ashes in the fireplace.

John Saul's Suffer the Children has already demonstrated that children themselves can be used as both dolls and playthings. In David Campton's story "At the Bottom of the Garden" a novel variety is added: children being manipulated by a small alien playmate in the most grotesque manner. The fact that this non-human creature, which absolutely shuns adult human company, can take children apart and reassemble their limbs as it wishes is by no means the horrible aspect of the story; only adult interference with these difficult operations causes disaster. Eight-year-old Geraldine lives in a "natural" dependence on her parents (who more or less care for her physical needs, but never really talk or listen to her) and in a deliberate dependence on Ineed, who has already taken out and repaired the girl's deformed teeth and promises to improve other parts as well. In the garden, the "no-man's land" between her parents' and Ineed's worlds, Geraldine and Ineed meet regularly. The girl never tries to hide her friends or her activities from her parents; on the contrary, she calls attention to every detail, but they take no notice of her descriptions. Physical characteristics are employed as symbols in this connection: the constantly "flour-fogged spectacles"[14] of Geraldine's stupid, bustling, accident-prone mother stand for her "ever-cluttered mind" and the

blindness towards her daughter's affairs ("Mummy wouldn't notice if I
lost my head," 20). Ineed, on the other hand, literally wants to get
inside Geraldine's head to understand how her playmate's interior is
composed. Against Geraldine's expectations her parents do notice that
she has lost her head when they incidentally look out of the window
("There were two tiny figures by the hedge at the bottom of the garden. The height and distance made them look almost like dolls. One
figure was bent over the other," 20). For the first time they care
about their daughter and thus destroy her life, because they drive
Ineed away once and for ·all. Geraldine's mother, who has previously
compared her failures in the girl's education to the catastrophes of
her cookery, kneels by the remnants of her child as if "kneeling by a
piece of broken china, and waiting for someone to fetch a dustpan"
(21). Even now she fails to register Geraldine's silent attempts at
communication. –

Apart from the manifold possibilities which voodoo rituals offer
to the writers of horror fiction, there exists another very popular
occasion which authors frequently employ as a background for their
tales: Guy Fawkes Night. Both the historical Gunpowder Plot and contemporary customs and ceremonies are of great significance. The conspiracy of thirteen Catholic noblemen who intended to blow up Jacob I
and the Parliament on November 5th, 1605 (the day of the opening of
Parliament), the failure of their plan and their subsequent execution,
and the Parliament's decision to declare this day a holiday are well-
known facts of English history. Guy Fawkes, the intended executor of
the plot, has become the central figure of all celebrations, during
which human replicas ("guys") are used in various ways.

Human "guys" are a favorite topic in horror literature. John
Metcalfe's story "Funeral March of a Marionette," for instance, centers upon the nightly round of two small boys, who drag the handcart
with their guy through the snowy streets of London. Only at the very
end of the story are explicit proofs given that the figure is the
children's baby brother Gus, who, having undergone the cruellest forms
of (thoughtless) abuse, is dying of cold and exhaustion. The attentive
reader has been able to interpret several hints at the "doll's" real
nature right from the start; the boys' initial enthusiasm and delight,
but also their growing uneasiness (which could also be explained by
the deserted surroundings and the children's fatigue) can be seen in a
different, sinister light. The author skilfully employs visual and
acoustic effects to accompany the group's peregrinations through the
night life of the city—an adult domain which is for once taken over
by the numerous hordes of begging children. The adults' reactions to
the guy are even more horrifying than the children's indifference, because the boys simply regard their brother as an object that they must
return after making the highest possible profit from it. The adult
"benefactors," however, do not look at the guy at all; either
"blinded" by the snow, the city lights and other distractions, or too
drunk to comprehend the situation, they do not save the child that is
fully exposed to view and dying under their very eyes.

One of the most elaborate and profound examples, "Guy Fawkes
Night" by Richard Davis, happens to contain one of the most relentless
struggles between father and child as well. A twelve-year-old boy's
deadly hatred for his father, a country squire, leads the child to
cold-blooded murder. The historical meaning of Guy Fawkes Night must

be taken into consideration here: after all, the burning dummy represents the king rather than the assassin. When the boy David disguises
his father's (a nobleman's) unconscious body and sets him on fire in
front of the whole village community, one can perceive that this
patricide is a form of regicide, too. A friend remembers the "glorious
holocaust" forty years later: "Funny how important the night of the
Bonfire had become in his mind. Everything had changed that night. It
was almost like the end of an era."[15] David executes a tyrant who has
himself destroyed human life; he has ordered three poachers smoked out
("David had been present, but in the background, crying with fear and
pain for the wretches inside. They had stuck it out till the last
possible moment, and then three sorry-looking specimens, blackened and
scorched, their clothes half off their bodies, and wriggling with
pain, had emerged. One of them had later died in the cottage hospital," 49). Still a minor after the ruler's death, David does not continue the odious family tradition, and the children's dance around the
"funeral pyre" (53) is the last remarkable happening on this estate.

3. THE VICTIM

THE CHILD AS A VICTIM OF PARENTS AND TUTORS

> And I could see that child's one eye
> Which seemed to laugh, and say with glee:
> "What caused my death you'll never know--
> Perhaps my mother murdered me."
>
> William H. Davies, "The Inquest"[1]

In the course of the preceding chapters it has been pointed out in detail that, irrespective of plot and imagery, the child's representation in horror fiction remains practically uniform. One can notice, too, that even its heterogeneous functions as victim or victimizer do not bring about any decisive difference in appearance and demeanor. The following classification by functions is therefore mainly a formal one; it emphasizes important similarities rather than introducing additional criteria by which basic distinctions concerning the child's "nature" might be made. There certainly exists an interdependence between the child's unchanging features and the difficulties which sometimes lie in the definition of its true function. The poem "The Inquest" by William H. Davies clearly illustrates this particular problem. The four-month-old corpse that seems to wink at the reader in order to tease him does not quite correspond to his conception of an innocent, helpless victim: "One eye, that had a yellow lid,/Was shut--so was the mouth, that smiled;/The left eye open, shining bright--/It seemed a knowing little child" (16). The child seems amused at the jury's helplessness and dismay, and when the coroner pronounces the verdict--death by accident--its smile appears to harmonize with the mother's and express a perverse bond, a conspiracy between the two.

Setting up a catalogue of the most common parental offenses against their offspring, one observes that one of the worst crimes merely consists in the adults' carelessness and indifference, for these attitudes always cause disaster. Guy de Maupassant's tale "Le Baptême" is a particularly apt example. On the day of its christening a new-born child is exposed for hours to the icy winter wind. Waiting in front of the chapel, the relatives even undress the child, because it has to "wait for God all naked" ("C'était l'usage. Si on ne l'avait pas suivi, il serait arrivé malheur au petit"--"That was the custom. If they had not complied with it, some misfortune would have befallen the little one"[2]). The priest is equally cold-blooded and prolongs the ceremony ("in order to make that human larva suffer that was tortured by the cold, in the name of a merciless, barbarous God," 50). The child's doom is sealed when its parents, instead of hurrying home to warm it, get drunk and fall asleep in a ditch. The narrator has previously talked about savage tribes who were extinguished by alcohol; a "civilized" French family is obviously just as capable of self-destruction.

Maupassant frequently concentrates on the careless abuse of children's lives. In a tale with the significant title "La Mère aux monstres" he goes a step further, depicting the gradual development from "mere" thoughtlessness to commercialized cruelty: a beautiful woman who becomes pregnant at regular intervals does not want to look ugly in her condition and goes on wearing the tightest corsets until the moment of delivery. Having discovered that one can sell the hideously misshapen children as fairground freaks at a considerable profit, she starts "breeding" them deliberately. Of course Maupassant, who is a master of psychological insights rather than sensational descriptions, presents much subtler aspects of parental ignorance to the reader. In his tale "Une Veuve" a small boy's female relatives drive him to despair and suicide by playing a practical joke on him. They treat the child, who still likes to sit in his mother's lap, like a grown-up accomplished lover and suitor; the women do not bear in mind that the male members of the family, each of them a passionate lover, all ended their lives through suicide, and that the boy--though too young to love--has always seen himself as the heir of this tradition. Adult passion ruins the life of an unspoilt child that blindly tries to imitate his elders.

The second major crime against children is the parents' egoistic wish to keep their offspring to themselves by hiding them away from the outside world. The stories "Oh, Mirror, Mirror" by Nigel Kneale and "Jack-in-the-Box" by Ray Bradbury both deal with this topic, but the authors' basic conceptions show remarkable differences. The first example can, as the title suggests, be regarded as a nightmarish modern adaptation of various fairytale motifs: a young girl's aunt, who has kept the child within the boundaries of her house and garden and never allowed her to leave her property, has to take the ultimate measure of telling the girl that in her case the ugly duckling she has learned about has never turned into a swan. The woman gives her a mirror and explains to her that the child's white skin, pink cheeks, red lips, blue eyes, and golden curls would cause people outside to torture and kill her, because she is too ugly to bear (except for her Auntie, of course). People outside have thick hair and a dark and tough skin ("Brown skinned and hard, they are, with strong black hair. I'm one of them. So I can go out and talk among them"[3]). The girl's aunt takes advantage of the fact that the girl, who has grown up in a fairytale world, is impressionable enough to believe in a realm of ogres and demons outside. Reading between the lines of Auntie's terrifying prediction about how people will chase the girl, one can understand the adult's merciless attempts to possess the child for a lifetime. She is in reality the one who has experienced such persecution, and the house both live in is Auntie's fortress against her enemy, the outside world ("It's terrible to be different. But your Auntie's here. She understands. And there's a high wall, and nothing to be afraid of, if they don't see inside," 178). But the "enemy," beauty, is inside as well; Auntie's recommendation to add brown stain to the child's washing water (another popular motif) will make conditions bearable for "both" sides: "And when she looks in the mirror, she won't seem so different after all. She can pretend to be like me, can't she?" (179)

Bradbury's story is totally different (and more profound) with regard to the adult's motivation and the general atmosphere. Strangely

enough, the author has greater success in creating a fairytale realm
than his predecessor, without ever having to invoke the standard
formulas. Bradbury describes the most trivial objects the way children
grasp them with their basically different conceptions of size, proportion, and utility. As everything is revealed through a small boy's
eyes, the reader needs much time and imagination to become "acclimat-
ized" to this enchanted world of beauty and realize that it only consists of a house with many rooms, a lift, and a large garden.

The boy's mother wants to keep him safely by her side and warns
him not to go out, not because of any bad human beings, but because of
the cars that are responsible for her husband's death: "'Do you want
to see the Beasts that run down paths and crush people like straw-
berries?...Do you want to go out there?' she cried, 'like your father
did before you were born, and be killed as he was killed, struck down
by one of those Terrors on the road, would you like that!'"[4] The
mother's motives cannot be called entirely selfish; she is extremely
vulnerable herself and fears for her equally delicate son ("there she
would be, in her tower, silent and white, high and alone and quiet. It
was like passing a deserted greenhouse in which one last wild white
blossom lifted its head to the moonlight," 81). Her husband was her
god, and she passes this religion on to her boy: God the Father built
their World, and one day his son will inherit it. On each birthday the
boy may enter a new room, and on his eighteenth birthday he will be
"Man of the House, Father, God, Ruler of the Universe" (89). His
mother even splits herself into two personalities, stern Mother and
understanding Teacher, to make the boy feel less lonely. His birth-
days, however, are celebrated with shorter and shorter intervals between, and one morning Mother/Teacher is dead. The boy, who has always
wanted to know about the Beasts and Death ("Was Death a feeling? Did
God enjoy it so much he never came back? Was Death a journey then?"
93) is somehow glad to escape from his jail--like his Jack-in-the-Box.
People outside wonder at the strange child shouting, "I'm dead, I'm
dead, I'm glad I'm dead, I'm dead, I'm dead, it's good to be dead!"

Four children who are kept prisoners in the modern version of a
"strong and dark castle, ruled over by a witch and an ogre,"[5] are the
protagonists of the novel Flowers in the Attic by Virginia C. Andrews.
Its motto, "Shall the clay say to him that fashioneth it, What makest
thou?" (Isaiah 45:9), expresses the children's victimization through
their god-like grandparents, caused directly by the guilt of their
parents, whose marriage was based on incest. Seldom is the recurrent
idea of the "sins of the fathers" elaborated with such consistency.
The children's parents had to flee from the deceitful paradise they
had grown up in; after the father's death, the mother returns, hoping
to inherit a fortune. She allows the bigoted "rulers" to lock her
children up for years like lepers--to her original offense she thus
adds greed, neglect, and egotism. The children, "spawned from the
Devil," "evil from the moment of conception" (91), arouse their grandmother's wrath through their very beauty and must suffer all the terrors of her sadistic regime. Their mother's visits, which become rarer
and finally stop altogether, do not console them: "She looked so vi-
brantly healthy, so unbelievably happy, while we wilted and felt half-
sick from the oppressive heat of this room" (121). Indeed, the mother
absorbs all the vital energy the children are losing; she seems to
feed on it ("Momma was wearing pink--she did look lovely in pink. It

put roses in her cheeks, and her hair glowed with rosy warmth," 174).
Apart from the contrast between a life of imprisonment and freedom,
her growing vigor shows her successful efforts to reabsorb the powers
she has spent on her (now unwanted) offspring. She needs all the energy she can drain from her surroundings since she is courting again.
     Although the plot of the novel is by no means based on super-
natural phenomena, the vampiric imagery cannot be ignored. The older
brother and sister, who become surrogate parents for the small twins,
want to give their own health to restore theirs (174), and they eventually do so as a last resort: they make the starving, apathetic twins
drink from their own blood. They can rescue them for the time being,
though the whole incident leaves all four of them pale and listless.
Of course, the children's extensive suffering has consequences: one of
the twins dies from exhaustion. The second part of the novel, following an interval of several years of imprisonment, presents the older
children as a pubescent couple. And, as the ironic result of their
narrow confinement, the two commit incest--their elders' crime they
have always been warned against.
     Children are often abused as living pawns in the battle between
their parents. The parent's hatred for his or her partner is transferred to the more helpless offspring, the partner's Achilles' heel.
In this case the child is of course reduced to an object by its own
parent. Gustav Meyrink's "Die Urne von St. Gingolph," a simple but
meaningful tale, shows the essence of such a triangular relationship:
while a mother is kneeling in front of a cross, fervently praying for
the forgiveness of her adultery, her husband hides their child in a
huge grey urn nearby. The urn has many functions in the story--a
"physical" one, for instance: "Had that not been a soft wail, quite
close to her?...A wail, a painful wail which enshrouded her entirely,
which resounded above and beneath her--in the air--in the earth....Now
the wail sounds nearer-- --and louder; madness spreads its black wings
that will darken the sky-- --her entire brain is one smarting auditory
nerve."⁶ Hearing the wail of her offspring, the woman reacts like any
female animal and grows frantic, because the object of her maternal
instincts is so near and yet beyond her reach. The urn seems to punish
the murderer as well; a moonbeam which is reflected on its surface
creates a glowing red eye that stares at the man and makes him run
away in panic. Above all, however, the urn is a suitable place for the
physical reminder of the adults' former passion, which has burnt to
ashes. The child's lifeless remnants are covered by a lid that has the
significant shape of an "obstinate" cranium made of stone.
     In the novel Where are the Children? by Mary Higgins Clark a hus-
band takes steps which are even more drastic. Being a sadist by nature
and suspecting his wife of adultery, he premeditatedly kills their
children in a most cold-blooded manner and feigns suicide. From a safe
distance (a house called the Lookout) he witnesses with voyeuristic
delight how his wife, who is charged with the murders, is desperately
struggling to prove her innocence. For such absolute power over his
wife he has sacrificed his own children with pleasure.
     In one of Ray Bradbury's less refined tales, "The October Game,"
the author nonetheless ingeniously unfolds the detailed history of a
child's abuse from the very day of conception. The various turns in
the child's development (which seem to depend entirely on the opposing
magic spells of her god-like parents) are recorded like scores in the

battle between father and mother--at least by the increasingly enervated father. In the beginning he has realized his own principle,
absolute male predominance, by forcing the child on his wife. The
woman, his weaker opponent, has withdrawn from him since that moment.
She is convinced that her husband only wanted her to give birth to a
dark-haired son, the very picture of his father, or die. But she sur-
vives ("And in triumph!"[7])--she has taken the subtlest and cruellest
"revenge":

> Marion and Louise, the two silent denouncers of his viril-
> ity, his dark power. What alchemy had there been in Louise
> that took the dark of a dark man and bleached and bleached
> the dark brown eyes and black hair and washed and bleached
> the ingrown baby all during the period before birth until
> the child was born, Marion, blonde, blue-eyed, ruddy-
> cheeked?...she had produced a child in her own image...(228)

Instead of growing fond of his daughter, he bears the female "superiority" in his house for eight years, until he decides that one
"witch" must be punished through the death of the other; a children's
party on Halloween and a special "game" in the cellar (the "tomb of
the witch," 231) form the most appropriate background for such a
scheme.[8]

The Girl in a Swing, a novel by Richard Adams, deals with the
sacrifice of a child whose existence would thwart its mother's plan to
marry the man she loves. With his lengthy and tiresome account of the
author of Watership Down proves that a plot which is suitable for a
short story should not be employed for a novel of this size. The story
of the mysterious and voluptuous Karin, who enchants her lover like a
pagan goddess, kills her small daughter to follow him, and is finally
"reclaimed" by the girl's decaying corpse that has risen from the bottom of the ocean, is certainly fascinating in itself. Instead of
gradually preparing the reader for the gruesome climax, however, the
author infallibly undermines each promising episode with a long-winded
lecture on the history of English pottery.

Not death, but a girl's psychic destruction is the effect of a
mother's uncontrolled passion in Ruth Rendell's "The Vinegar Mother."
Like the mysterious plant that looks like a slice of liver and turns
good red wine into vinegar,[9] the child's mother turns the happy family
life into a nightmare for her unsuspecting daughter. Both "mothers"
are precious, demanding creatures, flourishing in the house (called
Sanctuary) and devouring the life inside. Both must never be touched
with metal, or they "will shrivel and die" (123). In the end the cuck-
olded father shoots his wife, while the child, who has meanwhile become a haunted girl with "dark circles round her old woman's eyes"
(136), stabs the vinegar mother "to death" with a knife.

Compared with this convincing account of emotional vampirism,
Charles Lloyd's "Special Diet," an example of physical vampirism, must
appear somewhat ludicrous. An eight-year-old girl who usually wears a
"jaunty red beret"[10] visits her mad grandmother, who asks a present of
her: "Just a cupful. One teacupful of your young healthy blood" (81).
Apart from the obvious fairytale motif, the traditional idea of blood
as the source of youth and health forms the basis of the story. A vampire's thirst and the greed of senile people are skilfully combined in

the grandmother's attitude. The reader can also discover some less
conspicuous literary allusions, like that to Dr. Seward's mental patient in Dracula, who, like Granny, begins his vampiric career by
eating vermin.[11] Moreover, the story reminds the reader of Vitezslav
Nezval's novel Valerie a týden divů (Valerie and the Week of Wonders),
in which a small girl is confronted with her grandmother's vampiric
tendency as well--though not as drastically.

All the child's adult relatives qualify as victimizers, though
parents certainly have a prominent position. In total contrast to the
fairytale, however, the wicked stepmother is not a very popular figure
in horror fiction. Characters like the evil stepmother in Barbara
Benziger's "Dear Jeffy," who tries to eradicate her husband's offspring one by one, are exceptions among the murderous next of kin.
Other persons in the child's immediate surroundings, like nannies and
baby-sitters, belong to the more "favored" victimizers. Evelyn Piper's
novel The Nanny and Dulcie Gray's story "The Babysitter" illustrate
that here children are also frequently treated as pawns in the
struggle between adults. In the latter work, above all, the baby is
reduced to a mere object that can be used to blackmail an opponent.
The baby-sitter kills her charge in order to manifest her superiority
over other people: "She'd always wanted to hurt a baby, to make it
suffer because it was helpless. Now was her chance and if somehow she
could involve Alice in what she did, Alice would be as helpless as the
baby, Alice would be utterly dependent on her, and would have to stay
with her for ever."[12] The benevolent "Uncle" in Walter Winward's
rather tasteless story "The Benefactor," on the other hand, aims his
actions directly at his small victims; once in a while he takes a
child out of an orphanage to save it from the corruption of adult age
by killing it in time. Charles Birkin's tale "The Last Night," dealing
with a girl in a hospital who is slowly put to death by a mad surgeon,
is equally insignificant, because the author revels in the details of
sadistic tortures and entirely neglects the artistic possibilities
which the setting offers him.

The relationship between two ageing spinsters and a small boy
which is depicted in Angus Wilson's "Raspberry Jam" shocks the reader
much more by the contrast between its initial innocence and the final
catastrophe. The story, which reminds one of the traditional image of
the American Southern belle (and the notion that most elderly Southern
ladies "have been away" at least once in their lifetime), is an ingenious mixture of the idyllic bond between the old ladies and the
child presented in Truman Capote's The Grass Harp, and the peculiar
horror of William Faulkner's "A Rose for Emily." The old ladies in
question live in constant struggle with their neighbors who regard
them as freaks and only tolerate them because of the money they gener-
ously spend on community welfare; the sisters' friendship for the boy
is the more sincere. They can give the boy all the love and understanding he has lacked in the company of his unimaginative parents.
This overall situation must inevitably lead to the incident which forever kills the child's affection and confidence. After several vicious
attacks from the outside world the ladies drink heavily for a whole
week, and by the time the boy arrives for tea they are "in a state of
mental and nervous excitement" that renders them "far from normal."[13]
As birds have eaten the raspberries which were meant to be a special
treat for their guest, the women consider all birds members of the

"conspiracy" against them. In the boy's presence they slowly torture a captured bird to death until it is "nothing but a sodden crimson mass" ("'Why, it's nothing now, it just looks like a lump of raspberry jam,'" 306). In their clouded state of mind they do not realize that they have crushed both a feeling and a human being that were as delicate as the bird.

"The Rocking-Horse Winner," one of D. H. Lawrence's best-known and most praised stories, is another excellent illustration of the fact that the victim may sometimes appear at least as weird and frightening to the reader as the cruellest victimizer possibly can. The reason for the boy's suffering and death seems quite trivial at first sight; his life is ruined by his hyper-sensitive reaction to the atmosphere in his home: "They lived in a pleasant house, with a garden, and they had discreet servants, and felt themselves superior to anyone in the neighbourhood. Although they lived in style, they felt always an anxiety in the house. There was never enough money. The mother had a small income, and the father had a small income, but not nearly enough for the social position which they had to keep up."[14] A haunting but unspoken phrase begins to fill the house, soon becoming an unbearable crescendo: "There must be more money! There must be more money! The children could hear it all the time, though nobody said it aloud. They heard it at Christmas, when the expensive and splendid toys filled the nursery. Behind the shining modern rocking-horse, behind the smart doll's house, a voice would start whispering: 'There must be more money! There must be more money!'" (791) The boy Paul, even more sensitive than his sisters, is told that luck is "what causes you to have money," and he decides to win his mother's affection by "being lucky."[15] He wants to attain luck on horseback: "...he would sit on his big rocking-horse, charging madly into space, with a frenzy that made the little girls peer at him uneasily. Wildly the horse careered, the waving dark hair of the boy tossed, his eyes had a strange glare in them. The little girls dared not speak to him..." At last he suddenly stops, forces his horse into the mechanical gallop and slides down--"'Well, I got there!' he announced fiercely, his blue eyes still flaring" (793).

Having recognized that he can foretell the winning horse at the races, he becomes his uncle's partner and wins a fortune. He cannot win his mother's love, however, because the money she gets makes her greedier still: "The house had been 'whispering' worse than ever lately, and, even in spite of his luck, Paul could not bear up against it" (799). At last the voices scream in ecstasy and frighten Paul terribly. Ironically the mother, who does not know the new source of money, reproaches her son for wasting his energy with riding a wooden horse (he is too old for a rocking-horse--at least too old to use it as a toy[16]). Trying to quieten the voices, Paul goes on madly riding his horse, his blue eyes blazing; when he breaks down, he is still "tossing ceaselessly on the pillow." Paul is certainly an uncanny boy, but the reader must bear in mind that the rhythm of his insane gallop is only the response to the wilder rhythm of the chant around him. The child appears like an apocalyptic rider, but he is in fact a Christ figure who sacrifices his life in practicing the religion of his elders--the worship of Mammon. He has inspired the servants in the house with religious awe all the time; his mother's heart, however, has "gone, turned actually into a stone" (804).

THE CHILD AS A VICTIM OF ITS ENVIRONMENT

> And many minutes later she vaguely sensed the brief ride
> into the chilly operating theater, where her head was fixed
> in a stainless steel clamp and her mouth forced open to make
> way for the anesthetic tube. Then the nearness of her death
> became absolutely an overpowering reality, and the child
> wanted to tell these people that she would not fault them if
> it came to pass--unaware that they had not intended to care.
>
>   Terrel Miedaner, <u>The Soul of Anna Klane</u>[1]

It is often difficult to draw clear lines between the domestic
sphere, people and relationships that belong to it, and the outside
world which influences family life in manifold ways. Lawrence's "Rocking-Horse Winner" is driven to insanity by the "voices" inside his
home, unaware that these commands (commandments) come from beyond his
direct surroundings, that they are dictates of public life. In Davies'
"The Inquest," which deals with the most "intimate" form of murder,
the jury--public opinion--is directly involved and indirectly accused
of aiding and abetting the mother's crime. The child's role as a universal victim, which has become most obvious in the discussion about
peer groups, is responsible for the difficulties that lie in defining
private and public spheres of influence. As parents only form a small
part of the great mass of guilty adults, their particular offenses are
contributions to the general sin and corruption of adult life accordingly.

Most of these crimes (war, the persecution of nonconformists, the
abuse of nature, but also the breaking of the Ten Commandments, or the
seven deadly sins) are deeply rooted in human nature; their timelessness does not call for any concrete reference to time and place within
a tale. Therefore, the majority of short stories do not contain any
specifications in this respect. For obvious reasons a novel requires
at least a broadly defined setting (as, for instance, the era of Depression in <u>The Night of the Hunter</u>); but authors simultaneously employ various means which prevent the reader from linking the child too
closely to the setting in which it appears (the child's ethereal, un-
earthly presentation in the above novel produces this particular effect). In horror fiction the child must never be regarded as embedded
in any special historical context. Social criticism plays--perhaps
much against the layman's expectations--an immensely important role in
horror literature. The accusations of human vices and wrongdoings,
however, are both subtly hidden and much more general than, say, the
exposure of contemporary cruelties in Dickens' novels (some of which,
like the childhood episodes in Victor Hugo's <u>Notre Dame de Paris</u> or
<u>L'Homme qui rit</u>, admittedly contain classic Gothic elements). It is
also notable that the main forms of victimization imply death, total
physical destruction on the one hand, and purely psychic damage on the
other hand, whereas the broad field between these extremes is usually
ignored. Authors rarely dwell upon the description of continual physical suffering; they prefer to depict extended periods of psychic and

mental torture instead. Child victims in horror fiction retain their physical beauty and purity till death. The dirt and filth of their surroundings do not stain them--except in a figurative sense.

Social criticism in horror fiction is not chiefly, let alone exclusively, aimed at the situation in which the respective work is written. If a special historical event (the American Civil War, for instance) is explicitly mentioned in a story, the symbolic implications may well exceed the limits of this particular epoch. On the other hand, writers frequently take incidents of their own epoch as starting-points for fictional works: Jeremias Gotthelf's most famous tale, _Die schwarze Spinne_ (The Black Spider), which does not include any references to historical facts or figures, must, as Klaus Lindemann points out in his convincing analysis, be regarded as the author's expression of the general fear after Napoleon's reign and between the revolutions. To the critic's mind the myth of evil serves as an interpretation of (concrete) historical catastrophes, and also as a justification of a restorative policy and an idealization of static societies.[2] The story itself, which belongs without doubt to the ghastliest works ever written, centers upon all-embracing themes of human existence--birth, life, and death, and man's weakness in the struggle between God and the Devil.

The equally ancient central motif of a bargain with the Devil effectively illustrates that a human being does not "give birth" to children alone, but that "pregnancy" may also result in the rise of chaos and corruption. The Green One has sealed a pact with the most daring woman of a peasant community and given her a kiss on the cheek as the final affirmation. He provides the peasants in time with the payment in kind they owe their master, and now people try to deny him his reward, the soul of the first new-born child. The child that was meant for the Devil is baptized before he can receive it. During another woman's pregnancy it becomes clear that the Devil's kiss implanted his evil seed in his partner's cheek, a monstrous spider, which brings forth its own offspring at the moment of the second christening:

> In the house they began to cheer the renewed victory, the Green One's powerlessness, his assistant's futile efforts; but outside lay Christine, thrown to the ground by an unbearable pang, and in her face labor pains began to rage no woman in childbed had ever experienced before, and the spider in her face rose and swelled and burnt like fire through her bones.
>
> Suddenly Christine felt as if her face were going to burst, as if red-hot coals were born in it, came alive, swarmed across her face, across each limb, as if the whole of her face came alive and swarmed, burning hot, across her entire body. There, in the pale flash of lightning, she saw innumerable tiny black spiders, long-legged, poisonous, running across her limbs, out into the night...the spider settled down again, became once more an almost invisible spot, and with dying eyes gazed after its infernal offspring, which it had brought forth and sent out as a sign that the Green One was not to be joked with.[3]

Tortured by the Devil's seed, the human beings decide to sacrifice a child of their own, and even the baby's father agrees to the plan. A brave priest can save this child's soul, though its body must perish through the contact with the Devil; a courageous mother is even able to captivate the spider in a knot-hole. At this point of the story the ambiguity concerning the rise and decline of human morals and the re-petitive structure of human history becomes obvious: the beam with the knot-hole is used for a beautiful new house. There it serves as a per-manent warning, which is of course finally laughed at. Human beings can only be convinced by evidence, and they get it by removing the plug from the hole.

Gotthelf expresses the spirit of his age in very general terms, to be sure; his tale, however, is easily comprehensible for any modern reader. Swift's merciless satire "A Modest Proposal," on the other hand, which was written as a specific attack on a specific social situation ("the present deplorable state of the Kingdom"⁴), includes truly horrible implications that scarcely affect the modern reader very much, for he may consider some bygone epoch in a far-off country as a detached onlooker. Pieces of advice like "I rather recommend buying the Children alive, and dressing them hot from the Knife, as we do roasting Pigs" (516) evoke pleasant shivers, but hardly concern or shame within the reader (which they certainly would if the numerous hints at the historical background did not impede his fantasy).

The fact that writers of horror fiction underline the universal meaning of the child's appearance, and that they deliberately suppress references to the (actual) events which caused them to write a story in the first place, is demonstrated most plainly by Ambrose Bierce's "Chickamauga." Without doubt the American Civil War and the author's active participation in it directly inspired him to write his <u>Tales of Soldiers and Civilians</u>; in contrast to the other stories in the col-lection, "Chickamauga" does not contain a hint at this particular war at all--except for the title. Neither the setting nor the fighting armies are identified in any way; the incident in question could hap-pen anywhere and at any time.

The story of the small boy who goes astray in the wood near his parents' house, falls asleep, and awakes to watch a grotesque pro-cession of maimed and mutilated soldiers moving towards an eerie red glow in the distance (the burning ruins of the boy's own home), be-longs to Bierce's major achievements. The nameless child protagonist, a deaf-mute, has inherited the "lust for war" of his forefathers ("this child's spirit, in bodies of its ancestors, had for thousands of years been trained to memorable feats of discovery and conquest;" "the warrior-fire survived; once kindled, it is never extinguished"⁵). Being "the son of an heroic race," the boy indulges in imaginary battles, delights in various "postures of aggression and defense," and kills his invisible enemies with incredible ease. When "real danger" in the shape of a rabbit threatens him, he flees in panic, "calling with inarticulate cries for his mother, weeping, stumbling, his tender skin cruelly torn by brambles, his little heart beating hard with ter-ror--breathless, blind with tears--lost in the forest!" (28) As Stuart Woodruff points out, Bierce took a profound interest in the implica-tions of heredity: "If Bierce's characters lack psychological complex-ity, a partial explanation is that Bierce was more concerned with certain generic human traits than with specific or idiosyncratic qual-

ities."⁶ The statement might well be applied to the majority of
writers who concentrate on the child in horror literature.

The boy is both a victimizer and a victim: the "merry spectacle"
of war, to which the agonized soldiers contribute like the "painted
clown whom he had seen last summer in the circus" (30), excites and
delights the child (who is both ignorant and deaf); he plays cruelly
with the men and displays a merciless "childish curiosity." The cruel
aspects of war which concern him directly (his devastated home and his
horribly disfigured dead mother) reduce the strong, mighty, brave
warrior of his fancy to the weak creature he actually is. The pathos
which lies in the boy's sudden and total disillusionment ("His little
world swung half around; the points of the compass were reversed," 33)
does not contradict the main idea of the story that the child carries
in him the very same instinctive forces which lead the wounded soldiers on through the forest and which have destroyed his own world.
The boy's "innocent" games of war are gradually replaced by the sight
of real war and the final contact with it.

Two motifs are closely linked with the concept of heredity that
determines the tale: the reversed positions of child and adults and
the interchangeability of human beings and animals. The boy becomes
the leader of the soldiers, who "were men, yet crept like babes" (30),
and he does not recognize their human nature at all, but regards them
as "great black beetles," pigs, dogs, and bears. His final reaction to
his mother's death shows his own share of subhuman qualities: he emits
"a series of inarticulate and indescribable cries--something between
the chattering of an ape and the gobbling of a turkey--a startling,
soulless, unholy sound, the language of a devil" (33).

A literally soulless child whose deplorable condition is caused
by the ignorance and arrogance of society is the last victim in this
chapter. Though Terrel Miedaner's The Soul of Anna Klane, the story of
a ten-year-old girl who suffers from a brain tumor and is forced to
undergo surgery despite her own and her father's protests, seems to
deal with a rather limited kind of problem, it is in fact the basis of
an exceedingly profound essay on one of the most universal topics: the
human soul and its vulnerability. Enwrapped in an entirely fantastic,
thrilling plot, the pros and cons of a philosophical, even theological
discussion strike the reader with their full impact.

The presentation of the child Anna has various essential functions in the novel; during no phase of the action can she be considered a "normal" child, but in contrast to other works in which the
small protagonist is no child-"character" at all, Anna's appearance is
neither incidental nor unintended. The author takes advantage of the
usual "flatness" of depiction; with a child protagonist he is all the
more able to demonstrate the difference between a human being with a
soul or without a soul. At the beginning of the novel Anna is a child-
prodigy, who has both her own body and brain under perfect control.
Her superior intelligence is accompanied by innocent charm, a fine
sense of humor, and wisdom--an unusual combination of qualities indeed, especially in a child. The novel starts with a conversation between her and her beloved father; the high level of this communication
is to disconcert (and intimidate) the reader and prepare him for the
dramatic change in the child's pattern of behavior.

Having sensed a growth in her brain, Anna consults a physician
and, though she has meanwhile found a way to stop the growth inside

her through sheer concentration and will-power, she cannot stop the concerted action of doctors, policemen, and judges, who are deaf to her pleas because she is a minor. Her unforeseen appearance at the court where her destiny will be decided (she has escaped from the hospital for this occasion) bears a high symbolic value: "Although she had no need of it, Anna did not resist as the officer shrouded her body with the heavy robe. As it did not seem right to cover this child in black, he arranged the cloak with its purple lining facing outward, then stepped away as she thanked him for his trouble."[7] Anna's subtle ways of argumentation make her audience feel deeply ashamed, but her fate is sealed by "common sense":

> The judge turned to Anna. "I'm afraid you'll have to leave us. Don't worry, now," he smiled benevolently. "We'll do the best thing for you."--She stood up, letting the purple robe fall about her feet. "I think you will do what you believe is right," she said sadly. "And if that turns out not to be the best thing for me, well, I invite you to my funeral." Quickly, before he could answer or react, Anna bent forward and kissed him. (36)

The operation (during which "all the monsters and goblins of her preschool imagination" become "as real as life, conjured into existence by the magic of a surgeon's wand," 52) destroys the child's psyche and leaves her a soulless creature. Ironically enough, Anna's condition now pleases every adult, because she is so reassuringly "normal" for her age: a bored, listless girl who is only interested in the "flickering colors on the video screen" of her television set. The reader, who has grown used to the "person" Anna, is appalled at her condition. The public within the novel has to learn the truth as well. For this purpose Anna's father, who has recognized his child's spiritual death, minutely arranges an impressive scene; in front of the responsible surgeons and psychiatrists he tells his daughter to shoot herself with a gun. As the child has no volition (she is a "remarkably well-balanced child" in the doctor's opinion, but a mere zombie for her father), she obeys the command without the slightest hesitation.

Apart from the fundamental question as to the nature of the human soul, Anna's story serves as a fascinating allegory of the relationship between the child and its adult environment. Basically self-sufficient, the child is "adjusted" and corrupted. Her father's efforts cannot reverse this process. One may ask what guilt a father can bear who loves his daughter as much as Anna's father loves her: after all, he himself constructed and developed the "incredible million-dollar probe" which destroys his child's brain.

4. THE "EVIL INNOCENT"

THE POSSESSED CHILD

> Klein reached down to check her pulse. "Now, let's see what
> the trouble is, dear," he said gently. And abruptly was
> reeling, stunned and staggering, across the room from the
> force of a vicious backward swing of Regan's arm as the girl
> sat up, her face contorted with a hideous rage.
>   "The sow is mine!" she bellowed in a coarse and powerful
> voice. "She is mine! Keep away from her! She is mine!"
>
> William Peter Blatty, The Exorcist[1]

From the earliest origins of Gothic literature the most essential point of interest has been the struggle between good and evil
forces within the human soul. This inner bifurcation, which has found
its clearest expression in the Doppelgänger motif employed in Mary
Shelley's Frankenstein, Poe's "William Wilson," or Stevenson's tale of
Dr. Jekyll and Mr. Hyde, has always been restricted to adult protagonists. If the child (considered basically "innocent" by nature) was
involved in any conflict between good and evil, it served at best as a
pawn in other people's schemes, as illustrated in Gotthelf's tale.
Evil attacked the child as an outward force, and adult human beings
(sometimes assisted by heavenly powers) had to rescue the helpless
creature whose life and soul depended on the success of their mission.
Basically, this situation has never demonstrated any remarkable
variation. Authors have taken it for granted that the choice between
good and evil requires knowledge of both. Though the figure of the
"evil innocent" has grown, especially within the past two decades,
more and more popular, in this particular respect it hardly provides
an equivalent of the Doppelgänger. Unlike that classical type, the
child is never fully conscious of the harmful things that happen
through it--sometimes to it--and notably has no awareness of any meta-
morphoses within its own soul. The term "evil" is problematic in any
case: its most widespread popular meaning ("morally depraved, bad,
wicked, vicious") can in its strict sense not be applied to the child,
although the mere monstrosity of its "crimes" may easily lead an indiscriminate observer to do so. Other major meanings of the word
("doing or tending to do harm;" "causing discomfort, pain, or trouble;
unpleasant, offensive, disagreeable") are without reservation suitable
for the phenomenon under discussion.
"Innocence," on the other hand, can be an equally deceptive term
in this context, and precisely because the expression seems to be perfectly clear. The implications "freedom from sin, guilt, or moral
wrong," "freedom from specific guilt," or "freedom from cunning or
artifice" are accepted without hesitation and even appear somewhat
trivial. The initial and (considering the Latin origin) principal
sense, harmlessness and innocuousness, complicates matters consider-

ably.

Since the publication of the first famous representative of the "evil innocent," Henry James's <u>The Turn of the Screw</u> (1898), there has occurred a significant retrogression with regard to the complexity of the child's characterization. Critics have pointed out in detail how the author succeeded in presenting two flawless angelic creatures (through the eyes of the narrator) and simultaneously two small human beings who sometimes "kick over the traces" like all flesh-and-blood children. In his narrative James plays freely with the child's traditional image and, to some extent, exposes the absurdity of this conception. One has to read carefully between the lines of the Governess's account in order to recognize that Miles and Flora are not possessed by spirits, that they are neither "evil" nor "innocent" in a conventional sense.[2] They have, as Muriel Shine puts it, rather "become instruments of their elders' hostilities and aggressions, tools adults use to destroy each other;" they are "victims of a morally deficient adult world."[3] The basically simple story of the woman who has to accept full responsibility for her orphaned charges and whose over-anxiety and incomprehension of the children's behavior lead her to believe that the two are dominated by the ghosts of their wicked and depraved former tutors, fascinates the reader mainly because of its ambiguity. The Governess presupposes absolute purity in her charming, beautiful charges, yet she sees evil lurking behind every word they say and each trifling offense they commit. The wickedness which the woman senses is merely the reflection of her own knowledge of evil and the corruption that comes to every adult human being.[4]

Miles's self-concept as a "little man," above all, and his attempts to realize this concept finally bring about his doom. Wishing to get attention from the woman who is responsible for him (since his uncle has abandoned him), he tries to cope as best he can with an adult who makes extraordinary demands upon him. Since the Governess never explicitly states what she really is demanding of him, the child is forced to rely on his intuitive insights and must "fail." He cannot yet grasp the concept of masculinity the **woman** subconsciously applies to him; the sexual fantasy that lies hidden beneath the Governess's frantic effort to subdue and possess the boy becomes most explicit near the deadly finale:

> Miles stood again with his hands in his little pockets and his back to me--stood and looked out of the wide window through which, that other day, I had seen what pulled me up. We continued silent while the maid was with us--as silent, it whimsically occurred to me, as some young couple who, on their wedding-journey, at the inn, feel shy in the presence of the waiter. He turned round only when the waiter had left us. "Well--so we're alone!"[5]

Contemporary versions of the "evil innocent" do not appear nearly so enigmatic as their predecessors, and the numerous stories which are obviously written after the Jamesian "fashion"--invariably containing a governess with full responsibility for her charge(s), absent or dead parents, and ghosts--can by no means rival the ambiguity of <u>The Turn of the Screw</u>. Modern authors display a pronounced tendency to simplify the nature of their child protagonists. In most cases the appearance of ghosts is not meant to be explained away; the child is actually possessed by evil spirits. Strangely enough, Henry James "anticipated modern psychology" in his deep concern for the child's behavior,[6] whereas "post-Freudian" writers ignore the possibilities of child psychology.

The problem of sexuality, on the other hand, has become a major point of interest in connection with the evil innocent. Since sexual activities of any kind are generally taboo, authors gladly employ evil spirits to give the "aberrations" of their child protagonists a plausible justification. Thus, children may practise incest and masturbation or rape their relatives, always remaining "detached" observers of their own actions. Few writers combine the influence of evil forces with the underlying possibility that the child's own sexual desires may have awakened (which means it is pubescent). Theodus Carroll's novel Evil is a Quiet Word is a fascinating, highly original illustration of this idea. At first sight the plot seems to be a reversal of the "classic" pattern: a male employee has to protect a thirteen-year-old girl, whose parents are abroad, from the harmful influence of two ghosts. He is all alone with the child and a housekeeper (who shows a remarkable resemblance to James's Mrs. Grose); the ghosts he sees, however, are not merely the manifestations of his fantasy, because numerous other people have noticed them before. The "ghostly" plot and the child's sexual awakening do not exclude, but parallel and reinforce each other in a very efficient way.

Though Max, the gardener, is not the narrator, the events are chiefly related from his point of view--in order to show that, strangely enough, he is the actual victim in the novel. The author makes ingenious use of the gardening motif, which, although often employed as a symbol of fertility and sexuality, does not appear hackneyed. Max, a man in his late twenties, is a tender, vulnerable, chaste person with the pure heart that supposedly only children possess. In his subconscious mind he is infinitely afraid of his sexuality; he does not suppress it consciously because he is not really aware of it at all. During his one year at a university, when he was majoring in horticulture, his mother died under mysterious circumstances, and Max had to spend some time in a mental home afterwards. There, ironically, his sanity was restored by the gardening lessons his psychiatrist gave to him. Max can "handle" spade and seeds now, but, as his charge Clarissa suggests, he resembles a friar who cultivates the garden of a monastery.[7] The concept of the chaste gardener (which is quite successfully pointed out in Robert Duncan's "The Market Gardeners" or Jerzy Kosinski's Being There, too) also implies the cultivation of a pupil's mind; Clarissa wants to become Max's pupil, but the girl already "knows" much more than her tutor.

Through the permanent contact to the spirits of two dead children, a boy and a girl who were sexually abused by their uncle, and through the experience with her own developing body Clarissa has not lost her innocence, but shows an interest in sexual affairs which frightens Max to the core. Of course he ascribes everything to the dead twins and keeps the girl company all the time to protect her from evil. As the girl, who is indeed unaware of the powers that guide her (both those of the spirits and of her own body), has chosen Max as her "instructor," their close relationship must destroy him. One day before her parents' return the girl actually rapes Max. The man does still not comprehend Clarissa's feelings for him, but now he can hear the ghostly train the girl has always told him about. The locomotive, which often serves as a sexual symbol as well (for instance in Tennessee Williams' A Streetcar Named Desire), is used in the climactic scene of the novel: Max sees the fatal train that threatens to crush Clarissa, standing on the rails with the twins beside her, and perishes himself in his attempt to rescue his charge.

In comparison with the unique ambiguity of the preceding novel, William Peter Blatty's The Exorcist appears rather flat and unimaginative. Though the novel (and the subsequent film) launched a vogue, drawing public attention to the phenomenon of exorcism, neither the plot nor the representation of the eleven-year-old girl Regan contribute any original aspects to the theme under discussion. The novel rather serves as a (negative) example of the fact that some authors abuse the phenomenon of the evil innocent in order to give their pornographic descriptions an additional cheap thrill. In the beginning Regan is a "perfectly" amiable child, flawless in every respect; during the possession (which develops gradually, but soon covers every trace of the "original" child--except her body) Regan may indulge in all kinds of obscenities; after the exorcism she is her "real self" again and does not even remember the previous incidents. No interaction has taken place; the demon was merely a visitor.

Laurence Grafftey-Smith's story "The Locket," a genuine ghost story, is also based on a girl's possession, but here the erotic element is only subtly hinted at. The girl Penny, an extremely impressionable child to begin with, has retired with her parents to a lonely estate in the country. Since her earliest infancy she has been prepared for a musical career, but her music has begun to drain her of her vital energy, and she must abstain from it for a while. The "vacuum" in her receptive mind is soon filled by the influence of a ghost, the spirit of a lascivious villain who, during his lifetime, used to kidnap and abuse small boys and girls, and who killed his wife in a bestial manner. Through this ghost Penny is sexually "initiated," and her demeanor changes in a way nobody can understand; her vicious, knowing look frightens her relatives most. When the unwitting narrator gives the girl an antique locket he has come across, the secret relationship alters dramatically: the power of Penny's locket, which originally belonged to the ghost's wife, makes the spirit kill the girl, too. When her parents find her, the corpse is covered with red marks, disfigured by the "burning kisses" of the lustful fiend.

Another interesting sexual allusion is made in Graham Masterton's novel The Revenge of Manitou. This work is embedded in the Cthulhu mythology invented by H. P. Lovecraft, as are numerous modern horror novels. Although Lovecraft himself did not take much interest in children--with, perhaps, the exception of his tale "The Dunwich Horror"--a considerable number of stories written in the tradition he established contain child protagonists (Robert Bloch's "Notebook Found in a Deserted House" is the fictitious diary of a small boy who relates his dangerous contact with Yog-Sothoth and Nyarlathotep). The Revenge of Manitou deals with a whole class of children who are possessed by the spirits of twenty-two great Indian medicine men. Under the leadership of the Lovecraftian wizard Misquamacus, the spirits want to use the bodies of their hosts to conjure one of the mightiest gods and take revenge on the white population throughout America. The

eight-year-old Toby, who harbors their leader, forms the center of
attention. He was chosen both because he is the descendant of a traitor (the "sins of the fathers" are involved again) and because, as a
child, he is open-minded by nature. In his normal condition Toby is
the usual nice boy, playful and naive; the age-old, cunning look that
distorts his features while the ghost speaks through him shocks his
parents all the more. In order to show his power, the spirit in Toby's
body commits rape "by proxy": he makes a sheet move about and violate
Toby's mother in the very presence of the boy's father. The strong
oedipal suggestion is reinforced by the father, who, although he knows
that his son is possessed, addresses the boy: "Toby! Toby! It's your
mother! It's your mother!"[8]

The configuration of the peer group is ingeniously combined with
the notion that both Indian rituals and the child's play are determined by a certain amount of innate savagery. Ironically enough, the
children's unwitting parents can at first not distinguish between
both; when the group assembles for a gruesome ceremony that includes
the cruel torturing of lizards (a ritual which the reader can witness
in detail, but which the adults, significantly, only watch from afar),
this appears perfectly "natural" for children. The same can be said
about the children's wild dances--and the fact that the appointed day
of the class picnic is chosen as the day of apocalypse is indeed the
height of irony. The children themselves are not affected by the
activities of their bodies. After each "seizure" they return to the
"surface" as if awakening from a trance. It is indicated, however,
that they must be rescued in time: the spirits are "growing" within
them and accumulating energy; in the final phase they will "spread
their wings" (101) like moths leaving their chrysales. Since the but-
terfly is an old symbol of the soul, this image forms an interesting
variation on the fact that in horror fiction children do not reach
adulthood in the course of a gradual development--only the spirits
which will leave the children's bodies are not (or no longer) their
own.

Apart from the "traditional" possession by spirits there can be
found novel, "contemporary" forms of control through superior forces.
The child protagonist of John Coyne's The Searing, for instance, who
is generally considered autistic, literally functions on a different
wave-length: extraterrestrial beings implanted a data bank in her
brain which, however, got out of control and leaves the girl a mixture
between a human being and a defective robot. With a mere touch she can
kill a person, while "sudden bolts of violent light"[9] flash and blaze
in her retinas, flashes which remind one of a malfunctioning machine.
Her childish self does not mean to harm, but the lack of communication
makes it impossible for her to warn anybody. The attempts at communication she does make are impressive enough; she draws a sign with her
own blood, or she wildly screeches into the microphone of a tape-
recorder, a message which is later deciphered as "Help me, Sara,
before I kill you" (202)--the perfect expression of "innocence," helplessness, and incalculable dangerousness.

THE CHILD AS CATALYST OR MEDIUM

> ...she thought that Danny might be the one the hotel really
> wanted, the reason it was going so far...maybe the reason it
> was _able_ to go so far. It might even be that in some unknown
> fashion it was Danny's shine that was powering it, the way a
> battery powers the electrical equipment in a car...the way a
> battery gets a car to start. If they got out of here, the
> Overlook might subside to its old semi-sentient state, able
> to do no more than present penny-dreadful horror slides to
> the more psychically aware guests who entered it....But if
> it absorbed Danny...Danny's shine or life-force or spirit...
> whatever you wanted to call it...into itself--what would it
> be then?
>
> Stephen King, <u>The Shining</u>'

The second main category of the "evil innocent" can be distinguished from the possessed child through the fact that the child in
this case is not manipulated by outer forces, spiritual or "mechanical;" the power which leads it to commit or release harmful acts is
an innate one. A further subdivision has to be made as to the quality
of this particular power, because its nature is directly connected
with the child's representation. If the child possesses an innate
power which is beyond its conscious control, it is depicted as a victim of the energies it sets free; a child that abuses its superhuman
abilities because it does not yet comprehend the consequences of its
actions is endowed with many of the features that usually characterize
the child-monster, although it is basically as "innocent" as the other
type.

Five-year-old Danny, the protagonist in Stephen King's <u>The
Shining</u>, has an extraordinary psychic capacity, which manifests, above
all, in his "shining," the ability to send and receive thoughts over
extreme distances. When he and his family arrive at the Overlook Hotel
in the mountains of Colorado, where they will spend the winter cut off
from civilization, an inevitable process sets in. The hotel, a conglomerate of all the thoughts, emotions, intrigues and crimes its
guests have deposited in it in the course of nearly a century, wants
to absorb Danny's power. Danny's father, the caretaker of the Overlook, is bribed by its ghosts to give them his son as a sacrifice;
after a long and fierce emotional struggle he decides to kill Danny,
who is rescued in time by another "shiner" the boy has called from
Florida.

Like each of King's novels, <u>The Shining</u> is a complex work of art
which must be understood on various levels. The symbolic dimension is
the most interesting and elucidating among them; although the author
makes use of several traditional symbols, he intertwines them in a
highly original manner. The house as an image of the human psyche,
with the various rooms representing parts of the brain, has been employed in countless literary works from Poe's "Fall of the House of
Usher" to Gustav Meyrink's <u>Golem</u>. In King's novel the hotel with its

significant name stands, among many other things, for the corrupted, haunted mind of Danny's father. The secret papers in the cellar, the big old boiler of the central heating which finally explodes and destroys the whole building because its pressure is no longer controlled, the ghosts in the rooms and the rats beneath the roof all testify to the run-down state of the (superficially) magnificent hotel which has received too many destructive guests. The wasps' nest on the roof which Danny's father smokes out and gives his son as a present is another symbol of the human brain and its dangerousness: the boy takes the supposedly empty nest to his room and is nearly stung to death at night—the innumerable holes in the nest still swarm with deadly creatures. Danny's father is the caretaker of the house, but feels like its master; his relation to his son is the same. His readiness to sacrifice his son to the hotel coincides with his wish to dominate him completely: when he comes for him with a mallet, he only announces a thrashing.

The fact that Danny's psychic energies are the catalyst through which the machinery of evil is set in motion is expressed by another vivid symbol. This image, the great clock in the ballroom, is a direct reference to Poe's "Masque of the Red Death" and the ball Prince Prospero and his guests are having until the clock strikes twelve and the Red Death holds sway over all. The ghosts in the hotel have long been waiting for the signal to unmask, but the clock only starts ticking after Danny has turned the little silver key ("For an adult it would have been uncomfortably small, but it fitted his own fingers perfectly"[2]) to wind up the fatal mechanism: "It was as if the whole place had been wound up with a silver key. The clock was running. The clock was running. He was that key, Danny thought sadly" (284).

Robby, the nine-year-old boy in John Saul's Cry For the Strangers, functions as a catalyst, too. When he and his parents and sister settle down in a small New England harbor town, Robby's presence triggers off an evil development. The ghosts that have been sleeping on the shore are roused by the boy's arrival, and a series of grisly murders begins. The only aspect which makes Robby's catalytic function stand out from other examples of its kind is the fact that, strangely enough, Robby's parents have chosen their domicile on the beach because the boy seems to find peace there. From the day of his birth the child has suffered from hyperkinesis, and during the last three years before the action starts he has nearly disrupted the family with energies they could not handle. The spirits, however, need his surplus energy to perform their evil actions, and in the end they "absorb" the boy completely.

The child that possesses an innate super-power and does not control it (or at least not according to adult standards) usually appears as an entirely different species. Its own parents hate it for its power and the permanent dread it causes with its unpredictable caprices. One of the most famous stories dealing with such an untamed— and untamable—creature is Jerome Bixby's "It's a Good Life." Three-year-old Anthony is the uncontested ruler over a whole village, because he can read people's thoughts and change objects of every size and kind. His harmful activities have continued since the very moment of his birth, "since that day three years ago when Anthony had crept from her womb and old Doc Bates—God rest him—had screamed and dropped him and tried to kill him, and Anthony had whined and done the thing. Had taken the village someplace. Or had destroyed the world and left only the village, nobody knew which."[3]

Basically Anthony is a "normal" child, not wicked by nature, but dominated by his quickly shifting moods, his sympathies and antipathies. For his "friends" he tries to fulfill every secret wish, but of course he cannot know the right way: "That was if he liked you. He might try to help you, in his way. And that could be pretty horrible. If he didn't like you...well, that could be worse" (80). Anthony senses the hostility which surrounds him and likes to retire into a nearby cornfield, where he has created a special microcosm for the animals that live there, for he feels "in all the tiny minds around him the desire—or the instinctive want—for this kind of resting place, and that kind of mating place, and this kind of place to play, and that kind of home" (84). He obviously has a positive capacity, but he is somewhat embittered by the homicidal thoughts adults have had in his presence for a long time—until he "thought them all into the cornfield" (his childish euphemism for graveyard). He is not so particular about the way he treats certain other animals, making, for instance, a rat eat itself and die from pain.

Apart from his psychic powers, the only feature which distinguishes him from others is his "bright, wet, purple gaze" which becomes redder in relation to his anger. Anthony never shares the company of other children; they are strictly kept away from him (from the "nice, nice goblin," 90) because they do not control their thoughts, either, and are thus defenceless in a double way. The adults of the village try to keep their minds completely blank in the boy's presence—a defense which often proves highly insufficient. The second method of both defense and consolation is their novel way of thinking that everything is "good" (hence the title of the story), "nice," "fine" and in perfect order. When Anthony kills one of the grown-ups during the dreaded "TV-show" (a pantomime the boy presents for his own delight), everything is still "just swell," even though the others must hold the widow's arms and legs and prevent her from screaming. After all, "everything had to be good. Had to be fine just as it was, even if it wasn't. Always. Because any change might be worse. So terribly much worse" (88).

Peter Oldale's "The Problem Child" is based on similar conditions: through telekinesis a baby can draw objects in its own direction when it cries very loudly, thus endangering itself and others. Only little Rosie's mother perceives her daughter's latent ability and asks her doctor about the phenomenon. It goes without saying that the mother is considered mad: like innumerable other mothers in horror fiction, she is suspected of a subconscious aversion to child-bearing in general and to her own child in particular, since a mother's fear of her offspring often coincides with her overwhelming fear of responsibility. In most of these stories the child is a new-born infant, and the mother has just been released from hospital, with the full weight of her duty coming down upon her. Authors frequently take this situation as the basis of an ambiguous development which leaves the mother's environment (and sometimes the reader) in doubt concerning the true source of the evil occurrences (Ray Bradbury's "Small Assassin" and Gerhard Amanshauser's "Entlarvung der flüchtig skizzierten Herren" serve as excellent examples in this respect). Rosie, in any event, does have supernatural powers, and when she and her father

leave the mental home where Rosie's mother is confined on the fifth
floor, the baby draws her through the very "unbreakable" window pane
and is literally buried beneath her corpse.

The title of Lewis Padgett's story "When the Bough Breaks" obviously refers to the old nursery rhyme about the cradle that comes down
when the burden becomes too heavy. This is the case in the Calderon
family, which consists of father, mother, and a baby with the significant name Alexander. Three diminutive creatures from the future visit
them one day to give lessons to the infant, who will be the founder of
their race and their beloved leader. Unfortunately, Alexander learns
too quickly to employ his super-powers and tortures his parents day
and night, for he has not yet developed a conscience and is as relentless as any other child at his age. The unnerved parents cannot be
comforted by the creatures' devotion and adoration (since the beings
at the same time encourage their son to continue with his experiments); the prospect of having to bear the situation for years to come
makes them "break the bough" deliberately. They eliminate their son by
giving him an object the creatures have forbidden him to play with,
and all of a sudden Alexander "has never existed." Only his shoes
remind the grieving parents of his former presence.

5. THE MONSTER

> Paul lives with his Mummy Burnell now but he seems to be
> getting pale again. Though he loves his Mummy Burnell she is
> a very fleshy lady and his appetite is growing every day,
> his little front teeth getting sharper.
>
> M. S. Waddell, "The Pale Boy"[1]

The reader of horror fiction who comes across the word "monster"
instantly associates this term with the most familiar representatives
of this "species": vampires, ghouls, werewolves, and zombies. In the
Twentieth Century each of these types has been provided with forms of
offspring that differ considerably from their elders. The nature of
diminutive monsters not only contradicts the principles which underlie
the literary existence of their adult equivalents; they also form an
obvious exception because they are usually on excellent terms with
their adult relatives and have a marked liking for domestic life.

One of the first notable vampire stories in which children play a
prominent role is Joseph Sheridan LeFanu's narrative "Carmilla"
(1872); the child in question, however, remains a passive victim of
vampirism: the narrator experiences her first encounter with the vampire Carmilla when she is only six years old, during a peaceful night
in her nursery. Many years later she meets the beautiful lady again,
who, since she is not subject to any process of aging, has not changed
at all. Carmilla clearly fulfills the two important requirements that
determine a vampire's nature: she belongs to the undead, and she subsists on blood.[2] Furthermore, like many vampires she is endowed with a
wonderful erotic charm which her victims cannot resist. These basic
traits are often drastically altered or altogether ignored if the vampire is a child. M. S. Waddell's "The Pale Boy" illustrates the possibility that a vampire child can have its peculiar charms, which have
little to do with a grown-up's sexual attraction but which help the
child to accomplish its aim in a very similar manner. When the orphan's foster-mother takes the boy in her arms for the first time and
is kissed on the cheek ("it was a curious kiss and it made her
start"[3]), she is obviously filled with near-erotic spasms as well.
This excitement takes a different direction in the woman, who has been
grossly neglected by her husband: "'After that, what could I do?' she
said to her husband....The poor mite, she said to herself, starved of
affection, and she ran her hand almost caressingly over the two tiny
scars his teeth had made on her cheek" (25-26). The woman develops
motherly feelings (and something more) for want of a lover, and the
tiny boy's beauty strengthens her desire. The boy, for his part, does
not act out of any erotic motives (he does not despise ugly Daddy
Burnell as a feast at all); he rather shows the special mixture of

playfulness, curiosity, and cruelty "normal" children are supposed to display, too. In his case, however, these traits of character are accompanied by the innate abysmal malice of all vampires, big or small.

The reader can discern other basic peculiarities in the monstrous offspring's representation in horror fiction. The combination of horrible and comic effects within a story, above all, is a feature which frequently goes along with the child-monster's appearance and thus distinguishes it from both adult monsters and human children. The quotations above suggest that "The Pale Boy" is not meant to be taken seriously, nor is there any special "message" hidden beneath the comic surface. There do exist stories, on the other hand, in which the comic devices underline the satirical impact. The tale "My Mother Married a Vampire" by Ronald Chetwynd-Hayes belongs to this latter category. The very first sentences, which refer to the title ("She did. I ought to know because--the vampire--was my father and what that makes me is anyone's guess. A humvam maybe"⁴) indicate to some extent what the reader may expect: the "humvam" is both a human and a humorous vampire. The narrator tells the reader about his childhood experiences with his father ("his profession was a messy one and she was rather afraid he might be mistaken for a butcher"), whom he always considered a waiter because he worked at night, "immaculately dressed in a well-pressed dinner jacket and smelling of rose-water" (131). The unwitting boy uses swear-words like "cross," "priest," "angelic," and similar expressions whose mere mention makes his father so sick that he has to be revived with "red stuff." The idea which underlies these incidents--namely the fact that a vampire child does not know by nature what it has to do and must be initiated first--reminds the reader of the film <u>Dracula père et fils</u>, a typical representative of the seventies: here the vampire serves mainly as an object of ridicule, and his erotic appeal only emphasizes this function through the effect of contrast. In his early childhood the vampire's (Christopher Lee's) son eliminates his mother by exposing her to full sunlight; this accident is the result of childish play and ignorance.

The vampire's son in the short story is just as "innocent" as his equivalent in the film. He brings home a clergyman who is even more dangerous than his ecclesiastical garments suggest: the man belongs to the dreaded "B. Squad," whose main aim is the destruction of vampires. The rigorous, brutal proceedings of this group are the object of criticism in this narrative. Though the action is set in England, the "Bleeny" and their relentless persecution of "dissentients" remind one quite strongly of the methods employed in totalitarian states: every harmless-looking neighbor may be a spy; a convict's family has to witness the execution; the members of the Squad like to torture the relatives, and while "the underlings might be crude, unthinkingly cruel," "high authority would be coldly efficient": "Exterminate. Erase. Blot out....Right, lads, down in the cellar. Bring your kit" (141). Furthermore, references are made to communists and to the next victim waiting at the teaching college. The ending reveals that not even the most ardent persecutors are immune against the "public diseases" they try to exterminate; the B. Squad Commander is bitten during the execution he performs, catches the "virus," and is caught by his subordinates, who fight over their "fallen chief" like "dogs over a succulent bone" (143). Still very "respectful," however, they politely request him to take the most convenient position (for all parties concerned) for being impaled in the prescribed manner he knows only too well.

The possibility that vampires propagate like human beings (and with human beings) contradicts all traditional "laws" of vampirism; yet this alteration has become a prevalent factor during the past decades. The existence of a child-vampire, however, may also originate after the conventional fashion, through the bite of another vampire. Anne Rice's remarkable novel Interview With the Vampire, which generally abounds in innovative ideas, follows the tradition at least in this particular respect. The five-year-old girl Claudia is a fragile human child, and, significantly, just bereaved of her mother when the vampire Louis feeds on her. Louis, the narrator of the novel, is a perfectly likable figure, always in doubt as to the real nature of a vampire, the motives, passions, and "morality" which should lead on a creature like himself. Ironically enough, he is drawn to the child not by bloodthirstiness but by his compassion for the wailing, helpless girl. When he feels the child's peculiar, bird-like heartbeat ("the rapid, tenacious heart of the child, beating harder and harder, refusing to die, beating like a tiny fist beating on a door, crying, 'I will not die, I will not die, I cannot die, I cannot die...'"5), he is torn between his hunger and his wish to caress--his bite is the expression of both feelings. The girl, on the other hand, who becomes a vampire as well, is not half as moderate and gloomy as the man who "made" her: when she is told to drink blood for it will make her strong, she is as greedy as an animal ("...she wouldn't let go. With her fingers locked around his fingers and arm she held the wrist to her mouth, a growl coming out of her," 92); yet, being pulled away from her nourishment, she shows the "most innocent astonishment." The girl has not greatly changed despite her new form of existence; she still looks like an angel with her white dress and golden curls, and she still asks for her "Mamma." Nonetheless, Louis is attracted by her physical beauty in a sensual way:

> I found her on my lap, my arms around her, feeling again how soft she was, how plump her skin was, like the skin of warm fruit, plums warmed by sunlight; her huge luminiscent eyes were fixed on me with trusting curiosity....She was the most beautiful child I'd ever seen, and now she glowed with the cold fire of a vampire....She was not a child any longer, she was a vampire child. (94-95)

Louis knows that Claudia's mind will develop, whereas her body will always remain that of a child.

At the beginning of the girl's vampiric career her mind is a child's mind as well; she has no recollection of her brief human life and, unlike Louis, knows no restraint: "...little child she was, but also fierce killer now capable of the ruthless pursuit of blood with all a child's demanding....Mute and beautiful, she played with dolls, dressing, undressing them by the hour. Mute and beautiful, she killed" (98). Although Louis detests the killing of humans, he does not feel repelled by Claudia's childish ruthlessness, because her greed, her grace, and her cruel desire to play with her game before the kill have a perverse quality of "liveliness" about them. To watch her kill is chilling: "Like a child numbed with fright she would whisper her plea for help to her gentle, admiring patrons, and as they carried her out

of the square, her arms would fix about their necks, her tongue between her teeth, her vision glazed with consuming hunger" (101). Then
she leads her victims to the doll shop or the café where they give her
"steaming cups of chocolate or tea to ruddy her pale cheeks, cups she
pushed away, waiting, waiting, as if feasting silently on their terrible kindness." Claudia is to remain the "demon child" forever, but
her soul inevitably becomes a woman's, and one day the transition is
indicated most clearly--Claudia wants a coffin of her own.

   One of the most horrifying scenes presenting a vampiric attack
launched by children is to be found in Stephen King's novel 'Salem's
Lot. The town Jerusalem's Lot is gradually contaminated by vampirism,
and though the victims form a cross-section of the population,
children play a major role in the work, both as vampires and as exterminators. The ghastly effect of the encounter in question is to a
great extent due to the concerted action of a whole horde of children,
who, close to midnight, lure the driver of their school bus to his
vehicle they have occupied. Through the preceding events the reader is
prepared for the worst, whereas the man, awakened by the continual
honking of the bus horn, is merely suspecting a prank. His faulty es-
timation of the situation is the more grotesque since it extends to
the distribution of power. He has always been a hated tormentor of his
charges and feels prepared for their mischief like a soldier at war:
"You could read it in their eyes. He had learned that standing guard
at the repple depple in the war;" "He felt tough and coldly competent.
This was infiltration, just like the Army."[6] When the driver carefully
approaches his bus, intending to punish the "little bastards," the
"miserable little sneaks" who have intruded themselves upon the sign
of his authority, the driver's seat, he is welcomed: "The kid sitting
in the driver's seat with both hands plastered on the horn ring turned
to him and smiled crazily. Charlie felt a sickening drop in his gut.
It was Richie Boddin. He was white--just as white as a sheet--except
for the black chips of coal that were his eyes, and his lips, which
were ruby red.--And his teeth--" (380-81). A worse surprise awaits the
driver as he looks down the aisle:

> Was that Mike Philbrook? Audie James? God Almighty, the
> Griffen boys were down there! Hal and Jack, sitting near the
> back with hay in their hair. But they don't ride on my bus!
> Mary Kate Greigson and Brent Tenney, sitting side by side.
> She was in a nightgown, he in blue jeans and a flannel shirt
> that was on backward and inside out, as if he had forgotten
> how to dress himself.--And Danny Glick. But--oh, Christ--he
> was dead; dead for weeks!

The door is closed shut, and the horde get out of their seats like
one, closing in on their victim, who in vain tries to "reconcile" with
the formerly powerless enemies: "'No,' he said, trying to smile. 'You
kids...you don't understand. It's me. It's Charlie Rhodes. You...
you...' He grinned at them without meaning, shook his head, held out
his hands to show them they were just ole Charlie Rhodes's hands,
blameless..."

   Nearly all of the novel aspects that concern the vampire child
can be applied to the "ghoulish" offspring as well. In Eastern mythology the ghoul is a demonic spirit who robs graves and feeds on the

corpses in them; the "Arabian Nights," above all, contain numerous hints at such creatures (the "Story of Sidi Nouman," for instance, centers upon a beautiful ghoul-girl). No allusion whatsoever is made to happy ghoul families who live in perfect domestic harmony, to their "human" forms of propagation, and to their idiosyncratic sense of humor. All this is rendered possible whenever ghoul-children appear in a story. Ray Bradbury has even created a diminutive cycle on this theme; the tales "The Homecoming," "Uncle Einar," and "The Traveler" all deal with the Elliott family, which consists of hundreds of members spread all over the world. The central characters of this clan do not live in vaults at all, but are respectable members of human society. The butcher and the undertaker ("a dealer in cold-cuts traded for another of the same"[7]) belong to them, and their children even attend school regularly. The main child character, Timothy, has great problems, because he is different: he does not like blood and corpses, spiders and snakes, and he is even afraid of the dark. Being a "freak of nature," he is still loved by his relatives. Timothy feels like an outsider for he is mortal, but his mother comforts him: "We all love you. No matter how different you are, no matter if you leave us one day....And if and when you die, your bones will lie undisturbed, we'll see to that. You'll lie at ease forever, and I'll come visit every Allhallows Eve and tuck you in the more secure'" (160).

Bradbury describes his family from an insider's point of view, as most authors do who deal with monster communities. There is certainly a ludicrous element in the author's narration, but these comic devices never overshadow the general morbid, melancholic atmosphere which determines much of his work. Morag Greer's "Under the Flagstone" reminds the reader to some extent of Bradbury's presentation. The first half of the story includes vivid descriptions of the beautiful decay that surrounds the graveyard domicile of the ghoul family, and the child protagonist, Ira, is introduced:

> Grey shirt and trousers smeared with dirt, delicate, pale, angelic face lightly flushed with the sun, the little boy sat on another heap of fresh soil, holding in one small hand a human shin bone to which were attached a few scraps of skin and flesh....He raised his eyes, which till then had been demurely lowered, and golden lights welled up from the fathomless pupils and flickered across the pale lilac irises. Full red lips drew back in a lopsided grin, revealing sharply pointed ivory white teeth.[8]

Like all of his kind, Ira is friendly with his human prey in order to lure his victims to the family, where, of course, his heart really lies. The second half of the story is a mere mockery of the promising start. One may get the feeling that the author has restrained herself up to this point only to strike the reader with the full impact of a repugnant and primitive account of the feast: she does not content herself with the depiction of the "normal" ghoulish meal, but takes obvious delight in the slow, agonizing dismemberment of a living woman who lies on the family's dinner table.

Ronald Chetwynd-Hayes's story "Why?" whose title refers to the most commonplace and enervating utterance children (human and ghoulish offspring alike) are capable of making, is widely dominated by its

comic effects. Apart from a few "stage directions," the entire tale
consists of dialogues, the ghoul-child's initial and final conversa-
tions with her mother and her talk with a grave-digger. To make sure
that the reader can guess at the nature of the monsters and is prepared for the ambiguity of the second "scene," the author drops sufficient hints at the ghoul-mother's outward appearance: "'Mummy, why is
your face all lumpy and green?...And your nose...is so like a lump of
blue fungus. You must know that blue and green do not really go together. After all grass does not grow in the sky....Why did you become so very ugly, Mummy?'"[9] Of course the small girl is sent out to
play after such impertinent remarks; outside she unnerves the friendly
and patient human being with similar questions. The grave-digger does
not believe her when she points at her home, because a churchyard is
"hardly the place for a beautiful little girl" like the "Missy" (74).
After a time, however, the man grows angry at her, and she has to call
her mother, who comes running on all fours. The girl cannot refrain
from making comments about the terrified man's complexion ("'Mummy,
he's going green like you'") and upon his fate: "'Mummy, are we going
to eat the nasty man?'" (78)

Apart from several narratives dealing with fairies and their
(sometimes) evil offspring (as, for instance, Robert Kirk's 17th-
century account "The Secret Commonwealth"), the literary representation of child-werewolves bears some significance in this context.
Robert Stallman's novel <u>The Orphan</u> illustrates the drastic changes
this mystic figure may undergo in literature if the werewolf's "human
half" is still a child. The werewolf, a human being who turns into a
wolf at night (especially during full moon), is widely considered a
physical expression of the wish for a bestial sexuality which is not
restrained by any moral scruples.[10] Though most werewolves are adult
males, one can as well find female specimens, as in Clemence Housman's
"classic" tale "The Were-Wolf," or male adolescents like Saki's
"Gabriel-Ernest."

Robert Lee Burney, the five-year-old narrator and protagonist of
Stallman's novel, differs remarkably from all these werewolf characters. He can choose every animal form he wishes and is able to shift
at any hour, day and night. The greatest alteration can be found in
the dual personality inside Robert: the boy harbors two different
beings who are aware of each other's presence, live "side by side" and
try to suppress one another. The "wolf ego" is the original one, and
the reader can deduce from furtive remarks that the boy Robert first
comes into being when the wolf is cornered by humans and must allow
the shift for his own safety: "Robert got to his feet, dizzy with
birth, and stepped from behind the hay. The light crashed in his eyes.
He was crying and shivering, naked."[11] The human part of Robert is a
completely harmless, ignorant, and vulnerable creature that does not
know evil at all; through the contact to human beings and the love he
receives he grows stronger, until he can make "bargains" with the wolf
in him and finally even subdue him. The age-old idea of the struggle
between good and evil arises again, though the situation cannot be explained in such simple terms. The wolf is not "all bad" to begin with;
he is a grown-up beast that enjoys hunting and killing, but he never
harms human beings. In a crucial situation he even rescues the family
who has fostered the boy, giving up the security of his camouflage.
Moreover, all erotic allusions refer to the boy, who takes great de-

light in the shape of a motherly woman he comes across. Love
strengthens the boy and even softens the wolf to some extent; the
beast's instincts begin to deteriorate, and the wolf is aware of it:
"Perhaps I too am becoming civilized and will soon be eating Red Heart
dog food in three delicious flavors out of a can" (76). "Civilization"
is the keyword of this novel, whose imagery also stands for the ad-
justment of the individual to civilized society--and in a way for the
development of any human child. The inevitable shift of power is
additionally emphasized through the break within the novel: the first
part is revealed through the eyes of the beast, whereas the second
part is narrated by the boy, Robert.

The most recent among the "classic" monsters is without doubt the
zombie, the walking corpse. The rise of this species in horror fiction
and especially in the horror film was initiated by William Seabrook's
report on Haitian voodoo magic (1929). In his detailed description
this expert mentioned creatures that were resurrected from their
graves or whose souls were taken by voodoo sorcerers. Zombies could be
the individual victims of a sorcerer's wrath, or they were simply
summoned because they provided cheap labor; in any case, their "revived" bodies did not harbor spirits nor minds but were manipulated by
remote control.

The earliest notable horror films centering upon zombies, Victor
Halperin's _White Zombie_ (USA 1932) and Val Lewton's _I Walked With a
Zombie_ (USA 1943), followed rather faithfully the observations made by
Seabrook and the original beliefs in the nature of the walking dead.
When the theme was taken up again in the horror film of the seventies
(a series of international productions started in 1968 by George
Romero's _Night of the Living Dead_), the zombie's characteristics
underwent a remarkable change symptomatic of a basically different attitude among directors and audience. First of all, the "genesis" of
the new zombie no longer has anything to do with sorcery; instead, the
reasons for the resurrection of corpses are radioactivity, pollution,
and an excess of chemical (i. e. artificial) _fertilization_: problems
of increasing topical relevance. Furthermore, from the almost mechanical object of voodoo magic the zombie has developed into a being that
is, at least partly, led on by internal drives--the urge to kill and,
above all, to eat human flesh. One can argue about the question as to
whether this blend of zombie and ghoul is an improvement or a deterio-
ration; in any event, the replacement of comparatively aesthetic
figures (the heroine of _White Zombie_ being the sleeping beauty _par
excellence_) by Romero's rotting heaps of flesh is obviously meant to
satisfy spectators with a penchant for an over-explicit presentation
of physical abominations. Although the impending screening of Stephen
King's novel _Pet Sematary_ threatens to pay tribute to this develop-
ment--after the film _Creepshow_ this will be another instance of col-
laboration between the author and George Romero--the novel itself is
even more profound than the rest of King's fiction. In fact, it almost
entirely denies its reader the pleasurable thrills he is accustomed
to: the spots it touches are too tender, and the relationship between
reader and protagonist is too intimate to bear. _Pet Sematary_ is an
emotionally depressing, intellectually rewarding novel; its motto,
"death is a mystery, and burial is a secret," does not impede the
author's imaginative excursions into the nature of grief, mourning,
and despair.

Pet Sematary presents one of the world's smallest zombies, two-
year-old Gage, whose second span of life shows parallels both to the
voodoo revival and the existence of the modern ghoul-zombie. The circumstances of his re-creation and the plot he is involved in, however,
could not have been invented for anything but a child-monster. Gage's
father, a physician, violates the laws of life and death, and the son
he restores to unnatural, soulless life returns only to bring death
and insanity to his parents. When Louis Creed buys some real estate in
Maine he is not aware that the old Micmac burial ground that is part
of his land has great magic powers: whatever or whoever is buried
there comes to life again and returns to its owner. From an old neighbor he learns the truth about the place, which is separated from the
adjacent ground by a seemingly insurmountable barrier. Even before
that he is instructed that although the territory belongs to his
property he does not own it.[12]

The power over life and death would mean an immense temptation to
every human being; for a physician it is also a professional challenge. To the mind of Louis's neighbor, doctors have already been very
successful in banishing the phantom of death from daily life: they
just wave their "magic wand" (61) and everything is alright. Yet the
Indian site is stronger than this modern "medicine-man;" as if to mock
him, it gives him the illusion that he has the direct power to overcome death, though in reality he scarcely has the power of decision.
In contrast to most scientists who manipulate life in horror fiction,
Louis Creed is (despite his name) an atheist--at least in the beginning. He does believe, however, in a superior force called metabolism,
the "body clock" that must not be rewound. He is also aware that, in
considering the crucial step, he is "thinking about a dark blasphemy"
(254); and he cannot help comparing himself to Jesus, who called forth
Lazarus, and of course to God, who will resurrect the dead on the day
of the Last Judgement. It is significant that in order to reach the
Micmac cemetery one has to cross the "Little God Swamp;" Louis feels
exhilarated like a small god when he enters the magic area.

Death and fertility have always formed an inseparable union which
manifests in countless rites practised by all cultures on earth. They
are two sides of one coin, and their correlation is a perfectly natural one. As soon as a human being interferes with the rhythm of life,
the same union becomes a perversity. Only God may harvest the seed he
has sown in his graveyards without disturbing the balance. The idea of
the cemetery as a place of tillage is very common; the German language, which has quite a large vocabulary in all matters concerning
death, knows the obsolete expression Gottesacker. The implication of
semen and fecundity contradicts the explanation (given in the novel)
that the inscription over the place which gives the book its title is
only a childish mis-spelling.

Both the cat which serves as the "guinea-pig" for Louis Creed's
experiments and his small son are run over by trucks loaded with
chemical fertilizer; the thought that this is no mere coincidence even
occurs to Creed himself: he perceives "dramatic unity" (142) in this
detail. During the boy's official funeral Creed must think of
"planting Gage" (237). Like a nineteenth-century Resurrection Man
Creed exhumes the small body and buries it in the Micmac ground. Before that, still in the funeral hall, Gage is nearly "resurrected"
when his relatives, demented with grief, have a fight and cause his

coffin to topple over and open. It is this unbearable grief, mirrored
in the despair of his next of kin, which finally makes Creed commit
the sacrilege.

The physician's emotional state partly excuses the crime but cannot overshadow the fact that he challenges the cosmic order. He literally throws down the gage to nature, and his son is the pawn in this
forbidden enterprise. To make things worse, Creed unconsciously regards his endeavor as an act of primary procreation: he carries the
"lifeless clay" (310) of his son for whose animation he alone is responsible. Moreover, he has been warned of the possible drastic change
in a revived person's behavior, and he feels prepared for both a
mental retardation and a murderous disposition in his son. In both
cases he would (after a thorough diagnosis, of course) kill his own
son--a self-righteousness which borders on megalomania. The equipment
to deal out death is in his black bag, the ominous black bag of a
physician or that of a magician. Ironically, the returning Gage takes
a scalpel from the very same black bag and kills his mother with this
instrument. When Louis needs it to cut fabric, his train of thought--
taken literally--forms an ironic hint at the misuse of the surgeon-
conjurer's kit: "A hell of a way to treat good instruments," but "none
of the knives in the house" would "do the trick" (390).

The Gage-thing which haunts its parents no longer has anything to
do with their alert, happy child of the past. It is a lurching creature which smells of the grave, a lump of dead flesh with moss on its
blond curls and burial suit. Nevertheless, it has retained most of its
former beauty, and, naturally, all its childish attributes. This accounts for the grotesqueness of the final scenes: Gage "piping" in a
babyish, but perfectly understandable voice, with "its mouth hung
open, baring small milk teeth" (382). Popular superstition always has
it that someone who returns from the dead changes into an evil being--
thus, primitive funeral rites are rather established to prevent such a
return, instead of encouraging it. Gage forms no exception in this respect. He recognizes his parents and is conscious of his surroundings;
his intelligence and mode of expression, however, are no longer those
of a two-year-old but determined by sadistic cunning. The clash between this small assassin, armed with the scalpel, and his overjoyed
mother is unavoidable:

> She cried his name and held her arms out. He ran to her and
> climbed into them, and all the time one hand remained behind
> his back, as if with a bunch of posies picked in someone's
> back meadow.
> "I brought you something, Mommy!" he screamed. "I brought
> you something, Mommy! I brought you something, I brought you
> something!" (390)

The reader is spared the description of Gage's cannibalistic activities.

On the last happy day of Gage's human life he and his father flew
a kite, a large vulture, which was snatched from their control by an
air current. This carrion bird has been hovering over its prey ever
since. Louis Creed knows that he must kill his son, although he can
never undo his crime. Discovering Gage's tiny footprints on the
kitchen floor, he realizes his guilt: "In his mind's eye he could see

them tracing a path across the entire country--first to Illinois, then
to Florida--across the entire world, if necessary. What you bought,
you owned, and what you owned eventually came home to you" (394).

   In the preceding collection of child-monsters one type is missing: a creature composed of parts of dead bodies, made after the Frankenstein "fashion." Apart from rare stories like Gustav Meyrink's "Das
Wachsfigurenkabinett," in which a single living child is remodeled by
a mad sorcerer/scientist and turned into Siamese twins (one bigger
creature that holds the foetus of his "brother" in his arms), a genuine childish equivalent of Frankenstein's creature has not (yet) been
developed. Another contemporary monster, however, can be compared to
it in at least one respect: the clone-child's "production" is also
based on human material, though only one cell is needed. Since the
clone usually assumes the exact shape and structure of the human being
who provided the nucleus, it is not its outward appearance which makes
the monster; the monstrosity lies, as in Mary Shelley's novel, in the
blasphemous wish to create human life in one's own image. The second
great sin, which is connected with the first, is the scientist's
striving for the total control of the future, an aim which he tries to
achieve by manufacturing masses of identical units. The rise of
totalitarian systems, the increasing interference of governmental
authority in biological experiments, growing ideological uniformity
and many other modern problems surely serve as a background for the
clone motif in literature. As the intentions of scientists and politicians need not be entirely condemnable in each case, authors do not
always depict them as villains; their ambitious projects, however,
seldom develop the way they planned them, but get out of hand instead
and soon come back at their inventors like boomerangs.
   The lyrics of the song "Genetic Engineering" by G. A. McCluskey
only consist of a few lines interspersed with several catchwords, but
the overall idea cannot be expressed in a clearer way. Between the
first stanza (which starts with the lines, "These are the little
children/Their future in our hands"[13]) and the closing mock-repetition
("These are the little children/Their future in their hands") the combinations "creature/JUDGEment" and "butcher--ENGINEER" attract one's
special attention. The most significant words, however, are repeated
over and over again: "Frankenstein's Monster." The idea of revolution
which stands behind this song has become prevalent in horror fiction
and forms an obvious answer to anti-Utopian works like Aldous Huxley's
Brave New World, in which the clones develop strictly in accordance
with the governmental design and rebellious thoughts are reserved to
the few individually raised human specimens.
   Kate Wilhelm's novel Where Late the Sweet Birds Sang is an ingenious combination of all basic ideas discussed above: the clone-
children turn on the scientists who "made" them; but they were planned
as separate entities and thwart their creators' efforts by forming independent peer groups (with all the typical features mentioned before)
on their own account. The beginning of the novel can be regarded as a
perfect recapitulation of all major points of interest concerning
human sins and their consequences. The similarities to the story of
Noah's ark strike the reader at once: the head of a large family has
been reading the signs that announce the extinction of mankind (including plague, famine, nuclear infection, inflation, and looting) and

has long provided for a place of refuge. He is the grandfather of the main line, the Sumners (a significant name in this connection), and the ruler over a dynasty whose members are "all part of the same river that flowed through the fertile valley,"[14] which means part of the evolutionary chain. They have all been trained and educated for special tasks, and when their leader summons them, they are prepared for all eventualities. After a great rain which destroys most of their surroundings the members of the family may leave their sanctuary; the "dove" that informs them of the development is, in their case, Grandfather Sumner's "man in Richmond." They find out that after a nuclear catastrophe all human beings (including the family) are barren, and that no child has survived. Thus, they have to produce clone-children in the image of each member of the clan. (The manufacture of the offspring is announced as follows: "'You know how we are getting our meat. You know the cattle are good, the chickens are good. Tomorrow, ladies and gentlemen, we will have our own babies developed the same way,'" 44.) Soon they recognize that they are raising creatures for whose novel form of existence they have not been prepared in any way: the adults cannot bear the memories conjured up by the "younger versions" of themselves, and they are frightened by the resemblance ("Hilda had strangled the small girl who looked more like her every day," 47). They are even more disquieted by the fact that their offspring keep strictly to themselves. The inevitable separation sets in; the members of the community begin to distinguish between "elders" and "offspring," and the adult scientists ask themselves why they consider their offspring "inhuman": "'Remember that old cliché, generation gap? It's here, I reckon'" (47).

Passion, pity, emotions, and individual souls no longer exist for the children; group thinking and group welfare determine their activities. As they can read the elders' thoughts, they are superior to them and assume power, whereas the adults become useless and are finally exiled for life. The pattern which underlies Kate Wilhelm's novel does not differ much from the fundamental principles that can be found in most stories dealing with peer groups. Basically it does not matter at all if children are born "individually" or produced in a cloning process, for the offspring's development is predictable in each case.

The old cliché of a generation gap, which was hinted at above, is also the key to the majority of works dealing with "extraterrestrial" offspring. On closer examination the reader may often realize that the hostile alien children who try to overthrow the human race are nothing but the projection of another, more immediate dread--the fear of human children and the future they are about to shape in their own fashion. The most famous literary example, John Wyndham's The Midwich Cuckoos, contains enough unmistakable hints at such a sublimation; the actual theme of the novel is the adaptability of a seemingly firm society (and civilization in general) to novel, unpredictable circumstances.

Despite the numerous casualties among the citizens of Midwich and the rather brutal ending, one can observe that the first part of the novel, concerned with the alien children's procreation, birth, and infancy, is an obvious satire on the sleepy, backward village life which is not only typical of England. When Midwich falls asleep through the influence of an extraterrestrial field of force, the living conditions have hardly changed at all; the village has always been a "sleeping beauty."¹⁵ During the sleep "its men and women, its horses, cows, and sheep; its pigs, its poultry, its larks, moles and mice" (25) all lie still (as in the fairytale); after the incident the narrator concedes that Midwich is "as near awake again" as is "natural to it" (45). Midwich has hitherto "lived and drowsed upon its good soil in Arcadian undistinction for a thousand years" (12), and its leading feature has always been the fact that it was a place "where things did not happen."

The stagnant, precisely regulated "life" of Midwich may well be compared to a similar form of existence in the borough of Vondervotteimittiss, the setting of Poe's comic tale "The Devil in the Belfry." In this borough sixty houses form a perfect circle around the belfry, which contains the mechanism that keeps the community going--because, on close examination, the whole village is situated on the very face of a clock.¹⁶ Every trifling "activity" is steered by the big clock in the center, until one day a strange bohemian with a fiddle disturbs both the peace and the mechanism of the clock; when the clock strikes thirteen instead of twelve, the whole orderly life of Vondervotteimittiss suddenly turns into tumult and uproar. The houses of Midwich form a perfect circle around the church as well, and the mysterious field of force, following the outlines of the village, is shaped like the cover of a cheese plate, which means that Midwich has (for a short while) a "hemisphere" of its own. The satiric elements in the novel are not so much aimed at bourgeois habits as at the mental and evolutionary sleep of civilized mankind.

During the course of the action Midwich must rely on itself exclusively, at first because the government tries to hush up the whole affair and isolate the village, later on because the "Dayout Children" themselves prevent any human contact with the outside world, and, all in all, because army and Air Force cannot handle the problem at all. They seem totally out of date: during the sleep, for instance, they use birds in cages which must help the soldiers, who with their technical equipment look like "mechanized Galahads" or eighteenth-century generals "watching a battle that was not going too well" (35).

The "heroes" of the novel, the narrator with his wife and Professor Zellaby with his family, are significantly newcomers and, in various respects, outsiders of the community. The narrator is outside the village during the sleep, and his wife, who accompanies him, does not give birth to a Dayout child afterwards. The Zellaby family moved to Midwich years ago and are comparative strangers, too; moreover, Zellaby's wife is pregnant with her husband's child, and his daughter loses her Dayout child in time. Professor Zellaby, a sage with a fool's cap and the author's mouthpiece, always seems to make the most trifling and unsuitable remarks, but becomes the savior of the whole village since he is the only far-sighted and consequent person in Midwich. One of his first soliloquies in the novel interestingly begins as follows: "We don't seem to be good at integrating novelties with our social lives, do we? The world of the etiquette book fell to pieces at the end of the last century, and there has been no code of manners to tell us how to deal with anything invented since" (18). After the sleep he gives himself an answer he cannot quite believe in: "And it simply came, and did nothing, and went away again, and had no effect on anything?" (50) For Zellaby the Dayout affair is a universal breaking test for civilized mankind; his wife also realizes that after the births all citizens "have been placed outside the conventions."

The most important idea behind the whole plot is once again hidden in an aside of Zellaby's:

> The Zellabys, feeling no doubt that we had passed through disquietment enough for the present, took pains to keep the conversation on subjects unrelated to Midwich and its troubles....I appreciated the effort, and ended the meal listening to Zellaby discoursing on...the desirability of intermittent periods of social rigidity for the purpose of curbing the subversive energies of a new generation, in a far more equable frame of mind than I had started it. (153-54)

Since the entire novel has an allegorical meaning, the drastic measures chosen in the end must not be taken literally. It is clear that a generation which threatens to overthrow an established form of human coexistence by developing new concepts cannot be exterminated root and branch. It is notable, however, that other "nests" of Dayout children are destroyed in time: an Eskimo tribe kills the golden-eyed babies at once, because anything unusual is a danger to tradition and convention, which are precious to "savage" races; in the Soviet Union a whole city is destroyed, since not even the germs of a novel development are tolerated there.

In Zellaby's opinion civilization had to be invented, for "Mother Nature" is "ruthless, hideous, and cruel beyond belief" (112); on the other hand, civilization is a kind of decadence, granting the individual too many rights and lacking the will to survive. Though Zellaby is a very humane person, he knows that the Dayout children have to be destroyed, since they do have an instinct of self-preservation which is stronger than any other motivation and must inevitably collide with the principles of civilization. This problem and its final solution appear equally paradoxical and correspond to Zellaby's inner conflict. He kills the children with a bomb to defend society and prove its will to survive; thus acting according to the "law of the jungle," he sacrifices his own life (which means he deliberately suppresses his own instinct of survival) for the benefit of the community. Zellaby is by no means a ruthless killer. On the contrary, he has been the children's teacher for a long time and is the only one to have "come as near friendship with them as possible" (208). Sympathizing completely with his pupils, he feels obliged to exterminate the danger growing within society, the "fifth column" (115).

Curiously enough, in several other works dealing with genuine extraterrestrial offspring the alien children are not presented as monsters at all. Jack Williamson's novel The Moon Children, for instance, contains three astronauts who discover a secret alien military base on the moon, lose both the contact to their own comrades and consciousness, and return with "alien seed." Their wives give birth to three children who, though they have special abilities and forms of "internal" communication, remain extremely vulnerable and must be protected from human society. On the other hand, there exist numerous examples of the fact that "earthly" children need not be more human than aliens and frequently collaborate with hostile forces from outer space. In most of these cases the children prepare a world-wide revolution, a complete overthrow (and sometimes extirpation) of the human race; and again this revolution is an answer to the sins of the adult "rulers." In Gerhard Amanshauser's "Entlarvung der flüchtig skizzierten Herren" ("Unmasking of the Hastily Sketched Gentlemen") both mother and child are depicted as uncanny creatures--they are outsiders because the unmarried mother cannot (and does not want to) comply with the rules of social life. In contrast to other women in the maternity ward, who look like fat, pink, happy animals, she wears a black gown which underlines her pale complexion. Back in her "home," which she has neglected for years, she leaves the child in the charge of an elderly woman. The baby is extremely quiet, but in order to keep it that way the television set has to work day and night. For the child's mother (and for innumerable other parents as well) this seems to be quite an agreeable solution. The baby, however, deciphers its own secret messages from outer space, transmitted through this "human" medium, and begins to produce sticky threads in enormous quantities, like a spider that is going to enshroud the whole planet.

The most dreadful specimens of alien human children can be found in Ray Bradbury's "Zero Hour," a story which has many features in common with The Midwich Cuckoos. Here the younger children, who are still impressionable, inventive, and merciless enough to betray their parents for the fun of a game and for the aliens' promise of absolute freedom ("the older ones, those ten years and more, disdained the affair"[17]), have started to play "invasion." They even tell their parents every detail about their friends from Jupiter, the appointed hour of occupation, and the ways the children help them with their endeavor--and, of course, the parents chuckle over their offspring's vivid imagination. They live in a society that feels perfectly secure ("'We're impregnable,' said Mom in mock seriousness," 182); "arm in arm, men all over earth" are "a united front" (180). Listening to the special terms the children repeat in front of them, the adults patiently "elucidate" the meanings: "'What's lodge-ick?'--'Logic? Why, dear, logic is knowing what things are true and not true'" (183). Ironically enough, the grown-ups are the ones who explicitly call their children a "fifth column"--mockingly, naturally. Only after the female adult protagonist has overheard her daughter announce that the older children, whom the little ones hate worst, will be killed first, does she grow suspicious:

> Children and love and hate, side by side. Sometimes children
> loved you, hated you--all in half a second. Strange
> children, did they ever forget or forgive the whippings and
> the harsh, strict words of command? She wondered. How can
> you ever forget or forgive those over and above you, those
> tall and silly dictators? (185)

The arrival of Satan's offspring on earth is the theme of two of the most popular twentieth-century horror novels: Ira Levin's Rosemary's Baby and David Seltzer's The Omen. Although both are notable for their suspense and psychological refinement, the children presented in them do not contribute any novel aspects to the image of the child in horror fiction. Two factors which rather concern the adult environment of the new-born Anti-Christ, on the other hand, are worth examining in some detail. The first, which becomes clearest in Rosemary's Baby, is in a way already indicated in The Midwich Cuckoos: the average mother's instinctive, unconditional, physical affection for her child, a love that can neither be diminished by the woman's knowledge of her baby's descent nor by its obvious dangerousness. Professor Zellaby observes this primitive pattern of behavior in the Midwich mothers' attitude towards their "offspring": "'If they had horns, tails, and cloven hooves Miss Ogle, Miss Lamb, and a number of others would still dote on them.'"[18]

The same can be said about Rosemary, the heroine of Ira Levin's novel. Although she has found out step by step that the friendly neighbors of the New York apartment house she and her husband live in belong to a sect of devil worshippers who have made her become Satan's mother, the love for a child she has never seen gives nearly superhuman energy and courage to this vulnerable woman who has always depended on others. During the months of her pregnancy she becomes more and more aware of the danger she is in, and, strangely enough, she draws strength from the existence of the Devil's child growing within her. Her own conception of "Andy" or "Jenny" is taking shape in the same measure, and she is willing to defend this clear conception of her own human child with all her might. Bodily reactions are infinitely stronger than Rosemary's reason; just as her body automatically begins to produce milk when she hears her child crying from afar, she feels compelled to care for Adrian, the son of the Devil, because he shows at least a certain similarity to a human baby. Thus, the final scene of the novel is more horrible than all preceding episodes which included murder, treason, and blasphemy. When Rosemary, who has disturbed the company at Adrian's "birthday party" with a butcher's knife, notices that "her son" is treated incompetently, she starts rocking the child's cradle and uttering baby-talk, reacting like any unreasoning mammal. The only condition she makes refers to the baby's name: when the devil worshippers agree to call the child "Andrew," her concept of maternity is secured, and the belief in this deep-rooted principle makes her ignore the terrible reality.

Like Rosemary, the parents of the Satanic child in The Omen are, at least in the beginning, not aware of their son's true origin. Damien's "mother" considers him her own child (who was murdered in a hospital in Rome), but the boy is a changeling, adopted by her husband, an influential ambassador and millionaire. Apart from several signs which betray Damien's beastly nature--only to the initiated few, of course--the boy is a beautiful child, whereas Adrian/Andrew has at least the "traditional" hooves, horns, and tail. Damien's parents and Rosemary are the victims of renegade priests or witches who have long prepared for the birth of the Anti-Christ. During a Black Mass Satan himself impregnates Rosemary,[19] whereas Damien's origin is not entirely explained, but forms an allusion to the Revelations of St. John.

At close view, the Devil and his Son function as the personifications of human evil. This does not appear original in the least since, after all, in most traceable human religions there have existed devils and demons, evil spirits who have to serve as physical projections of harmful powers in nature and evil qualities in man.[20] The Catholic Church has always advocated the personal existence of fallen angels and the Devil as their leader and God's antagonist. Since the Second Vatican Council (1962-65), however, both the Devil's personal representation in the Bible and the statements about his influence on human

acts have (officially) been ascribed to the evil disposition of man
instead. The destruction of this mythological tradition has obviously
found an answer in horror literature; the impoverishment of man's
beliefs, superstitions, and fantasies, together with his most "primitive" fears in an age of advancing "civilization," calls for a compen-
sation in fiction. Thus, the Devil is not only revived, but begets a
son, the physical sign of his unabated evil potency. In order to
underline the clash between our modern rational(istic) world and
medieval conceptions concerning the powers of darkness, Ira Levin
makes "his" Anti-Christ take shape in the very heart of New York,
whereas the leader of the witches is the descendant of an age-old
dynasty of devil worshippers. David Seltzer's Son of the Beast is born
in Rome and given to his foster-father in a Catholic hospital; on the
other hand, he grows up as the heir of a powerful American industrial-
ist and politician. Damien's foster-father is not religious at all;
only through one of the renegade priests does he learn the truth and
gradually accept it. Rosemary was brought up as a good Irish Catholic,
but has become indifferent and only starts praying again after she has
recognized the nature of her environment. Significantly, she once
gives a party attended by young actors and actresses where one of the
main topics of conversation is the question as to whether God has just
died, "in our time."[21]

The confrontation between the established Christian religion, a
Church which has degenerated into a soulless institution, and its
vigorous Satanic counterforce is a central theme in Rosemary's Baby.
The Satanists represent a cancer cell in the exhausted, corrupt body
of Christendom; their belief is not exactly the ancient, independent
religion Rosemary sees in it, but a kind of negative "confirmation" of
original Christian beliefs. The emptied shells of Christian customs
and rites are refilled by the devil worshippers, who take advantage of
the unbelief that grows even among the faithful. It is notable that
the year of Adrian's birth (1966, the "Year One") is also the first
year without an "official" devil.

Nevertheless, there is no open struggle between the opposing
forces. The mighty representatives of Christianity (which, in this
case, is synonymous with Catholicism) are too much interested in
secular affairs and too self-assured to grow suspicious. In the novel
they only form the dim background, whereas the action takes place in
the microcosm of Rosemary's "happy" home. The Pope is, in the truest
sense of the word, only perceived in passing: Rosemary dreams of him
as a tourist, with a suitcase in hand and a coat on his arm. In fact
Paul IV, who visits New York on the very day of Rosemary's impreg-
nation, is a constant traveler and an experienced showman; he celebrates a Mass in the Yankee stadium, and the tickets for this popular
occasion are much in demand. During the Holy Mass the Satanists have
their own feast, and Rosemary, who has been drugged, sees herself on a
yacht where only Catholics are admitted (among them the late President
Kennedy, who has recovered from his assassination). The Pope also
appears but, always in a hurry, he has no time to investigate Rosemary's situation.

From the beginning of her marriage Rosemary has been torn between
two extreme attitudes: that of her bigoted Irish family in the
country, industrious breeders each and all, and that of her husband, a

sophisticated atheist. She has chosen the liberal way of life New York offers her, but deep inside she feels like a traitor, the more because her relatives broke with her after her alliance with a Protestant. Rosemary's subconsciousness and conscience are more determined by her Catholic upbringing than she realizes; in her dreams she is scolded like a naughty child by the nuns who educated her. The baby she desires is not only a human being she can care for. It is also meant to redeem its mother from her "sinful" existence--carnality for its own sake, for instance. Rosemary thus pays her tribute to her prolific clan; the deep-rooted concept that motherhood is a respectable status which makes up for all one's faults leads her to welcome pregnancy as her individual perfection. The fact that Rosemary's personal savior is the potential destroyer of mankind shows another facet of the author's ironic attitude toward motherhood.

Damien's unwitting foster-mother also has her problems with motherhood. Dependent and extremely vulnerable since her childhood days, she feels that she is no match for her protective but ambitious husband. Bearing her husband's child means being worthy of his affection and becoming a "real" woman. A beautiful child is just the "appropriate issue, of the perfect marriage, of Robert and Kathy Thorn,"[22] and Damien surely meets this demand, since he is "perfect in every way," "an artist's rendering of what a human child should be" (15). Significantly, when compared to the newborn baby he is exchanged for Damien loses some of his attraction; the Thorn child looks like an angel lying beside its dark adversary ("two infants side by side: the blood-covered one, thick with hair, and the soft, white, beautiful one, its eyes gazing upward in absolute trust," 98). It is Robert Thorn's anxiety which makes him hastily agree to the secret adoption; his wife has already had two miscarriages, and her sanity is at stake. After four years it becomes clear that it is not "only 'goodness'" which comes "to the House of the Thorns" (71), and both parents live up to their ominous surname. The public, however, only sees the beautiful façade: on Damien's fourth birthday, during a magnificent party, a photographer remarks, "I don't know if we've got just the heir to the Thorn millions here, or Jesus Christ himself" (19). The fact that Robert Thorn, whom nature endowed with such an angelic son, tenderly fosters the child that was imposed on him is in a way paralleled by his bearing as a politician: being an idealistic diplomat who regards his task as a mission for the entire free world, he willingly becomes a slave to foreign forces if he feels that he can thus serve his purpose. In order to "save the world" he has developed, at least in the eyes of his wife, into a "whore," a noble-minded chessman controlled by his evil surroundings.

The fact that evil has its clearly defined physical center and outward projection does not mean that the aspect of personal human guilt and corruption is ignored. In Rosemary's Baby, in particular, the individual worshippers of evil are depicted; the "moloch" New York abounds with them, the whole city is undermined by them. Even Rosemary's husband collaborates with the sect, because the actor is offered a great career. Writers of horror fiction favor New York City as the ultimate expression of vice, corruption, and sin. Many aspects pointed out in John Shirley's novel Cellars remind the reader so strongly of Ira Levin's work that it deserves more attention than other, "genuine" examples of new-born devils (as, for instance, Ronald

Chetwynd-Hayes' "Cradle Demon," in which the underlying conception is ridiculed). Shirley's evil deity living in a subterranean lake beneath Manhattan is a mixture of Lovecraft's Cthulhu and the Moloch of the Old Testament. This monstrous god, however, does not demand children as sacrifices; on the contrary, his attitude is a perverse mockery of Christ's words "Suffer the children to come unto me." He loves children because he is a "playful child himself,"[23] a half-human embryo as tall as a house, who is sitting in his lake (his placenta) with crossed arms and legs like a statue. He controls the "upper world," the innumerable human beings who are willing to sell their souls to receive success, wealth, and earthly power in return; and he "invites" the children into his lower region since they can play the cruellest games, which he can enjoy with them. The children kill their parents to be with him underground, and they bring him the adult victims he needs. Painted like savages, they live in the sewer system, in cellars and subway stations, only emerging to the surface of the city to lure people into their realm. They are "having fun," for all their pleasures are authorized by a being superior to their parents.

The existence of a secret "Hades" beneath the visible center of corruption and crime, the symbolic meaning of subway tunnels, and the formation of adults and children by no means represent novel elements, but John Shirley makes the most of setting and imagery. Cellars is an exceedingly depressing novel, which makes the reader forget the fact that the hell depicted here is not a "Christian" one. In a discussion of Harlan Ellison's story "Croatoan," which deals with aborted fetuses that (after going "down the drain") live on in the sewer system of New York, Stephen King points out some connotations of this "underworld." To his mind the tale is based on "that myth of alligators under the streets,"[24] of beasts which, having grown from tiny pets into blood-thirsty creatures, are flushed down the toilets but go on existing "on the black underside of our society, feeding, growing bigger," waiting for the first unwary human prey. The sewer system is a "purgatorial world" of "Lovecraftian proportions," suitable for a writer who, at least in this case, is as "sternly moralistic" as an "Old Testament prophet" (374). The story begins with the male protagonist, an irresponsible Don Juan, flushing an aborted fetus down the toilet (an action which is quite familiar to him). The girlfriend who has had the abortion grows frantic and wants the child back; when the man levers up a manhole cover, he descends into a different world with roads and signs of its own. There he is awaited by masses of children who have mysteriously survived (and remained infants) throughout several centuries. All these children call the protagonist "father."

King calls the story a tale of "Just Revenge," which consists in the fact that the protagonist's dogged responsibilities have been waiting for him all along, like the corpse that returns from the dead to hunt down its killer. "Like the alligators of the myth, the fetuses have not died. The sin is not so easily gotten rid of. Used to swimming in placental waters, in their own way as primitive and reptilian as alligators themselves, the fetuses have survived the flush....They are the embodiment of such Old Testament maxims as 'Sin never dies' and 'Be sure your sin will find you out'" (375).

The stories in the following section give abundant evidence of the fact that the "average," "normal" human child may be a match for any alien, Satanic, or ghoulish offspring. Basically the majority of

"everyday monsters" can be placed in two categories: children who are
born and brought up in the usual (harmless) fashion, but start running
wild at a certain moment because their elders have committed an un-
pardonable offense; or children who at bottom remain "ordinary" boys
and girls whose more unpleasant childish traits are exaggerated in a
grotesque manner. Many plots are actually determined by a single
"ruling passion." Thus, thoughtless curiosity which gradually assumes
pathological dimensions may lead to vivisection and sorocide (as in
A. G. J. Rough's "Playtime" or "Sugar and Spice"); the protagonist's
crimes in a story by Patricia Highsmith are due to her efforts to live
up to the title and become "A Perfect Little Lady." A prototype of the
former category is "Wally," the infant hero of Conrad Hill's satire,
who is made to starve by his fitness-crazed parents and one day comes
to think of them in terms of "steaks."

    The children in Ludwig Hirsch's ballad "Die gottverdammte Pleite"
belong without doubt to the first category. Their ghastly murders are
the immediate reaction and response to the adults' corrupt way of
existence. All children turn into homicidal creatures after (during an
army maneuver in a wood near the border) an innocent rabbit has been
squashed under a tank. Now the formerly stable bourgeois life with its
rites and conventions is brought to an end: while her parents are
having a sophisticated conversation with her piano teacher, the child
Lisa drags her dog into the room, grinning with a blood-smeared mouth,
for she has just torn out the animal's throat. The seven-year-old boy
Thomas has always been fond of his grandfather and the old fairytales
he knows, but the child decides that the old man's electronic pace-
maker fits better in his own model train. After these examples of
individual "childish" behavior, the idea of the children's world-wide
revolution and revenge is introduced ("Yes, our little ones, our
little ones have declared war on us; declared war on you, mother, on
me, father"). The universal extent of the offspring's running amuck
finds ingenious expression in the following stanza, which also evidences the parents' helplessness:

    Armed to the teeth and shaking with fear
    The candle casts shadows, the cellar wall is dancing
    Thus we are sitting down there, weeping tears, bitter tears
    Our little ones outside are scorching the earth
    The rivers are boiling, the oceans vaporizing
    Up in the sky, even the Little Bear does not sleep any more.[25]

The direct cause of this holocaust, the rabbit's death, has a symbolic
function which is revealed at the end of the ballad. Man has created
an illusion of peacefulness and harmony, which he taught his children
and with which he has kept them quiet for ages; during the display of
his own murderous tendency he destroys this illusion and cannot prevent his offspring from emulating him. One can easily guess that the
fateful rabbit was the Easter bunny.

    The lyrics of another contemporary song also express the idea of
the child's running amuck as an answer to its parents' corruption. The
child in Ian Craig Marsh's "Crow and a Baby" is a "baby/Who wanted it
all/Moved out of the doll's house/Moved out of the hall,"[26] and who
vows revenge to the adult world:

> With one wing on the town
> And a gleam in an eye of red
> Said "My father was a crow
> Now I want all fathers dead
> Find the fathers of this world
> Treat them as a fatal foe
> Put them in the deepest hole
> Then cover the pit with snow..."

Septimus Dale's story "The Little Girl Eater" demonstrates that children can be influenced by their elders' inventions in different, equally disastrous ways. Miranda, a very impressionable little girl, becomes a ruthless killer because she takes certain remarks too seriously which her adult companions carelessly drop in order to keep her at a distance. Her mother's lover has taken them out to the beach; the child's presence serves as a mere "excuse" for the unwitting, absent father, and thus she is soon sent away to play. Miranda discovers an injured man whose body is pressed down to the ground by a girder, and who cannot free himself. The girl's impression of the creature in the sand is rather based on her fairytale "knowledge": "He was a funny sort of man, not like her Daddy. She could only see his head and shoulders and his arms, the rest of him was hidden in a funny hole in the ground. Perhaps he lived under the pier and only came out like the crabs when he thought there was nobody about....He was making a curious noise, a gulping, sucking sound, and his fingers were bloody."[27] Nevertheless, the girl decides to tell the adults about her encounter. She describes the man in a child's terms, and the adults, who think that she uses the expression "bloody" as a curse, mockingly declare, "He's a little girl eater. He lives down there under the sea and when the tide is out he stays there, waiting for silly little girls who go playing there. Then he gobbles them up, just like that" (92). Miranda considers this a personal challenge. The fatal misunderstanding becomes most obvious when the girl, who is carrying a huge stone to crush the "monster," is addressed by "it": "You're a good little girl...I want you to do something for me, quickly" (93). Miranda acts quickly indeed, though not quite in accordance with the stranger's wish, because--like so many of her modern coevals--this girl is not easily fooled by a bogeyman. Her elders' selfishness and indifference, however, have made a murderess of her: "Miranda ran away. She was happy. Mummy would be pleased. She had killed the nasty little girl eater."

Since basically inconspicuous children frequently turn wild as an answer to their elders' wrongdoings, it appears quite plausible that several of them are subject to the same causality in a different way. Adults who feel guilty expect and suspect their offspring of planning a dreadful revenge which is out of all proportion to the offense. Described from an adult's point of view, the child must infallibly assume the dimensions of a monster. Sometimes the riddle of its true intentions is left to the reader's sagacity or remains altogether unsolved. Thus, the loving father in Alfred Gillespie's story "The Evil Eye" fears the worst because he feels incompetent: "Outside my window somewhere, I'm convinced, a small, nine-year-old bat girl named Elizabeth, my stepdaughter, is circling and circling and circling in for the kill."[28] Though he is ashamed of using expressions like "malignant, gargoyle, monster child" or "bat girl," he is intimidated by the strange creature whose silent resistance he cannot break. Another adult, the father in Alex Hamilton's "The Attic Express," has always tried to force his own ideas upon his son, even determining the child's play. Just for once he hands over control to the boy to arouse his interest in a new model train ("'I might as well be on the train itself. Think of me being on it, that's it, and run it accordingly... I'm in your hands, son...'"[29]). In his imagination he reduces himself to the size of the "plaything" he has become and is suddenly at the mercy of the formerly powerless child. Only now does he realize that mercy is the last thing he may expect: whether he is finally crushed by his son or by his own conscience, however, is left to speculation.

The young patricide in Philip K. Dick's "The Father-Thing" is not so easy to classify, either. The tale, superficially a pure science fiction story, is based on the "Body-Snatcher" fashion. Human beings are exchanged for their replicas, which have grown like mushrooms in secret places, developing like larvae, waiting to leave their cocoons and replace their human originals. Eight-year-old Charles is convinced that something has happened to his real father, because the "father-thing" that comes back from the garage where his father has been working appears perfectly different to the child. Charles has actually witnessed the "two fathers" talking to each other before, and when he looks for his original father he only discovers the empty skin the replica has hidden. The father-thing is after him now that he has found out the truth, but the boy's friends help Charles. The replica's actions are steered and controlled by a huge metallic bug in the garden, which the children can kill before the father-thing and the newly released "Charles-thing" are able to devour Charles.

Though a gripping tale taken at face value, "The Father-Thing" fascinates the reader mainly through the underlying symbolic impact. Charles' father has indeed greatly changed, because something from outside is "eating him up"--his working hours at the office, not a monster in the garden. The "ordinary look of a tired, middle-aged husband" has been replaced by an unwonted grimness, "something alien and cold"[30]: the outward sign of his frustration and aggression. Finally his "new self" has won, and, after sharpening his tools in the garage, he decides that his son "is going to have to learn a few things." It is clear that the boy, who is not accustomed to corporal punishment, considers this another infallible proof of the father's changed identity. Of course the father's altered behavior affects the whole family (and Charles wonders if perhaps "the whole world" is going to be transformed, 316); the development of these new, cold, humorless, emotionless personalities takes its time--though only about as much time as the ripening of the large, peculiar mushrooms.

A LA RECHERCHE DU TEMPS PERDU

> One dream threaded through the others like an elusively
> mysterious theme in a complicated symphony, and the scenes
> it depicted were sharply outlined, as though sketched by a
> hand of gifted intensity: a small girl, wearing a bridal
> gown and a wreath of leaves, led a gray procession down a
> mountain path, and among them there was unusual silence till
> a woman at the rear asked, "Where is she taking us?" "No one
> knows," said an old man marching in front. "But isn't she
> pretty?"
>
>   Truman Capote, "Miriam"[1]

The last category of child-monsters differs considerably from all
examples presented so far, since the adult who must face a representative of this kind has conjured it up himself by trespassing upon
foreign ground: the realm of his own childhood. As has been pointed
out in detail, the worlds of grown-ups and children are absolutely incompatible with each other; as soon as a human being has accomplished
the transition from one sphere to the other (by ways which remain a
mystery to the reader), he or she may not even cast so much as a furtive glance back at the territory just left. Every attempt at returning to one's origins, however, is severely punished and has disastrous
consequences, for--like the sleep of reason--nostalgia "breeds
monsters."

Although Truman Capote has written very few horror stories, these
contributions (as, for instance, "A Tree of Night" or "Master Misery")
belong to the best works of horror fiction ever created. His tale
"Miriam" reveals both the author's wonderful capacity to evoke an
atmosphere of dread, decay and beauty and his deep psychological insights. Mrs. H. T. Miller, sixty-one years old, lives all alone in a
New York apartment; she is a plain, inconspicuous woman, who only
cares for her canary, disturbs nobody and keeps her room in perfect
order. The first impression of domestic tranquility is destroyed by a
few subtle hints at Mrs. Miller's abysmal loneliness, a feeling which
is transmitted to the reader through the gloomy description of the
snowy, desolate streets of New York in February. The girl Miriam, who
is actually the projection of Mrs. Miller's anguished mind that is
looking for consolation in a dream of youth and beauty, appears for
the first time in front of the cinema where Mrs. Miller has queued up
to buy a ticket. The wish to see a film, the obvious attempt at an
evasion of reality, brings forth another, "physical" manifestation of
this desire, and although at first sight the girl seems to intrude
herself upon Mrs. Miller, one becomes gradually aware that it is the
woman who has called her into being. The girl's first shy request is
quite significant in this regard: she asks the woman to buy a ticket
for her, too, since otherwise Miriam would not be allowed to enter the
cinema. Mrs. Miller feels strangely elated, a bit "like a criminal,"
for she somehow realizes that she has transgressed the regulations.
The woman marvels at the "strange" fact that both have the same Christian name (Miriam has no surname at all) and at the girl's outward
appearance. Miriam looks--according to her literally ethereal origin

and nature--translucent and fragile and has white hair like an albino.

After this first encounter and Miriam's official admittance Mrs. Miller is no longer safe from her "brain-child." On an exceptionally bleak Sunday night, when the woman has lost her sense of time for all days seem alike to her, the child visits her. This time Miriam is much bolder, demanding food and even claiming the brooch Mrs. Miller once received from her late husband. The adult cannot comprehend her sudden appearance in the dead of night; only the reader perceives the irony in her remark that Miriam's mother must be mad to let the child roam about at this time and in this attire--a white silk dress and white fillets--since, after all, Mrs. Miller is her "mother." The child's comment on a vase with paper roses that "imitations are sad" is equally ambiguous. Mrs. Miller, who feels completely helpless and vulnerable in the girl's presence, is both attracted and repelled by her. Miriam is denied a goodnight kiss and maliciously destroys the vase; after she has gone the woman is totally exhausted and has to spend a whole day in bed. Torn between a deep fear of the child and a curious affection for her, she begins to make preparations for her next visit, but when Miriam actually arrives she at first refuses to open the door for her.

Miriam intends to install herself for good and, although Mrs. Miller has known this from the start, she feels shocked and calls her neighbors for "help." When they cannot find a trace of the girl or her trunks, the woman's feelings form an odd mixture of horror (for it dawns on her that she has only invented Miriam) and relief (for she is convinced that she has re-discovered her own reliable adult self: "Mrs. H. T. Miller"). Strangely enough, the mixture remains much the same after the woman has returned to her rooms and found Miriam waiting for her: she will never feel alone again, but she is no longer "her own master," for the terrible whims of a child will determine her existence from now on.

David Cronenberg's novel The Brood, though basically simple in structure and plot, is a particularly vivid illustration of the idea that an adult's subconscious mind can create child monsters if it is roused in critical situations. A psychiatrist has developed a novel therapy, according to his own book entitled "The Shape of Rage": his patients are hypnotized and "sent back" to their early childhood. Experiencing their childish frustration and hatred once again, they are to develop physical excrescences in order to get rid of their innermost complexes. This therapy proves extremely effective in the treatment of the psychiatrist's model patient, a young woman who was maltreated by her parents during infancy. After a number of hypnotic sessions the woman (who remains unaware of her bodily reactions) gives birth to a genuine child, the physical projection of her rage, who acts out the murder which "the child in her" wants to commit. Significantly, after these murders by proxy the woman feels much calmer and can talk about her "deceased" relatives without the former wrath, for she is a "self-possessed" adult now. Each child of her hatred, however, dies as soon as it has fulfilled its special mission: it has no bones (only cartilage), no brains or digestive organs, the gills which can be found in embryos, and it draws its energy from a store of nutritive liquid in its hump--being thus "constructed" for one murder only, it is not destined ever to return to its "mother."

The imaginary children in Guy de Maupassant's story "La Reine

Hortense" only terrify the relatives of an old woman who, on her
death-bed, unconsciously reveals a deep yearning she has been hiding
all her life. The spinster has always been considered a hard-hearted,
self-sufficient woman without any weaker spots, a woman of royal dig-
nity, as her nickname suggests. Immediately before her death her confused mind gives "birth" to children she must have been "pregnant"
with for quite a time: she begins to utter baby-talk, caressing
children who are visible to her only, but who have individual names
and qualities. This scene appears ghostly indeed, the more since both
the appalled relatives in the story and the reader are confronted with
a desperate, passionate love which can literally find fulfillment only
in death.

An adult who tries to retrace his earliest steps and solve mysteries which should better rest undisturbed is often likely to come
across a monstrous criminal who is a younger version of himself. This
is the case in a story by Sally Franklin with the ominous title
"'Quieta Non Movere.'" After twenty-five years the female protagonist
returns to the house where she grew up until she was ten; both her
aunts and most of the servants are still alive and have basically
hardly changed at all. Only the former cook no longer works for the
family--the young woman is told that she left about twenty-five years
before, too. Whenever the protagonist raises questions concerning the
cook she meets with the hysterical reactions of her relatives and
grows suspicious. Following a "hunch," she walks through the labyrin-
thine garden to the summer house where she spent much of her childhood. On this way "back" (which has an obvious symbolic function) she
comes past the sundial with the title motto and a pond:

> Kneeling on the grass and looking into the water, Georgina
> half-expected to see a little girl's face staring back at
> her; a child of ten with pink bows on the ends of her pig-
> tails, and freckles. Instead, the woman's face reflected
> there seemed strange, almost frightening, as though there
> was someone standing behind her, looking over her shoul-
> der...[2]

The woman begins to remember the cook more clearly now and also re-
calls her hatred for the woman. When she finds her body in the summer
house, she is convinced that her aunts were blackmailed by the cook
and disposed of her, but before she can call the police she must learn
from the gardener that she committed the murder as a child and lost
her memory through a shock. It was the man who, in order to warn her
discreetly, changed the original inscription on the sundial. The old
motto was not "Quieta non movere," but "Tempus fugit."

A story with a similarly meaningful title, "The Return" by Gerald
M. Glaskin, resembles the above example in various respects. An old
woman comes back to the place where she grew up with her family; only
in the very end does the reader learn that she burnt down the house
and the people in it and has been confined since that day in her
childhood. The author's "trick" which makes it possible to withhold
the essential pieces of information till the end of the story is the
fact that the woman does not directly return to the "charred-blackened
wreck of a house,"[3] but is lying in the grass by a river nearby,

spinning thoughts and looking into the water. Deceived by the stream
of her deranged consciousness, the reader must believe that she is a
child; only the pain she feels when moving quickly does not quite correspond with her "youth," and when she bends over the river (a vivid
symbol which has been used over and over again in connection with insanity) she sees a horrid "apparition":

> And as though thinking of old people had invoked a manifes-
> tation before her very eyes, there, deep down in the
> water...the face of an old woman appeared suddenly in the
> depths to peer sinisterly up at her, the mouth leering ugli-
> ly, and the eyes--the eyes--relentlessly seeking her own.
> (26-27)

The woman is convinced that she comes home for her birthday party, and
indeed this is another birthday of the child in her--for, as is revealed later on, she has already escaped several times, and when she
is finally taken back to the mental ward she invites the nurses to
wish her many "happy returns."

The fact that the protagonist covers a "physical" distance while
mentally retracing his steps to childhood is a recurrent motif in and
outside horror fiction. Richard Davis' "Guy Fawkes Night," which has
been discussed before, serves as an original illustration of this
motif: the patricide's best friend, who has become a distinguished old
gentleman by now, comes across the initial stimulus, a guy: "'They're
not like the guys we used to make,' he thought wistfully."[4] Then he
enters the bus that will take him "home," and, after he has paid his
fare, starts traveling back. Moving along the streets of London, he
unveils one by one the evidences which lead him to his destination,
the discovery of the truth beneath the guy the children burned many
years before. Shortly before he arrives ("'Hyde Park Corner!' He came
to himself with a start. Good Lord, he was nearly home") an inner
voice warns him to "go no farther": "What did it say? Leave well
alone, it was saying. Don't trespass. Some things it is better not to
know. Yes, but what?...Stop, said the voice. Stop!...You fool, said
the voice, proceed at your peril!" (66) Of course, the old man does
not stop and, finally at home, collapses: "'Are you all right, dear?'
The conductress was standing over him anxiously. 'You've gone a very
funny colour.' Jerry felt as if he answered through thick layers of
cotton wool. 'Y-yes. I'm all right, thank you.'--'Bit travel sick, are
you?'--'Yes, a bit--travel sick.'"

It is notable that mental projections of children can sometimes
also serve as victims who must endure the punishment their adult pro-
creators actually deserve. This is the case in Rosemary Timperley's
"Street of the Blind Donkey." The female protagonist has just killed
her husband (a truth which she has suppressed completely and which the
reader does not learn till the end) and returns to Belgium where she
spent the happiest time of her childhood: "Why did I come to Belgium
in my headlong flight? Because a child waits for me here, a child who
was myself long, long ago, when I came here on my first Continental
holiday with my parents."[5] Soon, however, she feels persecuted by her
husband, who has always treated her as his possession and would rather
see her dead than let her become an independent human being again.
Finally the projection of her husband destroys the projection of

herself: "The shadow turns into a man--a man with familiar broad
shoulders, thick neck, heavy jowl. He seizes the girl, flings her to
the ground, pinions her arms, holds her down. He rapes her, with fantastic speed and precision. Then he puts his hands round her little
neck and strangles her" (170). Only now does the woman comprehend who
the girl was whom she has met so many times in Belgium:

> I know who the girl was, or is. I know that there is no hope
> of returning to the world of childhood, even in the beauti-
> ful city of Bruges. For the child is dead. Garder killed
> her. I cannot bring her back to life again. She was the only
> part of me that did not belong to Garder, body and soul, and
> as long as he was alive in the flesh, he could not reach
> her....Hoping to escape from him, I succeeded merely in
> giving all of myself to him, for the murderer belongs in all
> eternity to the victim, and the victim to the murderer.

"A Red Heart and Blue Roses" by Mildred Clingerman points out another original possibility of a "way back home": a twenty-six-year-old
orphan is looking for a foster-mother and gradually becomes smaller
and smaller until he is an infant. Although this story abounds with
comic elements, it can hardly be compared with, say, F. Scott Fitz-
gerald's story "The Curious Case of Benjamin Button" (whose protagonist is born as an old man and undergoes the same physical regression),
because the horror in this tale is rather emphasized by the comic
effects. The facts given in the story are not quite reliable for two
reasons: the narrator is just regaining consciousness after heavy
sedation, and the lady who tells her the story of her "son" lies in
the bed beside her--in the psychiatric ward of a clinic. The cause for
the middle-aged lady's stay (who, by the way, looks "like everybody's
secret ideal of motherhood"⁶ with her full bosom and broad hips) is,
ironically enough, her subconscious fear of motherhood. After she has
been released, the nurse tells the narrator that her companion is
pregnant again. Thus one must read between the lines of her account.
Her story about the strange "sailor boy" who gives her own adult son a
lift (driving him, most significantly, all the way back to Phoenix),
is invited for Christmas, and decides to stay with his new "Mom" forever, may also be the expression of her wish to return to childhood--
to her own infancy and to that of her adult, self-sufficient children,
who are about to leave their house and their mother. At her "critical"
age, the woman feels infinitely afraid of a new baby, yet desires it
as a kind of protection against old age, a proof of her own comparative youth.

According to this spiritual conflict, the strange boy both in-
timidates her and moves her to tears of compassion. He clings to her
like a lap-dog, tries to keep the others away from "his Mom" and has
his arm tattooed: to the initial dripping red heart and blue roses he
has added "Mom, I love you." "He would get a job and take care of me,
always. Even if the 'old man' died I wouldn't have to be alone, ever.
Nothing could make him leave me, ever, ever, ever. I was his Mom. He
had chosen me. Out of the whole world, he had chosen me. I was his,
and he was mine, for the rest of our lives" (113).

The woman expels her "offspring," but from now on she is haunted
by apparitions of a boy with a big tattoo, who has grown younger each

time she sees him. Lately, however, the nightmare she has been having has changed: "It isn't a real nightmare anymore. It's just a dream about a gift. Something fragile and of great value, which somebody has brought to me after great exertions and dangers. I accept it, but with immense reservations. My fingers refuse to close around it. I drop it, and it breaks. But it doesn't shatter like glass. It just lies there and bleeds" (116).

Ray Bradbury's contributions "The Lake" and "The Playground" are determined by an all-embracing atmosphere of sadness and dread. The first example, above all, fills the reader with a deep feeling of nostalgia, a yearning for pristine love, "that love that comes before all significance of body and morals," "that love that is no more bad than wind and sea and sand lying side by side for ever."[7] The narrator of the tale has experienced this kind of love as a twelve-year-old boy. The girl he loved swam out into the water in May and never came out again. In September the boy goes to the beach, leaving his mother behind like a strange woman, calling out the name of his dead friend. On the following day he travels westward on the train (thus moving from his sunrise towards sunset), abandoning the "rivers of child-hood." He grows up, changes his "young mind for an older one" and gets married; but "like a memory, a train works both ways. A train can bring rushing back all those things you left behind so many years before" (66).

The narrator spends his honeymoon in the town where he grew up; everybody has changed, no one recognizes him anymore, but his return raises the dead beloved from the bottom of the lake. The life guard who carries the girl's corpse must show it to him, and although the sight is not pleasant, the narrator feels reunited with his companion of yore, leaving the strange adult woman behind: "I thought: people grow. I have grown. But she has not changed. She is still small. She is still young. Death does not permit growth or change. She still has golden hair. She will be for ever young and I will love her for ever, oh God, I will love her for ever" (68).

"The Playground," on the other hand, is not an idyllic place at all. A father who is to send his tender-hearted, fragile son to this horrible institution, this "immense iron industry whose sole product was pain, sorrow and sadism,"[8] refuses to torture the boy in such a cruel manner. In order to spare him he makes a bargain with the "evil spirit" of the playground; he proposes trading places with his own child: "'You want it to be true. I saw your eyes then! If you could trade places with Jim, you would. Save him all that torture, let him be in your place, grown-up, the real work over and done'" (200). When the man becomes a child again he realizes the monstrosity of his sacrifice; for a child "a year is like ten years," and he has to spend twelve of these eternities confined in the world's most relentless concentration camp: "This is Hell, this is Hell!"

CONCLUSION

Whenever children are dealt with in horror fiction, authors unanimously comply with the unwritten laws that determine the offspring's appearance. The worlds of children and adults never overlap, but if they collide the outcome of this contact is invariably a catastrophic one. Transitions from one sphere to the other, no matter in which direction, are strictly avoided or accompanied by disaster, death, and madness. Children and grown-ups remain different species who are unable to communicate with each other. The child's uniform, almost two-dimensional representation underscores its remoteness from adult understanding.

The patterns which underlie the child's appearance have not changed for centuries, and although actual historical events have often invited writers of horror fiction to introduce children into their works, the basic mechanisms of characterization (or rather standardization), plot, and imagery do not appear to be liable to any kind of alteration. A "stimulus" from real life like the atomic catastrophe of Hiroshima gave rise to countless literary manifestations; the patterns underneath, like the formation and depiction of groups, remain constant factors in each case. Comparing narratives from different epochs, written by authors who do not exclusively concentrate on horror fiction, the reader notices the significant parallels in the choice of symbols and images, as for instance in the child-processions described by Arthur Machen, Bert Brecht or Marcel Schwob.

As has been pointed out before, social criticism plays an important role in connection with the child's appearance in horror literature. The main targets have also remained the same throughout several centuries; apart from their timelessness, however, one may observe other peculiarities in the kind of social criticism expressed in this particular genre. The frailties and vices of mankind which have been so frequently attacked can never be abolished and are not really meant to be; the exposure of man's sins often adds to the "dramatic potential" of a literary work, but represents an end in itself: constructive criticism is contrary to the very nature of horror fiction. Positive solutions or the mere prospect of possible improvements in the future sometimes entirely destroy the gruesome effect of a narrative. Two recent film adaptations, Cujo (1983) and the episode "It's a Good Life" from Twilight Zone (1983) show this fact quite clearly.

The first example, based on Stephen King's novel, contains only one major deviation from the literary pattern; this alteration, however, spoils much of the original impact. The connection between the flesh-and-blood beast Cujo and the subhuman traits which determine the social life of an average American family no longer finds its ultimate expression in the victimization of the parents' only son. The boy is rescued in time, his family are reunited and promise to live happily ever after, but such a constrained positive ending distorts the impression of the symbolic chain which has been left intact up to this point. The altered film version of Jerome Bixby's story even offers a "didactic" basis in the truest sense of the word: the boy Anthony, who terrorizes his surroundings through the indiscriminate use of his innate super-power, finds an adult woman who is willing to adopt him

and teach him to control his abilities for the benefit of mankind.
This solution emphasizes the idea that Anthony is not responsible for
his actions and that his capabilities are not negative by nature;
theoretically the ending does not contradict the possibilities inherent in the figure of the "evil innocent," but the example clearly
demonstrates that the child's ambivalent disposition only produces a
deep effect if greater stress is laid on the "evil" component of its
nature. Broadly speaking, horror fiction abounds in a social criticism
which has to be determined by a basically pessimistic attitude and
which is not meant to provide the reader with a "way out" of the
horrible events.

The obvious "fruitlessness" of such accusations against adult man
leads the reader to assume that they are merely a literary side product, not earnestly directed at the author's actual environment, but an
indirect expression of processes within his own psyche. The exact
demarcation line between children and adults reminds one of another,
equally sharp distinction which can be found in the very origins of
Gothic literature. In her work Ghosts of the Gothic Judith Wilt points
out that Gothic fiction (which she calls, in reference to a phrase by
Charlotte Brontë, "this heretic narrative"¹) contains two other pairs
of opposing forces whose struggle is as fierce and everlasting as that
between children and grown-ups. The opponents are, on the one hand,
parents and their adolescent, more or less impotent offspring (the
most impressive example in this connection is certainly The Castle of
Otranto); analyzing their confrontation, the critic interestingly
speaks of the "demon energies released between the parent and child
figures, the great old ones and the young usurpers of life" (12), and
tries to find a psychological answer: "Some deep struggle for control
of the springs of being itself seems to be the issue, some struggle by
the parent to unmake or reabsorb the child and thus to stop time, keep
power, take back freedom and life where it has inadvertently been
given away." To the other category belong all those who fight and defy
their creator, either the almighty God of the Christian (especially
Catholic) religion, or a seemingly omnipotent human "representative"
who, like Victor Frankenstein, claims the power over life and death.

The child in horror fiction is obviously a worthy heir of the
Gothic "minor," since the war between parents and their offspring in
the former genre comprises both the struggle between two generations
and the confrontation of self-entitled creators with their self-con-
scious creatures. Close consideration reveals that through the introduction of children the original Gothic concept of "heresy" has been
saved from a total decline: generally modern horror fiction no longer
deals with the relationship between God and man (apart from some
recent attempts to re-discover the topic, especially in the horror
film), whereas the child carries within itself the potentiality of
becoming a god-like being like its parents, and even its most trifling
activities bear the seeds of rebellion. After all, a heretic is not an
atheist, and heresy requires the presence of one or more divine beings
whose superior power and authority are contested.

The idea of the child as a crown-prince who is as yet powerless
but waiting for his installation is most effectively expressed in Ray
Bradbury's "Jack-in-the-Box," the more because the boy's father is
absent, in another sphere:

"In the Beginning was God. Who created the Universe, and the
Worlds within the Universe, the Continents within the Worlds
and the Lands within the Continents, and shaped from His
mind and hand His loving wife and a child who in time would
be God himself..."[2]

Kenneth Grahame's "The Olympians" depicts (though it is not a genuine
horror story) the eternal struggle between children and their elders,
who are most significantly called Arcadians and Olympians; the ending
of the story indicates a child's mysterious transition from the state
of ideal simplicity and innocence to the realm of the gods, the
knowing, yet ignorant grown-up people.

Considering the above points one can say that the child in horror
fiction maintains to some extent the original Gothic tradition; though
it had no place in Gothic literature, it fulfills several functions
all on its own which were allotted to various characters, protagonists
as well as antagonists, in Gothic fiction. Thus the child is not only
an inheritor, but quite an advanced successor in this regard. Its
superior status becomes even more obvious if one takes into consideration that the demarcation line between the two great opposing forces,
children and adults, is puberty. The fact that this boundary is so
sharply defined and, furthermore, that it is both a borderline in
literature and a transition stage in real life suggests the idea that
the war between the two groups actually represents a struggle within
one single human being, who, in this case, is always the author. In
any case, the spheres in which both age-groups are confined strongly
resemble different force fields which cannot and will never overlap
and whose dimensions and peripheries are determined by their mutual
repulsion.

In horror literature these force fields appear almost physically
tangible to the reader; many of the peculiarities concerning the depiction of the child and its environment that have been pointed out so
far support the assumption that the goings-on between the groups are
rather the reflection of some inner tension or conflict than the
author's view and description of his actual physical surroundings. The
fact that writers of horror fiction tend to choose, with practically
no exception, puberty as an ultimate dividing line, that they "punish"
any transgression and trespassing of their characters by the same
drastic means, and, above all, that they all make their child protagonists appear as remarkably flawless but bloodless beings emphasizes
that the children in literature hardly have any models in real life.
Taken as outward projections of a psychic situation, the offspring
become, like Truman Capote's albino Miriam, quite plausible in their
strangeness.

Considering an inner conflict as it is hinted at above, one will
likely come to imagine a human being (and, in this case, the writer of
horror fiction in particular) as someone whose personality is split,
neatly divided into one adult "half"--that of God the Father--and one
childish "half" which would correspond to God the Son. Such a division
is strongly reminiscent of those principles of aestheticism which
Oscar Wilde chose as the preface to his most famous and, with regard
to his own doctrines, most elucidative work, The Picture of Dorian
Gray. His very first sentence, "The artist is the creator of beautiful
things,"[3] expresses, as soon as it is seen in relation to the plot of

the narrative, the starting-point of the basic struggle between creator and creature. Dorian Gray has to kill the painter Basil Hallward,
because he, a creature, must dispose of the parent-like artist in
order to be free to create his own work, to make an art of his life.
In a very similar fashion the child in horror literature is striving
for the abolition of the odious rule of its parents, never considering
the question of their personal guilt. Parents, on the other hand,
fight and destroy their offspring in order to "reabsorb" (as Judith
Wilt puts it in connection with the Gothic elders) their creatures and
the vital energy they have spent on them. Both "parties" know instinctively that their respective opponents will attempt anything in order
to defy--or defend--the established adult government which seems to
have been installed by nature itself. Adult reason fights against
childish open-mindedness and impressionability; strict, imperturbable
grown-up logic struggles with a child's imaginative capacity.

An inner conflict like the one in question certainly invites a
"Freudian" mode of interpretation. Indeed, many of Freud's psycho-
analytical theories (which, admittedly, have been used and abused
rather too often and appear somewhat worn-out nowadays) seem to support the idea that the author's "dual personality" accounts for the
idiosyncratic nature of the literary manifestations discussed so far.
Apart from the striking parallel that puberty is taken as a central
dividing line in Freud's theses and horror fiction alike, the most
important agreement lies without doubt in the psycho-analyst's conception of the permanent struggle against the image of the overwhelming
Ur-Vater. Other, seemingly minor points in his doctrines advance to
the center of attention if one examines several literary peculiarities
relating to the transition from childhood to adult age or vice versa
more closely. The fact that the thanatos drive or death wish must
frequently be seen in direct relation to the desire to return to
childhood again and the hope of finding peace in the levelling and
total elimination of all "adult" passion and tension surely finds a
proper expression in horror fiction. It has been pointed out in detail
that an adult person's wish to return to his or her origins is always
combined with disastrous and sometimes fatal circumstances; the desire
for transition and the apparent punishment go, so to speak, "hand in
glove." The most appropriate example may once more be found among Ray
Bradbury's contributions: the train in his story "The Lake" brings the
narrator back to his childhood and his former "young mind," and it
also reunites him with his dead childhood companion and simultaneously
separates him from his adult mate. But death, and especially the
girl's death in the waters of childhood, does not really appear horrible in this case; it is a means of rediscovering the "love that
comes before all significance of body and morals." The parallels mentioned so far, however, are but an indication of the large scope the
child in horror literature offers for psycho-analytic consideration.

If one imagines the artist, and the human being in general, as a
personality that is to some extent "split" into child and adult, creature and creator, the term "schizophrenia" might come to one's mind
sooner or later. To be sure, the expression "split personality" is
only a colloquialism for a complex phenomenon and a complicated state
of mind; nevertheless it is in any event interesting to observe that
physicians, scientists, and philosophers have recently begun to
examine the creations of schizophrenic artists as a possible key to

evolutionary, social and anthropological questions and, above all, as a clue to the mysteries of human creativity. Some modern statements about the correlation between schizophrenia and creativity (a correlation which has become common knowledge[4]) and about the possibility that slight symptoms of schizophrenia serve as an excellent basis for a creative artist may seem daring at first sight. If one considers, however, that the "typically" schizophrenic modes of expression are, like those of every "normal" artist, manifestations of the same basic creative functions of mankind in general (105), sentences like the following by Leo Navratil no longer merely appear as unfounded speculations but show the great potentialities which also lie in fields outside the scope of abnormal psychology:

In the future the term "schizophrenia" will not be restricted to matters of psycho-pathological concern. Perhaps the disease schizophrenia is only the psychotic borderline case of that supreme schizophrenia which functions as the foundation of all creativity and without which humanity is inconceivable. (112)

APPENDIX I:
THE CHILD IN THE HORROR FILM

> ...an infallible, two-part criterion for identifying screen
> monsters: (1) they move very, very slowly; and (2) when
> encountering obstacles, they have a pronounced tendency to
> lumber right through them, in preference to the simpler ex-
> pedient of just walking around.
>
> Robert F. Moss, Karloff and Company: The Horror Film[1]

The above "infallible" definition of screen monsters obviously
refers to those representatives which distinguish themselves by their
physical strength and extreme size, like, above all, Frankenstein's
creature, King Kong, or the gigantic antediluvian beasts invented by
the Japanese film industry. Of course, many of the most impressive
screen monsters do not fall under the two criteria--vampires, for instance, who rely on their erotic charms and hypnotic influence rather
than on brute force. Least of all, however, can the above description
be applied to child monsters, because children always remain physically weak and inferior to their environment and have to carry out
their evil intentions by means of camouflage, the formation of groups,
or special mental abilities. The motto of this chapter evidences the
fact that the rise of an entire novel monstrous "species" has escaped
the critics' attention up to the present time. The child—monster's
harmless coeval, the child—victim, has been generally neglected as
well.

Since the beginning of the 1960's, a number of very successful
motion pictures (Village of the Damned, 1960; The Innocents, 1961; Our
Mother's House, 1967; most prominently, Rosemary's Baby, 1968; Ben,
1972; The Exorcist, 1973; The Omen, 1975; and, most recently, several
adaptations of Stephen King's novels and stories) have centered upon
child characters. These few outstanding examples, however, have hardly
made the audience realize that one can retrace a long, continual tradition of horror films in which children play essential parts. The
particular films mentioned only form the "tip of the iceberg" and,
although critics have taken notice of individual representatives, they
have focussed their ideas and statements on plot, imagery, and technical matters rather than on the appearance of the child. One may explain this by the fact that the children's heterogeneous functions in
these films prevent both critics and spectators from recognizing those
basic similarities and principles which have become evident in the
discussion of the underlying literary works.

Examining the tradition of the child's appearance in the horror
film, one can state several important facts which might be a surprise
to the average spectator. During the first decade of this century,
when Gaumont and other pioneers began to produce horror pictures which
actually deserved this term, they already chose children as welcome
and qualified characters. Among the first short-short motion pictures
dealing with children there are representatives which "anticipate"
later famous film plots: for instance The Key of Life (Edison, 1910),
in which a kitten is reincarnated as a "human kitten" through Hindu
charms[2]--a story which reminds one quite strongly of the various Cat

People adaptations. Other films clearly illustrate that the social
constellations pointed out in connection with literary works have been
favorite topics of film producers from the very beginning. A child's
contact to a doll, for instance, is depicted in one of the first
traceable specimens, The Doll's Revenge (Warner Bros. & Eagle, 1907),
in which a boy destroys a doll meant for his sister. The parts reassemble, and the doll grows to a frightening size. Another doll
appears, and the two pull the boy apart and eat him.[3] Her Dolly's Revenge (Lux, 1909) has a more "harmless" plot: a small girl dreams that
her doll stabs her to death with scissors.

Guy Fawkes Night is another motif which was taken up over and
again in the early days of the horror film, but in contrast to the
preceding constellation this topic already disappeared by 1910. Fire
and explosives have always fascinated directors because of their obvious visual attraction. In connection with Guy Fawkes several peculiarities are notable: although the burning of the dummy is not reserved
for children in real life, it is a pure children's affair in the horror film. The equation "regicide = parricide," which, after all, is an
original idea in itself (cf. the story by Richard Davis), is perceptible as a substratum in each of the films. Father's Hat, or, Guy
Fawkes' Day (1904) and The Stolen Guy (1905), however, are not quite
so explicit as the very first example, The Gunpowder Plot (1900), in
which a boy puts fireworks under his father's chair (= throne) and
blows him to pieces. Another curiosity consists in the fact that these
early films, which undeniably present murderous offspring, mercifully
figure under the rubric "trick."[4]

Apart from numerous early contributions which center on children
and modified fairytale figures, bogeymen, ogres and witches, one can
observe that in a great number of films children were chosen as protagonists because they offered excellent possibilities to the inventors of trick techniques. Whether the genre of the horror film was
"invented" for the chances of innovation and originality it gave to
its pioneers, or whether technical novelties were introduced in order
to create horrible effects, is a question one can hardly answer definitely in retrospect.[5] In any case, the child's "innate" potentialities obviously made it a favorite object of experimentation. Its
size, above all, and the process of growing were topics of interest.
In the above examples including children and dolls, for instance, the
horror is based on the fact that the child initially has the same size
as its doll, but is "outgrown" by its own plaything and becomes an
object itself. Any form of manipulation concerning a baby's rate of
growth can be found in the early representatives of the horror film as
well: The Baby Incubator (Gaumont, 1910) is about a scientist's invention, an incubator which warms and animates a baby until he steps
out of it and begins talking. One can observe that the unnatural
"production" of human life enjoys great popularity in the early films,
an attraction which must mainly be ascribed to the "mere" visual impressiveness of the motif. Scientists and doctors revive children or,
unlike the Frankenstein fashion, form diminutive offspring by mixing
powders and liquids, shaping the mixture into a human replica and in-
spiring the "thing" (which reminds one much more of the Golem mythology), as in What It Will Be (Lux, 1910). Others accelerate an infant's
growth with special food (Dr. Growemquick's Feeding Powder, Walturdaw,
1911), or by "scientific" means, as in A Scientific Mother (Falstaff/

Mutual, 1915): at the age of two a child is as tall as any normal ten-year-old.

From the 1920's to the 1950's children frequently appear in horror films, but there no longer exists a particular trend or a main topic under which the individual films may be categorized. One can notice, however, that film producers have meanwhile definitely ceased to connect human offspring automatically with fairytale figures. As in the beginnings of horror literature, the child is presented as an emblem of innocence and purity and makes an ideal victim. Apart from a single major exception, My Friend the Devil (Fox, 1922), in which a boy wants to make supernatural forces kill his stepfather and thus becomes "responsible" for the death of his mother who is struck by lightning, the average child does not yet harbor wicked intentions. The screenplay of this example, by the way, is an exceedingly free "adaptation" of Georges Ohnet's novel Le Docteur Rameau; the entire plot of the film cannot be traced in the book at all. On the whole, however, the child remains "harmless."

One of the most famous episodes in the history of the horror film, the "flower scene" in the Frankenstein version of 1931, serves as a brilliant illustration. The girl Maria, the only human being unafraid of the creature, involves him in her play and gives him a flower, a token of her unbiassed friendliness and trust. Her unintended death, which upsets the creature, is in a way a reversal of the outcome of a comparable scene in Der Golem (UFA, 1920): here a small girl who is not afraid of Rabbi Löw's creature offers him an apple. The Golem (who has just escaped destruction) "trusts" the girl and picks her up; she toys with the emblem, takes out the shem which is the creature's source of life, and unintentionally "kills" the Golem.

In the course of the 1940's a number of interesting productions are released. The Curse of the Cat People (RKO, 1944), an indirect sequel of Cat People by Val Lewton (1942), is as much a melodramatic study of a child's loneliness as a conventional horror story. The child, a six-year-old girl, "keeps herself company with the ghost of her dead, formerly insane mother (Simone Simon, from the earlier film)."[6] Part of the fascination lies in the uncertainty as to whether the action is rooted in the introverted girl's imagination, an approach which appears quite commonplace nowadays but proves very effective in this particular earlier example. The script of The Fallen Idol (London Films, 1948), written by Graham Greene, is based on his own story "The Basement Room." The author's basic intention to depict a child's terrible awakening to human fallibility can be clearly perceived in the film as well. Basically, the underlying story is faithfully reproduced, but one can notice two deviations from the original plot: the boy thinks that the butler has committed murder and, in order to defend the man, withholds vital information; moreover, in the closing moments the boy runs into the arms of his returning family. On the whole the adaptation can hardly be categorized as a horror film, a change which is mainly due to the fact that the vivid imagery of the story (the oppressive fairytale symbolism and numerous Gothic elements, above all) is entirely ignored. Without these effects--which, ironically enough, seem much better suited for a visual medium--the tale is transformed into a successful melodrama.

A boy's utter helplessness and loneliness in mortal danger is the theme of <u>The Window</u> (RKO, 1948). Though in the very bosom of his family, a ten-year-old boy cannot rely on his parents, because they "collaborate" with the killers who are after him: the boy is known to his surroundings as a "teller of fantastic stories,"[7] and thus the plot of the film can be called a "classic up-dating of the boy who cried 'Wolf' once too often." The child witnesses a murder committed by a couple in the neighborhood; his parents punish him for making up horrible stories, and the boy entrusts himself to a police detective. Through this man (who cannot trace any signs of the crime) the murderers find out about the eye witness's identity and decide to kill the boy. The child's parents, with terrifyingly understandable logic, send their "naughty" offspring to the heart of danger to apologize for spreading lies. Only luck can save the boy, who is all alone among sensible, responsible, and "protective" adults.

In the course of the 1950's several new themes are introduced into the horror film and affect the appearance of children in a peculiar manner. Without doubt the effects of World War II determine the choice of topics. René Clément's macabre masterpiece <u>Jeux Interdits</u> (1952), which contains horror of a very idiosyncratic kind, is a vivid illustration of the fact that although the spectator may be aware of the historical background he can be enchanted by the timeless sublimity of a child's play--and a child's suffering--in a way which makes him forget the actual circumstances and perceive the universal meaning instead. After all, apart from the (admittedly gruesome) introductory scenes, in which the parents of four-year-old Paulette are killed, the film does not directly center upon the war. After Paulette has made friends with the peasant boy Michel, who takes her to his family, the children's secret occupation expresses the cruelties of adult man in an indirect but much more impressive manner. Starting with the dead dog that is Paulette's last reminder of her happy family life, the children arrange an animal graveyard and steal crosses from "human" cemeteries, the village church and a hearse. Paulette has not yet grasped the idea of death but takes great delight in the game, whereas Michel provides his girlfriend with new corpses by killing chickens. To their minds graveyards make the dead feel less lonely; with great devotion they build a genuine necropolis, with an old owl as mayor.

The children's earnest intentions that lie beneath their play form a total contrast to the adults' feigned reverence for "human" death and funeral rites. The village cemetery is shamefully neglected; expensive wreaths and crosses are only chosen to make one's neighbors feel envious, and during a funeral two grown-ups have a fight in the grave. When the children steal the crosses from the cemetery (during a nightly air raid), they are told that crosses are not toys. Indeed, for the children these emblems have an important function. Michel comprehends the total corruption of his adult environment after Paulette, whom he has come to regard as his sister, has been taken to an orphanage. He destroys the graveyard and the crosses and gives Paulette's silver chain to the owl, the embodiment of eternal wisdom, to keep for "a hundred years": the timeless significance of the entire film cannot be expressed more brilliantly than through this final gesture.

The second important topic which is introduced in the 1950's, the results of the experimentation with nuclear energy, has its effects on the presentation of children as well. Children may to some extent carry out experiments themselves (for instance in <u>Child's Play</u>, 1954) or become radioactive, as in <u>The Atomic Kid</u> (1954), quite a ludicrous representative in this respect. The most famous example, <u>These are the Damned</u>, is an adaptation of H. L. Lawrence's <u>Children of Light</u>. Produced in 1961, it signifies a culmination point in the long series of "hysterical science fiction movies of the decade that had just ended." Though David Pirie calls the film a mere "interplay of all the tensions and extravagances that had punctuated the apocalyptic visions of the 1950's,"[8] the picture is a rather faithful reproduction of the novel and an equally strong expression of the basic idea, the definitive separation of grown-ups and children through the guilt of adult man.

The numerous films in which children are involved in nuclear catastrophes may be considered as more or less immediate responses to World War II, Hiroshima, and the general development of atomic weapons. The third main trend which arises in the 1950's--children being endangered and influenced by extraterrestrial beings--is in some cases a subtler but more frightening answer to the above "sins." Jack Arnold's <u>The Space Children</u> (1958) explores, like many of his early films, "the conflicts implicit in the confrontation between man and the forces of another, alien world," which, in this particular case, is "that of childhood."[9] Again nuclear power is dealt with: a group of children whose parents work on an isolated missile project is contacted by an alien intelligence. Using the children's minds to channel its mental power, the alien sabotages the project, preventing the missile with its atomic warhead being launched into space. The children, who form a gang, wander into the caves surrounding their parents' camp and find in one of them a glowing brain that grows as its power becomes greater. The brain, which disposes of a brutal father when he tries to beat his child, is in John Baxter's opinion "an adolescent vision of revenge, a chance to 'get back' on the adult world," and, since all the parents are shown as argumentative, unfeeling and self-interested, the film must (at least to this critic's mind) "have widened inestimably the gulf between the generations."

Five years earlier, adults were already presented as zombie-like strangers who want to kill their small son (<u>Invaders From Mars</u>; Fox, 1953); they have been transformed by Martians, however, and are happily reunited with their child, the hero of the film. Nevertheless, the effect the strange parents produce within the spectator is not counterbalanced, let alone eliminated by this positive ending. In 1960, the adaptation of John Wyndham's <u>Midwich Cuckoos</u>, <u>Village of the Damned</u>, is released. Apart from minor changes (the children's eyes only glow golden when they unite their mental energies--an extremely impressive device; moreover, they are capable of mind-reading) the film closely follows the original, although the sequel, <u>Children of the Damned</u> (1963), expresses the idea of a "generation war of apocalyptic dimensions"[10] in a more drastic, nearly surrealistic manner. Strictly speaking, the latter film is not a sequel, since its action parallels the incidents of Midwich, drawing attention to the fact that "nests" of alien children are spread all over the world. In order to underscore this world-wide distribution of alien seed, the children who are brought together from different continents to be interviewed by UNESCO officials bear the distinctive features of the races they were born "into." On further consideration the inherent contradiction becomes obvious: being members of an extraterrestrial race, the children can hardly be liable to human genetic variations--after all, the Midwich children are identical units who do not resemble their respective "mothers." Nonetheless, this optical demonstration of a universal threat also serves as an unintended indication that the children rather represent the sublimated fear of human offspring.

An outstanding film of the 1950's, the adaptation of The Night of the Hunter (1955), deserves special attention in several regards. Charles Laughton's first and only attempt at directing reveals the actor's versatile genius and makes his audience deeply regret lost opportunities. The dreamlike atmosphere which permeates the entire work is nourished by numerous original visual and acoustic devices; the lullabies of the hunter (Robert Mitchum in one of his finest performances), whose melodious notes end in insane shrieks, contrast sharply with the pious singing of the children's foster-mother. In fact both adults sing the same choral "together," expressing perfectly different attitudes. The tattoos on the hunter's fingers, the words "L-O-V-E" and "H-A-T-E" with which he demonstrates the struggle between good and evil forces, belong to the countless symbols that have been assimilated in the most ingenious conglomerate of horror film motifs, Jim Sharman's Rocky Horror Picture Show (1975).

The 1960's are generally marked by a series of major adaptations. In The Innocents (Fox/Achilles, 1961), based on The Turn of the Screw, the atmosphere of menacing evil and veiled eroticism is successfully re-created, though for obvious reasons the ambiguity beneath the governess's narration can hardly be convincingly translated by visual means. Peter Brook's Lord of the Flies (1963), a masterpiece on the whole, could even have become more effective in Technicolor, since the black-and-white photography fails to represent the superficially paradisiac beauty and peacefulness of the tropical island and thus emphasize the development of human evil. The director's original ideas of gradually turning the choir boys' "Kyrie eleison" into a genuine war chant, and of showing a photograph of the class taken immediately before their "journey" (when they were all "normal" English boys) are only two examples of his overall ingenuity.

Apart from the interesting film versions of Let's Kill Uncle (1966) and Our Mother's House (1967), one can generally state the fact that since the end of the 1950's children have undergone an almost complete change from victims to victimizers. Moreover, a novel trend which is introduced by Polanski's Rosemary's Baby (1968) begins to take shape, a series of motion pictures which might be aptly categorized under the term "Catholic film." The numerous examples released in the course of the last decade (The Exorcist and Don't Look Now, 1973; The Child and The Devil Within Her, 1974; The Omen and Communion, 1975; Look What Happened to Rosemary's Baby, 1976; Obsession and Damien: Omen II, 1977) either deal with Catholic ceremonies and doctrines or have Catholic churches as main settings. Italy as the very heart of Catholicism is chosen in four of the films mentioned above.

Rosemary's Baby, an exceptionally faithful adaptation of Ira Levin's novel, is determined by the brilliant performance of Mia Farrow, who, with her short hair and young girl's dress, manages to look like a small child herself--which surely corresponds to the director's conception, for Rosemary in her vulnerability is the actual child of both novel and film. The final scene, in which Rosemary's "transformation" into Satan's mother is accomplished, does not (in

spite of its inner logic) convince Ray Bradbury, who would have preferred another solution:

> No, she runs out the door, into the elevator, and down into
> the street. The Satanists pursue, fearful and shouting....
> She turns, runs, turns again, down alleys, up streets until
> at last she reaches a church or (why not?) a cathedral....
> What will she do now?...Rosemary steps up upon the altar
> platform and holds the baby out and up in the air and at
> last, eyes shut, gathers courage to speak. And this is what
> she says: "O Lord, O God, O Lord God. Take back your Son!"[11]

Bradbury demands a clear answer to the question which torments him
most after seeing the film:

> For, after all, wasn't there a time, billions of aeons ago,
> when Lucifer stood by the Throne of God? Was he not an ac-
> cepted Angel? Was he not one of the Sons?...And, finally,
> then, does not God forgive? And dark-hooved child brought by
> blameless and sore-tried mother onto a cathedral altar on
> rainy night; could God refuse such needful prayers? Would
> not the Lord take back his ancient enemy and make of him
> once more a Son upon the right hand of the Throne?

Bradbury's reaction to this first major "Catholic film" is in a way
symptomatic of the average spectator's attitude toward--and need
for--this sub-genre. Via the horror film he expects to be provided
with a definitive answer to the evil and corruption of the world. It
is notable that in this respect it does not seem to matter at all if
the answer comes in the form of a consolation (as in The Exorcist) or
as the prospect of a total apocalypse or even hell on earth--the addition of a "Satanic" hell to the existent human version, as in The
Omen. (Curiously enough, the ending of the latter film forms the exact
reverse of Bradbury's wishful thinking: the father's attempt to stab
Damien to death with "holy" daggers on the very altar of a cathedral
is an Old Testament "version" indeed.) As long as there exist clearly
defined centers of both good and evil forces--God and the Devil--which
one must either shun or feel attracted to, the outcome of the struggle
itself bears little importance. Rosemary, however, is a heroine who
feels attracted to the wrong "party," accepting her son without hesitation or reservation; after all, it is the perversion of motherhood
which evokes the ultimate impression of horror within the spectator,
and the horror presented here is not so easy to cope with as in later
films.
    The Exorcist, for instance, has stirred many critics' indignation
because the solution the film offers appears a bit too simple to them:
the domestic harmony and peacefulness of an American (atheistic)
household is disturbed by a demon; all of a sudden parents and tutors
fall back on a God who has not been openly denied (let alone defied)
but simply ignored up to this moment. Damien Karras, the priest-
psychiatrist who becomes involved in the affair, is "more agnostic"[12]
than his "mundane" medical colleagues, but has to perform the exorcism
which turns all characters into faithful Christians. The expulsion of
the demon is, strictly speaking, no genuine exorcism at all (Karras

invites the evil spirit to take possession of him and thus commits suicide); but the priest's heroic death "made in Hollywood" brings relief and reassurance to an audience whose peace of mind is restored through the intervention of a (as the priest Karl Weber puts it) "deus ex machina"--in the creation of this deceitful sense of relief, however, the "diabolus ex machina" has an (at least) equally important share.

One has to admit that the child protagonist of a more recent outstanding production, Omen II: Damien (1977), makes it hard for the spectator not to sympathize completely with the "wrong side." Although Damien (Jonathan Scott-Taylor), the Son of the Devil, is only twelve years old, he casts a spell on his audience. One must "love" him for the agony he experiences, an agony no mortal being, not even the fiend, should have to suffer. In total contrast to The Omen, the horror of the sequel is not based on the evil activities of an inscrutable small stranger. As an infant Damien used his super-human abilities unconsciously, and although he did so under the guidance of evil nurses and other tutors, always acting as their unwitting tool, he remained a dread-inspiring, beautiful monster and the uncontested center of evil.

As a pubescent boy Damien evokes an entirely different impression, though the basic constellation has not changed at all: devil-worshipping guardians and infernal beasts surround, influence, and shield the Son of the Devil from both physical danger and the investigations of his persecutors. Damien is still unaware of his origin and destiny and even somewhat upset by the effects of his power. He has been well prepared for his position as a "crown prince" (both as his foster-father's successor and as Satan's representative) and must now be initiated into the secret of his true mission on earth. Confused by the human problems his puberty brings about, Damien misinterprets his tutors' furtive remarks concerning great changes in the near future. When he finally discovers the Devil's brand on his skin his reaction forms an obvious parallel to the sufferings of Jesus Christ: he accepts the cup of sorrow and becomes a martyr in his father's cause. His agonized cry "Why me?" reveals his attitude towards his position. Unlike his father, he cannot really choose the course he takes; though his actions seem to show his determination, he remains a marionette. He tempts his beloved foster-brother to share his evil empire, just as his father tempted Christ; when Damien has to kill his antagonist, however, the murderer suffers more than his victim.

Although the pubescent Damien remains the physical center of evil, the real horror now lies in the fact that his unwitting "fellow" beings, model citizens each and all, regard him as the messiah of the financial and political world. Indeed, the boy's education enables him to fulfill the expectations of these people (who are not professed devil worshippers, after all) to their perfect satisfaction. All steps in this education, the drill in a renowned military academy, even his physical training, pave his way for an "exceptional" career; his success as a football player is not the only hint at the prospect that the Son of the Devil is going to be an all-American.

APPENDIX II: FILMOGRAPHY

1900   The Gunpowder Plot. P, D: Cecil M. Hepworth. R: Gifford, British Film Catalogue (B.F.C.); with Cecil Hepworth (as Father).

1901   An Over-Incubated Baby. P: R. W. Paul. D: Walter Booth. R: B.F.C. "Child put into professor's incubator comes out old man."

1904   Father's Hat; or, Guy Fawkes' Day. P: Clarendon. D: Percy Stow. R: B.F.C. "Father poses as guy and children set him alight."

1905   The Stolen Guy. P: Hepworth. D: Lewin Fitzhamon. R: B.F.C. "Drunkard poses as guy until children put him on bonfire."

1906   Baby's Peril. P: Urban Trading Co. R: B.F.C. "Parents try to get loaded revolver away from baby."

The Horse that Ate the Baby. P: Clarendon. D: Percy Stow. R: B.F.C. "Horse eats baby."

1907   The Doll's Revenge. Warner Bros. & Eagle. R: Willis.

Mrs. Smither's Boarding School. Biograph. 12 mins. R: Willis.   Two pupils dressed as ghosts frighten teacher.

1908   In the Bogie Man's Cave. Méliès/Star. R: Willis.   The Bogey Man decides to fry a boy for dinner.

1909   Mother Goose. Edison. 5 mins. R: Willis. "Large spider of most ferocious aspect frightens Miss Muffet and picks up a small boy."

Her Dolly's Revenge. Lux. 5 mins. R: Willis.

The Bogey Woman. Pathé. 7 mins. R: Willis.   The Bogey Woman turns children into vegetables.

Father's Baby Boy. P: Clarendon. D: Percy Stow. R: B.F.C.   "Bovril" makes baby grow to enormous size.

1910   What It Will Be. (France) Lux. 6 mins. R: Willis.

The Freak of Ferndale Forest. Warwick. 9 mins. R: Willis.   Beggar transforms child into "hideous beast."

The Key of Life. Edison. 16 mins. R: Willis.

The Baby Incubator. Gaumont. 8 mins. R: Willis.

1911   *An Old-Time Nightmare*. Powers. R: Willis.   Dream: huge birds menace boy.

Dr. Growemquick's Feeding Powder. Walturdaw. 10 mins. R: Willis.

The Baby and the Bomb. P: Hepworth. D: Bert Haldane. R: B.F.C.   Baby saves procession by blowing up anarchist with his own bomb.

1912   *Nursie and Knight*. Than. 17 mins. R: Willis. "Boy slays dragon in dream."

1913   *The Haunted House*. Pathéplay. 17 mins. R: Willis.   Afraid to pass a "haunted house," a little girl has her father accompany her.

1915   *A Scientific Mother*. Falstaff/Mutual. R: Willis.

1916   *The Regeneration of Margaret*. Essanay. 35 mins. D: Charles J. Brabin. R: Willis; with W. Howard, Ernest Maupain.   Operation cures baby of birth defects.

1917   *The Valley of Beautiful Things*. Victor. SP: Fred Myton. P: Lule Warrenton. R: Willis; with Peggy Custer, Antrim Short, Elsie Cort. Witch uses fairy child to lure and rob travelers.

1920   *The Branded Four*. Select. Serial. R: Willis. D: Duke Worne; with Ben Wilson, Neva Gerber, J. Girard, W. Dyer.   Children branded at birth with mysterious marks that will only appear at maturity.

1922   *My Friend the Devil*. Fox. 100 mins. D: Harry Millarde. SP: Paul Sloane, from *Le Docteur Rameau* by Georges Ohnet. PH: J. Ruttenberg. R: Willis; with Charles Richman, Ben Grauer, Alice May, Robert Frazer.

1928   *The Man Who Laughs*. USA. Paul Kohner/Universal. Silent. 90 mins. D: Paul Leni. SP: Bela Sekely, J. Grubb Alexander, from Victor Hugo's novel. PH: Gilbert Warrenton. P: Carl Laemmle. R: Willis. Child whose face has been horribly disfigured joins traveling circus.

1931   *Frankenstein*. USA. Universal. D: James Whale. SP: John Balderston, Garret Ford, Francis E. Farragoh, from Mary Shelley's novel. PH: Arthur A. Edeson. R: Moss; with Colin Clive, Boris Karloff, Mae Clarke, Marily Harris (as Maria).

M. Germany. P: Nero Film. D: Fritz Lang. PH: Fritz A. Wagner. SP: Thea von Harbou. M: Edvard Grieg; with Peter Lorre, Gustav Gründgens, Otto Wernicke, Ellen Widmann, Inge Landgut (as Elsie).

1932   *Shail Bala*. India. Ranjit. R: Willis; with Miss Gohar, Bhagwandas.   Guru's black magic causes deaths of children.

1934   *Black Moon*. USA. 69 mins. D: Roy W. Neill. SP: Wells Root, from Clements Ripley's story "Haiti Moon." PH: Joseph August; with Jack Holt, Fay Wray, Clarence Muse.   Obsessed by voodoo rituals, a white woman almost sacrifices her own child.

1938   Oh, Boy. A.B.P.C. 76 mins. D: Albert de Courville. R: Willis; with Albert Burdon, Mary Lawson. A mysterious drug that is to make a coward self-confident causes him to revert gradually to a baby.

The Barefoot Boy. Monogram. 63 mins. D: Karl Brown. SP: John Neville. PH: Gilbert Warrenton. P: Harold Lewis; with Jackie Moran, M. Jones, Ralph Morgan. Children locate missing bonds in a haunted house.

1944   The Curse of the Cat People. USA. RKO. 70 mins. D: Gunther von Fritsch, Robert Wise. SP: DeWitt Bodeen. P: Val Lewton. PH: Nicholas Masuraca. M: Roy Webb. R: Moss, Butler; with Simone Simon, Ann Carter.

1945   Dead of Night. Great Britain. Ealing. 104 mins. P: Michael Balcon. D: Basil Dearden, A. Cavalcanti, Robert Hamer, C. Crichton. SP: John Baines, Angus McPhail, T.E.B. Clarke. M: Georges Auric. PH: Stan Pavey. R: Frank; with Sally Ann Howes, Michael Allan, Robert Wyndham. Episode "The Christmas Story": Young girl encounters crying child who turns out to have been killed years before by his sister.

1946   Get Along, Little Zombie. Columbia. 20 mins. R: Willis.

1948   The Haunted Castle. United Artists/Alliance. 91 mins. SP/D: Val Guest. PH: Leslie Rowson. R: Willis; with William Graham, Garry Marsh, A. E. Matthews. Children plan to "haunt" old manor house.

The Fallen Idol. Great Britain. London Films. 94 mins. D: Carol Reed. SP: Graham Greene, from his story "The Basement Room." PH: Georges Périnal; with Ralph Richardson, Michèle Morgan, Bobby Henry.

The Window. USA. RKO. 73 mins. P: Dore Schary. SP: Mel Dinelli. D: Ted Tetzlaff. R: Hammond; with Bobby Driscoll, Arthur Kennedy, B. Hale.

1949   The Rocking Horse Winner. Rank/Universal. 90 mins. D: Anthony Pelissier. Based on the story by D. H. Lawrence. PH: Desmond Dickinson. M: William Alwyn. P: John Mills. R: Willis; with Valerie Hobson, John Howard Davies, John Mills, Hugh Sinclair.

Myrte and the Demons. Great Britain/Holland. European Art Union. 73 mins. D, P: Paul Schreiber. SP: Gyles Adams. PH: Bert Haanstra. M: Marinus Adam. R: Willis; with Myrte Schreiber, John Moore, Sonia Gables. Wood demons seek to destroy girl, turning her playmates to stone.

1952   Jeux Interdits. France. P: Robert Dorfmann. D: René Clément. SP: Jean Aurenche, Pierre Bost, René Clément, from a novel by François Boyer. PH: Robert Juillard. M: Narciso Yepes; with Georges Poujouly, Brigitte Fossey, Amédée, Suzanne Courtal.

1953   Invaders From Mars. USA. 20th-Century Fox. 77 mins. PH: John Seitz. P, D: William C. Menzies. SP: Richard Blake. M: Raoul Kraushaar. R: Willis; with Helen Carter, Arthur Franz, Jimmy Hunt.

The 5000 Fingers of Dr. T. USA. 85 mins. D: Roy Rowland; with Tommy Rettig, Hans Conried, Peter Lind Hayes, Mary Healy. In this grotesque musical, a small boy who hates his piano teacher dreams of him as an evil tyrant who has kidnapped 500 children and prepares them for a gigantic concert.

1954   Child's Play. Group 3/British Lion. 68 mins. D: Margaret Thomson. SP: Peter Blackmore, from a story by Don Sharp. PH: Denny Densham. M: Antony Hopkins. R: Willis; with Mona Washbourne, Carl Jaffe, Peter Martyn, Dorothy Alison.   Children produce "atomic sweetmeat, Bangcorn."

The Atomic Kid. Republic. 87 mins. D: Leslie Martinson. SP: John F. Murray, Benedict Freeman, from a story by Blake Edwards. PH: John L. Russell. R: Willis; with Mickey Rooney, Robert Strauss, Whit Bissell. A boy, caught in an atomic blast, becomes radioactive.

1955   The Night of the Hunter. United Artists. 93 mins. D: Charles Laughton. SP: James Agee, from Davis Grubb's novel. PH: Stanley Cortez. M: Walter Schumann; with Robert Mitchum, Billy Chapin, Sally Jane Bruce, Shelley Winters, Lillian Gish.

1956   The Bad Seed. Warner Bros. 127 mins. P, D: Mervyn LeRoy. SP: John Lee Mahin, from the play by Maxwell Anderson and the novel by William March. PH: Hal Rosson; with Nancy Kelly, Patty McCormack, Henry Jones, William Hopper, Eileen Heckart, Jesse White.

1957   Secret of the Golden Hill. (Thanamalai Rahasyam.) India-Tamil. Padmini. D, P: B. R. Pantulu. SP: C. Annamalai, Lakshmanan. R: Willis; with S. Ganesan, M. V. Kajamma.   Sorcerer casts spell on parents of boy reared by elephants.

Macabre. USA. 73 mins. Allied Artists. P, D: William Castle. SP: Robb White. PH: Carl Guthrie. M: Les Baxter. R: Frank; with William Prince, Jim Backus, Jacqueline Scott.   A doctor is suspected of having let his wife die; a plot is mounted to kill him by fright by making it appear that his small daughter has been buried alive.

El Vampiro Negro. Argentina. 77 mins. D: Roman V. Barreto. PH: Anibal Gonzalez Paz. SP: Barreto, Alberto Atchebehere. M: Eric Landy; with Olga Zubarry, Roberto Escalada, Nelly Panizza.   A psychopath terrorizes an Argentine city, murdering small children.

1958   Space Children. Paramount. 69 mins. D: Jack Arnold. SP: Bernard Schoenfeld, from a story by Tom Filer. PH: Ernest Laszlo. P: William Alland. M: Van Cleave. R: Baxter, Willis; with Michael Ray, Jackie Coogan, Adam Williams, Peggy Webber, Sandy Descher.

1959   Female Cobra. (Nagin.) Pakistani. Hayat. 118 mins. D: Kalil Quaiser. R: Willis.   Two dangerous supernatural reptiles disguise themselves as children and terrorize the countryside.

Daughter of Lightning. (Anak ng kidlat.) Filipino. Tamarawa. D: Mario Barri. R: Willis.   "Woman struck by lightning becomes pregnant. Daughter of union, potentially dangerous, has control of lightning."

Have Rocket, Will Travel. Columbia. 76 mins. D: David L. Rich. PH: Ray

Cory. SP: Raphael Hayes. M: Mischa Bakaleinikoff. R: Willis; with Moe
Howard, Larry Fine, Annalisa. Encounters with robots, giant spiders.

1960   Village of the Damned. MGM. 81 mins. P: Ronald Kinnoch. D: Wolf
Rilla. SP: Rilla, George Barclay, S. Silliphant, from John Wyndham's
The Midwich Cuckoos. PH: Geoffrey Faithfull. R: Pirie, Butler; with
George Sanders, Martin Stephens, Barbara Shelley, Michael Gwynn.

The Snake-Woman. United Artists. 68 mins. D: Sidney Furie. SP: Orville
Hampton. PH: Stephen Dade. M: Buxton Orr. R: Willis; with Geoffrey
Danton, John McCarthy, Susan Travers.   A pregnant woman is injected
with snake venom; she dies giving birth to a cold-blooded baby.

Peeping Tom. Anglo-Amalgamated. 109 mins. P, D: Michael Powell.
SP: Leo Marks. PH: Otto Heller. M: Brian Easdale. R: Frank; with Carl
Böhm, Anna Massay.   Father's voyeuristic, sadistic experiments with
his small child pave the way for the son's mental deformation.

1961   These are the Damned. Columbia/Hammer. 87 mins. SP: Evan Jones,
from H. L. Lawrence's Children of Light. D: Joseph Losey. PH: Arthur
Grant. P: Anthony Hinds. M: James Bernard. R: Pirie, Baxter; with Macdonald Carey, Shirley Ann Field, Oliver Reed, James Villiers.

Curse of the Werewolf. Great Britain. Universal/Hammer. P: Anthony
Hinds. D: Terence Fisher. SP: John Elder, from The Werewolf of Paris
by Guy Endore. PH: Arthur Grant. M: Benjamin Frankel. R: Pirie; with
Oliver Reed, Clifford Evans, Michael Ripper.   After the rape of a girl
by a beggar, her child grows up to be a werewolf.

The Innocents. Great Britain. Fox/Achilles. 99 mins. D, P: Jack
Clayton. SP: Truman Capote, W. Archibald, John Mortimer, from The Turn
of the Screw by Henry James. PH: Freddie Francis. M: Georges Auric.
R: Butler, Cinema; with Deborah Kerr, Martin Stephens, Megs Jenkins.

1962   Love Not Again. (koija koi nasuna koi.) Japan. Toei. 100 mins.
D: Tomu Uchida. SP: Yoshitaka Yoda. PH: Teiji Yoshida. R: Willis; with
Hashizo Okawa, Michiko Saga, Sumiko Hidaka.   White fox transforms her-
self in the shape of a woman who gives birth to a boy child.

1963   Lord of the Flies. Great Britain. 85 mins. D, SP: Peter Brook.
P: Al Hine, Lewis Allen; with James Aubrey, Tom Chapin, Surtees Twins.

Children of the Damned. MGM. 81 mins. P: Ben Arbeid. D: Anton Leader.
SP: Jack Briley. PH: Davis Boulton. M: Ron Goodwin. R: Pirie; with Ian
Hendry, Alan Badel, Barbara Ferris, Lee Yoke-Moon.   UNESCO investiga-
tors try to communicate with six "super-children" brought to London
from different countries.

1964   The Bad Seed. Turkey. Pesen/And Film. D: Nevzat Pesen. From the
play by Maxwell Anderson and the novel by William March. R: Willis;
with Lale, Alev Oraloglu.

1965   I Kill, You Kill. (Io uccido, tu uccidi.) France/Italy. Metro-
polis/Gulliver. SP, D: Gianni Puccini. SP: also Filippo Sanjust, De

Concini, Boschi. PH: Marcello Gatti. R: Willis; with E. Riva, Jean-Louis Trintignant, Dominique Boschero. Episode "Bitter Games": three children cause all the "bad" people they know to die mysteriously.

The Nanny. Great Britain. Hammer. D: Seth Holt. SP: Jimmy Sangster, from Evelyn Piper's novel. PH: Harry Waxman. R: Moss; with Bette Davis, William Dix, Wendy Craig. Boy suspects nanny of having killed his small sister, plans to punish her and is nearly murdered himself.

Bunny Lake is Missing. Great Britain. 107 mins. D: Otto Preminger. SP: John and Penelope Mortimer, from a novel by Evelyn Piper. M: Paul Glass. PH: Denys Coop; with Keir Dullea, Carol Lynley, Suki Appleby. A woman's brother, jealous of her love, destroys all evidence of her child's existence and finally tries to kill the four-year-old.

1966 Kill, Baby, Kill. (Operazione paura.) Italy. Europix. 83 mins. D: Mario Bava. PH: Antonio Rinaldi. SP: Bava, R. Migliorini, Roberto Natale. M: Carlo Rustichelli. R: Willis; with Giacomo R. Stuart, Max Lawrence, Erika Blank. Baroness haunts people to death with apparition of her dead child.

Let's Kill Uncle. Universal. 92 mins. P, D: William Castle. SP: Mark Rodgers, from Rohan O'Grady's novel. PH: Harold Lipstein. M: Herman Stein; with Nigel Green, Linda Lawson, Mary Badham, Pat Cardi.

Picture Mommy Dead. USA. 88 mins. Embassy. PH: Ellsworth Frederick. SP: Robert Sherman. D, P: Bert Gordon; with Don Ameche, Martha Hyer, Susan Gordon. A girl is haunted by visions of her dead mother.

Miri. (Star Trek episode; 1st season) SP: Adrian Spies. PH: Jerry Finnerman. M: Alexander Courage; with Kim Darby, Jim Goodwin, John Megna.

1967 Hamelin. Spain. Prades. 105 mins. D: Luis Delgado. SP: R.P. Carpio. PH: Godofredo Pacheco. M: A. Waitzman; with Miguel Rios.

Our Mother's House. Great Britain. Heron/MGM. 105 mins. P, D: Jack Clayton. SP: Haya Harareet, Jeremy Brooks, from Julian Gloag's novel. PH: Larry Pizer. M: Georges Delerue; with Margaret Brooks, Pamela Franklin, Mark Lester, Dirk Bogarde, Sarah Nicholls.

1968 Rosemary's Baby. USA. Paramount. 134 mins. D: Roman Polanski. SP: Polanski, from Ira Levin's novel. PH: William Fraker. P: William Castle; with Mia Farrow, John Cassavetes, Ruth Gordon, Maurice Evans.

Der kleine Vampir. Germany. Rob Houver Film. 80 mins. D, SP, M: Roland Klick. PH: Robert van Ackeren; with Sascha Urchs, Sieghardt Rupp, Hans Kallen. Nine-year-old kills his baby sister without reason and causes his family to commit crimes in order to cover his traces.

And the Children Shall Lead. (Star Trek episode; 3rd season) PH: Jerry Finnerman. SP: Edward J. Lakso; with Melvin Belli, Brian Tochi, Mark Robert, Pamelyn Ferdin. Being promised freedom from parental supervision, a group of children help a demonic superior being to kill the adult explorers of a deserted planet. They are the catalyst that has resuscitated the being and the medium through which it can act.

Night of the Living Dead. USA. Image Ten. 96 mins. D, PH: George A. Romero. SP: John Russo; with Judith O'Dea, Duan Jones, Karl Hardman. A small girl, wounded by a zombie, is nursed by her parents. She turns into a zombie, too, and devours the adults who are unable to kill her.

1969   Daddy's Gone A-Hunting. USA. 108 mins. D: Mark Robson. M: John Williams. SP: Larry Cohen, Lorenzo Semple. PH: Ernest Laszlo; with Carol White, Paul Burke, Scott Hylands. Psychopath tries to force his former girlfriend to kill the child she has with another man.

The Illustrated Man. Warner Bros. 103 mins. D: Jack Smight. SP: Howard Kreitsek, from Bradbury's "The Veld," "The Long Rain," "The Last Night of the World." PH: Philip Lathrop. M: Jerry Goldsmith; with Rod Steiger, Claire Bloom, Robert Drivas, Tim Weldon, Don Dubbins.

Valerie and the Week of Wonders. (Valerie a tyden divu.) Czechoslovakia. 85 mins. Barrandov. D: Jaromil Jires. SP: Ester Krumbachova, from V. Nezval's novel. PH: Jan Curik. M: Lubos Fiser. R: Willis; with Jaroslava Musil, Helena Anyzkova. Girl's grandmother is a vampire.

1970   The House that Dripped Blood. Great Britain. Amicus. 101 mins. P: Max Rosenberg, Milton Subotsky. D: Peter Duffell. SP: Robert Bloch, from "Sweets to the Sweet" and other tales. PH: Ray Parslow; with Peter Cushing, Christopher Lee, Ingrid Pitt, Chloe Franks.

Hands Off Gretel. (Hänsel und Gretel verliefen sich im Wald.) Germany. Pohland. 82 mins. SP, D: F. Gottlieb. PH: P. Schloemp. R: Willis; with Barbara Klingered, Francy Fair, Dagobert Walter. Featuring a "witch-countess," complete with the inscription "Dracula" over her fireplace.

Satan's Skin. Great Britain. 93 mins. P: Peter Andrews, M. Heyworth. D: Piers Haggard. SP: Robert Wynne-Simmons. PH: Dick Bush. R: Frank; with Patrick Wymark, Linda Hayden. The discovery of a bizarre skull leads to the formation of a Satanic cult among the local children.

I Drink Your Blood. USA. 82 mins. D, SP: David Durston. PH: Jacques Demarceaux. M: Clay Pitts; with Bhaskar, Jadine Wong, Ronda Fultz. Small boy wants to avenge his sister's rape, kills rabid dog, prepares cake with the beast's blood and divides it among his victims who turn into bloodthirsty maniacs.

1971   The Brotherhood of Satan. USA. 92 mins. D: Bernard McEveety. SP: William Welch. PH: John A. Morrill; with Strother Martin, Charles Bateman. Group of Satanists kidnap children to reincarnate in their bodies.

The Last Child. ABC-TV/Aaron Spelling. 75 mins. SP: Peter S. Fischer. D: John Moxey. PH: Arch Dalzell. M: Laurence Rosenthal. R: Willis; with Van Heflin, Michael Cole, Harry Guardino. In the future a population control law dictates that a baby must be killed.

The Nightcomers. Great Britain. Scimitar/K-L-K. 96 mins. P, D: Michael

Winner. SP: Michael Hastings, inspired by <u>The Turn of the Screw</u>. PH: Robert Paynter. M: Jerry Fielding. R: Pirie, Frank; with Marlon Brando, Stephanie Beacham, Thora Hird. "Two young children are intrigued by the sado-masochistic sexual games played by their governess and the gardener in turn-of-the-century England. They become corrupted and finally kill the two adults" (Frank).

<u>Night Hair Child</u>. Great Britain. Leander Films. 89 mins. P: Graham Harris. D: James Kelly. SP: Trevor Preston. PH: Luis Cuadrado; with Mark Lester, Hardy Krüger, Britt Ekland. Sadistic twelve-year-old murders his mother and makes sexual advances on his step-mother.

<u>Dead Time/Whoever Slew Auntie Roo?</u>. Great Britain. P: Samuel Arkoff, James Nicholson. D: Curtis Harrington. SP: Robert Blees, James Sangster. PH: Desmond Dickinson. M: Kenneth Jones; with Shelley Winters, Mark Lester, Chloe Franks. A contemporary version of "Hänsel und Gretel": A small boy and his sister maliciously dispose of the owner of the "Gingerbread House," a deranged (though harmless) lady who keeps her daughter's mummified corpse in the nursery.

1972   <u>Ben</u>. USA. Cinerama. P: Mort Briskin. D: Phil Karlson. 92 mins. SP: Gilbert Ralston, based on characters from Stephen Gilbert's <u>Ratman's Notebooks</u>. Sequel to <u>Willard</u>. PH: Russell Metty. M: Walter Scharf; with Joseph Campanella, Lee Harcourt Montgomery. Small invalid boy prefers to live in the garage and makes friends with the rat-"leader" Ben.

<u>Tales From the Crypt</u>. Great Britain. 95 mins. SP: Milton Subotsky. D: Freddie Francis. PH: Norman Warwick. M: Douglas Gambley; with Ralph Richardson, Joan Collins, Chloe Franks. 1st episode: Small girl opens the door for "Father Christmas," a lunatic escapee, while her mother is barricading the windows.

<u>Nothing But the Night</u>. Great Britain. 90 mins. P: Anthony N. Keys. D: Peter Sasdy. PH: Ken Talbot. SP: Brian Hayles, from John Blackburn's novel. R: Frank; with Christopher Lee, Peter Cushing, Diana Dors. Children from an orphanage are injected with the life essence of dead trustees from the institution to perpetuate their existence.

<u>The Other</u>. USA. 100 mins. P, D: Robert Mulligan. SP: Thomas Tryon, based on his own novel. PH: Robert L. Surtees. M: Jerry Goldsmith. R: Frank; with Uta Hagen, Diana Muldaur, Chris and Martin Udvarnoky. Angelic ten-year-old is apparently possessed by the spirit of his evil older brother, who leads him to commit mutilation and murder.

<u>Au rendez-vous de la mort joyeuse</u>. France/Italy. 80 mins. D: Juan Buñuel. SP: Pierre Jean Maintigneux, Buñuel. PH: Ghislain Cloquet; with Françoise Fabian, Jean-Marc Bory, Yasmine Dahm. Married couple with small daughter move into house in a lonely wood; the child's "wild talent" is the possible reason for the subsequent "haunting."

1973   <u>The Exorcist</u>. USA. Warner Bros. 122 mins. D: William Friedkin. SP: William Peter Blatty, from his novel. P: Blatty. PH: Owen Roizman, Billy Williams. M: Krzysztof Penderecki, Mike Oldfield. R: Frank;

with Ellen Burstyn, Max von Sydow, Lee J. Cobb, Linda Blair.

Don't Look Now. Great Britain/Italy. 110 mins. D: Nicholas Roeg.
P: Peter Katz. SP: Allan Scott, from Daphne du Maurier's story.
PH: Anthony Richmond. M: Pino D'Onaggio. R: Moss, Frank; with Julie
Christie, Donald Sutherland. Parents get in spiritual contact with
their dead daughter through a blind medium; running after a tiny fig-
ure clad like his child, the father faces a dwarf who cuts his throat.

Tales that Witness Madness. Great Britain. 90 mins. P: Norman Priggen.
D: Freddie Francis. SP: Jay Fairbank. PH: Norman Warwick. R: Frank;
with Jack Hawkins, Donald Pleasence, Georgia Brown. "A young boy of 6
who lives with his constantly quarrelling parents creates an 'imaginary' tiger which turns out to be only too real."

Dark Places. Great Britain. 91 mins. D: Don Sharp. SP: Ed Brennan,
Joseph van Winkle. PH: Ernest Steward. M: Wilfred Josephs; with Robert
Hardy, Christopher Lee, Joan Collins. Ex-mental patient inherits a
house and is soon haunted by the laughter of dead children.

The Boy Who Cried Werewolf. USA. Universal. 93 mins. P: Aaron Rosenberg. D: Nathan H. Juran. SP: Bob Homel. PH: Michael Joyce. M: Ted
Stovall. R: Frank; with Kerwin Mathews, Robert Wilke. Young boy is
attacked by werewolf; father later changes into wolf man.

Andy Warhol's Frankenstein. (Carne per Frankenstein.) Italy/France.
Cinecittà. 95 mins. P: Carlo Ponti, Andrew Braunsberg. SP: Paul
Maurissey. PH: Luigi Kuveiler. M: Claudio Gizzi; with Joe Dallesandro,
Udo Kier, Nicoleta Elmi, Srdjan Zelenovic. Baron Frankenstein's
children Eric and Marika emulate their father, starting with the
slicing of dolls, then continuing their experiments with humans. As
true "embodiments of beauty," they are made in their father's image.

1974   Chi Sei?. (GB: The Devil Within Her.) Italy. 109 mins. P: O.
Assonitis, Giorgio C. Rossi. D: Oliver Hellman. SP: Sonia Molteni.
PH: Robert d'Ettore Piazzoli. M: Franco Micalizzi; with Juliet Mills,
Richard Johnson, Gabriele Lavia. Young woman is impregnated by the
Devil; the child is to take the place of a moribund disciple.

The Living Dead at the Manchester Morgue. (Fin de semano para los
muertes.) Spain. As a result of pest "control," corpses are revived
and new-born infants bite mothers and nurses in a hospital.

1975   The Omen. USA. 112 mins. 20th-Century Fox. P: Harvey Bernhard.
D: Richard Donner. SP: David Seltzer. PH: Gilbert Taylor. M: Jerry
Goldsmith; with Gregory Peck, Lee Remick, Harvey Stephens.

Communion. USA. 105 mins. P: Richard Rosenberg. D: Alfred Sole. PH: Ed
Salier. SP: Rosemary Ritvo, Sole. M: Stephen Lawrence; with Brooke
Shields, Linda Miller, Mildred Clinton. Two small sisters represent a
Cain-and-Abel relationship: Karen enjoys her mother's love and prepares herself for her first Holy Communion; Alice has fallen from
grace and celebrates devilish rites in the basement. During the Communion Karen is slaughtered.

Cria Cuervos... Spain. 110 mins. D, SP: Carlos Saura. P: Elias Querejeta. PH: Teodoro Escamilla. M: Federico Mompour. R: ZOOM, 28 (1976); with Geraldine Chaplin, Ana Torrent. Though not a "straight-forward" horror film, the work contains countless Gothic elements. A small girl believes that she possesses the power over life and death, suggests putting her grandmother to death, and pours a "poisonous" powder into her aunt's drink. The title refers to a Spanish saying: "Feed the ravens, and they will pick out your eyes."

Quién puede matar a un niño? (Is It Right to Kill a Child?) Spain. 105 mins. D: Narciso I. Serrador. P: Manuel Perez. SP: Luis Penafiel, from The Game by J. J. Plans. PH: José Alcaine. M: Waldo de los Rios; with Lewis Fiander, Prunella Ransome, Antonio Iranzo, the children. Couple spend honeymoon on island that seems mysteriously deserted. Children have taken over power, murdering all adults in sight. The topic of "revenge" is illustrated by a prologue: Korea, Vietnam, Biafra, Nazi terrors.

I Don't Want to Be Born. Great Britain. 94 mins. P: Norma Corney. D: Peter Sasdy. SP: Stanley Price. PH: Kenneth Talbot. M: Ron Grainer. R: Frank; with Joan Collins, Eileen Atkins. Woman spurns dwarf and is cursed; she gives birth to a savage, strong baby that is possessed.

The Premonition. USA. Galaxy Films. D, P: Robert A. Schnitzer. SP: Anthony Mahon, Schnitzer. PH: Victor C. Milt. M: Henry Mollicone; with Sharon Farrell, Edward Bell, Ellen Barber. Psychopath plans to kidnap her daughter living with foster parents; her insane lover kills her and carries the child away. Via telepathy the foster mother searches for the child.

The Child. Italy/Germany. 90 mins. P: Enzo Doria, Dieter Geissler. D, SP: Aldo Lado. M: Ennio Morricone; with George Lazenby, Anita Strindberg. In this film Venice seems to swarm with small children, who represent the (possible) future of the moribund city. A fake priest, disguised as a veiled lady, kills the prettiest of them to spare them the corruption of adult life.

It's Alive. USA. Warner/Larco. 91 mins. P, D, SP: Larry Cohen. PH: Fenton Hamilton. M: Bernard Herrmann. R: Frank; with John Ryan, Sharon Farrell, Andrew Duggan, Guy Stockwell. "A woman gives birth to a terrifyingly strong and murderous mutant baby after taking inadequately tested drugs during pregnancy."

1976   The Little Girl Who Lives Down the Lane. Canada. Rank. 92 mins. P: Zev Braun. D: Nicolas Gessner. SP: Laird Koenig, from his novel. PH: René Verzier. M: Mort Shuman; with Jodie Foster, Martin Sheen, Alexis Smith, Scott Jacoby. Highly self-sufficient thirteen-year-old girl lives alone, kills her intrusive mother, disposes of her curious landlady, and poisons a child molester who knows her secret.

Something Wicked This Way Comes. Paramount. P: Hank Moonjean, Peter V. Douglas. D: Jack Clayton. SP: Ray Bradbury, from his novel. M: James Horner. PH: Stephen H. Burum; with Jason Robards, Jonathan Pryce.

The Haunting of Julia. Great Britain. 95 mins. P: Peter Fetterman, Alfred Pariser. D: Richard Loncraine. PH: Peter Hannan. M: Colin Towns.
SP: Dave Humphries, from the novel Julia by Peter Straub; with Mia
Farrow, Keir Dullea, Samantha Gates.   Feeling responsible for her
small daughter's death, the protagonist abandons her husband and buys
an old house. A séance and several apparitions gradually reveal to her
that the house is possessed by the spirit of an evil girl who made her
playmates kill a boy in the nearby playground. The woman's recent loss
and longing make her become the dead girl's instrument--like the
child's mother, she has "murdered" her daughter. Finally the woman
openly "receives" the girl and is killed by her.

The Pit. USA. 93 mins. P: Bennet Fode. D: Lew Lehman. PH: Fred Guthe.
SP: Ian A. Stuart. M: Victor Davies; with Sammy Snyders, Jeannie
Elias, Jennifer Lehman.   Twelve-year-old outsider finds a pit in the
wood with carnivorous monsters in it. He provides his "friends" with
human flesh by pushing his enemies into the pit, until he meets a nice
girl who leads him into the wood and pushes him into another pit where
her friends live.

Look What Happened to Rosemary's Baby. (TV) USA. D: Sam O'Steen.
SP: Anthony Wilson. R: Frank; with Patty Duke Astin (as Satanic
child), Ruth Gordon.   The made-for-TV movie sequel to Rosemary's Baby
follows the activities of the Satanic child as she (!) grows up.

Friday the 13th/The Orphan. USA. D, P, SP: John Ballard. PH: Beda F.
Batka. M: Teo Macero; with Mark Owens, Peggy Feury.   The story is
closely based on Saki's "Sredni Vashtar." The boy's efforts to main-
tain his personality are reinforced by his strong bond with his dead
father, a hunter of big game.

Dracula Père et Fils. France.   As a child, Dracula's son kills his
mother by exposing her to daylight.

Cauchemars. France/Canada. 91 mins. P: Nicole M. Boisvert. D: Eddy
Matelon. SP: Matelon, Alain Sens-Cazenave, Myra Clement. R: Frank;
with Alan Scarfe, Randi Allen.   "A young girl is possessed by the
spirit of her dead aunt."

1977   Demon Seed. MGM/United Artists. P: Herb Jaffe. D: Donald
Cammell. SP: Robert Jaffe, Roger O'Hirson, from a novel by Dean R.
Koontz. PH: Bill Butler. M: Jerry Fielding; with Julie Christie, Fritz
Weaver.   The wife of a leading inventor is raped by her omnipotent
home computer; she gives birth to a being that first looks like a
robot, then cracks its "shell" and appears human beneath--until the
baby begins to speak with the computer's deep masculine voice.

Omen II: Damien. USA. 20th-Century Fox. 102 mins. P: Harvey Bernhard.
D: Don Taylor. PH: Bill Butler. M: Jerry Goldsmith. SP: Stanley Mann,
Michael Hodges, from a story by Bernhard and characters by David
Seltzer; with William Holden, Jonathan Scott-Taylor (as Damien).

Obsession. USA. Columbia. 98 mins. D: Brian de Palma. P: George Litto,
Harry Blum. SP: Paul Schrader. PH: Vilmos Zsigmond. M: Bernard Herr-

mann; with Cliff Robertson, Geneviève Bujold, Wanda Blackman (child). Husband loses wife and daughter after kidnapping; years later the daughter returns to take revenge on her father. Flashbacks to her infancy reveal that she considers him guilty of neglect.

Audrey Rose. D: Robert Wise. SP: Frank de Felitta, from his own novel. P: Joe Wizan, Felitta. M: Michael Small; with Marsha Mason, Anthony Hopkins. The premise of the film is that a soul can be reborn at almost the instant of its physical death, and the tension derives from the struggle between the father of the deceased child and the parents of his reincarnated daughter who refuse to believe in such phenomena.

The Uncanny. Canada/Great Britain. 85 mins. P: Claude Heroux, René Dupont. D: Denis Heroux. SP: Michel Parry. PH: Harry Waxman. R: Frank; with Peter Cushing, Chloe Franks, Katrina Holden. Episode "Quebec Province": young girl is tormented by her small selfish cousin and, with black magic and her cat, shrinks her enemy and crushes her.

The Manitou. USA. 105 mins. P, D: William Girdler. SP: Girdler, Jon Cedar, Thomas Pope, from Graham Masterton's novel. PH: Michel Hugo. M: Lalo Schifrin. R: Frank; with Tony Curtis, Michael Ansara. Indian witch doctor reincarnates himself as a foetus growing on the neck of a woman and wreaks havoc in a hospital.

The Child. USA. 72 mins. P: Robert Dadashian. D: Robert Voskanian. SP: Ralph Lucas. PH: Mori Alavi; with Laurel Barnett, Rosalie Cole. Small girl has inherited her mother's mental disease and wickedness; she kills adults with the aid of animals and corpses she resurrects from the graveyard, until her nanny slaughters her with an axe.

Nero Veneziano. P: Luigi Borghese. D: Ugo Liberatore. SP: Roberto Gandus, Liberatore. PH: Borghese. M: Pino Donaggio; with Renato Cestie, Olga Karlatos. A man has visions of the Antichrist; when his girlfriend gives birth to a son, he recognizes the Devil's face.

1978   It Lives Again. USA. Warner Bros. 88 mins. M: Bernard Herrmann. P: Larry Larco. D, SP: Larry Cohen. PH: Fenton Hamilton. Sequel to It's Alive; with Frederic Forrest, Kathleen Lloyd, John P. Ryan. Organization of idealistic scientists try to prevent police from killing new-born human monster. In a secret research center they raise similar infants from all over the country to prove their harmlessness.

1979   Prophecy. USA. Paramount. 99 mins. P: Robert L. Rosen. D: John Frankenheimer. SP: David Seltzer. PH: Harry Stradling. M: Leonard Rosenman; with Talia Shire, Robert Foxworth. As a result of pollution, a woman will give birth to a monster.

The Brood. Canada. Mutual/Elgin. 91 mins. P: Claude Heroux. PH: Mark Irwin. D, SP: David Cronenberg. M: Howard Shore; with Oliver Reed, Samantha Eggar, Cindy Hinds.

The Shining. Great Britain. Peregrine Film. 146 (119) mins. P, D: Stanley Kubrick. SP: Kubrick, Diana Johnson, from Stephen King's novel. PH: John Alcott; with Jack Nicholson, Shelley Duvall, Danny

Lloyd.

The Boogey Man. USA. 82 mins. D: Ulli Lommel. SP: Lommel, Suzanna Love, David Herschel. PH: David Sperling, Jochen Breitenstein; with Suzanna Love, Ron James. Small brother and sister are terrorized by their mother's lover, who disguises himself as the Boogey Man and maltreats them. The boy finally stabs him to death.

The Changeling. Canada. Archway Films. 107 mins. P: Joel Michaels, Garth Drabinsky. D: Peter Medak. SP: William Gray, Diana Maddox. PH: John Coquillon. M: Rick Wilkins; with George C. Scott, Trish van Devere. A professor who has just lost his small daughter rents an old mansion and is contacted by the ghost of a child. The invalid boy was drowned by his father and replaced by a healthy changeling decades before. Only the impostor's death can appease the dead child's wrath.

When a Stranger Calls. USA. 97 mins. P: Melvin Simon, Barry Krost. D: Fred Walton. SP: Steve Feke, Fred Walton. PH: Don Peterman. M: Dana Kaproff. R: Frank; with Charles Durning, Carol Kane. A young baby-sitter is terrorized by a lunatic who murders her two small charges.

Halloween. Warner Bros. 91 mins. D: John Carpenter. P: Moustapha Akka. SP: Carpenter, Debra Hill. PH: Dean Cundey; with Donald Pleasence, Tony Moran. Six-year-old boy, disguised behind a bizarre mask, stabs his sister to death during Halloween, when horror and fun collide.

1980 Macabro. Italy. 90 mins. D, SP: Lamberto Bava. PH: Franco Delli Colli. M: Bava; with Bernice Stegers, Veronica Zinny. The child Lucy drowns her brother in a fit of rage because her mother has a lover.

The Children. USA. 90 mins. P: Carlton Albright. SP: Albright, Edward Terry. D: Max Kalmanowicz. PH: Barry Abrams. M: Harry Manfredini; with Martin Shakar, Sarah and Nathanael Albright, Gil Rogers. A poisonous gas cloud escapes from the nuclear power station "Yankee Power" and enshrouds a school bus. All children in the bus are transformed into zombies who return to their parents to embrace and kill them.

The Awakening. Great Britain/USA. 105 mins. D: Mike Newell. SP: Allan Scott, Chris Bryant, C. Exton, from a novel by Bram Stoker. PH: Jack Cardiff; with Charlton Heston, Susannah York. When an explorer opens the forbidden tomb of an evil Egyptian queen, his wife gives birth to a dead child; as the man touches the mummy's finger, the baby comes alive--with the spirit of the queen.

Inseminoid. England/Hong Kong. Jupiter Film. P: Richard Gordon, David Speechley. D: Norman J. Warren. SP: Nick and Gloria Maley; with Robin Clarke, Jennifer Ashley. A team of scientists on a distant planet discover the vaults of an extinct race. A female member is impregnated with a crystalline substance and begins to slaughter her colleagues, until she gives birth to murderous twins who kill all survivors.

1981 Omen III: The Final Conflict. USA. 20th-Century Fox. P: Harvey Bernhard. D: Graham Baker. SP: Andrew Birkin. PH: Robert Paynter, Phil Meheux. M: Jerry Goldsmith; with Sam Neill, Lisa Harrow, Mason Adams.

At the age of thirty-two Damien Thorn comes across a small boy who, after an initiation ceremony, becomes his most faithful disciple. Thorn has his followers kill all newborn infants for, like Herod, he tries to prevent the rise of the second Christ.

Basket Case. USA. P: Edgar Levins. D, SP: Frank Hennenlotter. M: Gus Russo. PH: Bruce Torbet; with Kevin Van Hentenryck, Terri Susan Smith. A woman gives birth to Siamese twins, a healthy boy and a beastly though intelligent freak. When the father has the "excrescence" removed from the side of his beautiful son and leaves it in the garbage the twins take deadly revenge on the man.

Venom. USA. 90 mins. D: Piers Haggard. SP: Robert Carrington. PH: Gil Taylor. M: Michael Kamen; with Klaus Kinski, Oliver Reed, Sarah Miles. A gang of kidnappers is besieged by the police in the victim's house. The child's pet, a black mamba, reduces the gangsters one by one.

1982 Kiss Daddy Goodbye. USA. 95 mins. D: Patrick Regan. P: Alain Silver. PH: George Bakken. M: David Spear. SP: Silver, Regan, Ron Abrams, Mary Stewart; with Nell Regan, Patrick Regan III, Fabian Forte. Small brother and sister with superhuman abilities are secretly educated by their father. When he is murdered the children turn him into a zombie both to keep up appearances and to kill the people they detest. Through their mental power they hold all living adults at bay.

Poltergeist. USA. MGM. 114 mins. P: Steven Spielberg, Frank Marshall. D: Tobe Hooper. SP: Spielberg, Michael Grais. PH: Matthew Leonetti. M: Jerry Goldsmith; with Craig T. Nelson, Heather O'Rourke. Speculator abuses former churchyard as a building site. The inhabitants, especially the children, get into evil contact with the ghosts.

Death Valley. USA. Universal. 86 mins. D: Dick Richards. P: Elliott Kastner. SP: Richard Rothstein. PH: Stephen H. Burum. M: Dana Kaproff; with Paul le Mat, Catherine Hicks, Peter Billingsley (as Billie). Small boy becomes the main witness in a case of triple murder and is chased by the killer and his insane twin brother. All adults around him unwittingly betray him and force him to rely on his own abilities.

Creepshow. USA. P: Richard Rubinstein. D: George Romero. SP: Stephen King. PH: Michael Gornick. M: John Harrison; with Fritz Weaver, Stephen King, Joe King (as Billy). The frame story deals with a boy who is forbidden to read "Creepshow" comics and who therefore tortures his father to death with a voodoo doll--a toy he has ordered with a "Creepshow" coupon.

1983 Cujo. USA. Warner Bros. D: Lewis Teague. P: Daniel H. Blatt, Robert Singer. SP: Don Carlos Dunaway, Lauren Currier, from Stephen King's novel; with Dee Wallace, Danny Pintauro, Daniel Hugh-Kelly.

Twilight Zone. USA. Warner/Columbia. D: Steven Spielberg, Joe Dante, George Miller, John Landis. P: Spielberg, Dante. M: Jerry Goldsmith. Third episode: SP: Richard Matheson, from "It's a Good Life" by Jerome Bixby. D: Dante; with Dan Aykroyd, Albert Brooks, John Lithgow.

1984   Children of the Corn. USA. P: Donald Borchers, Terrence Kirby. D: Fritz Kiersch. SP: George Goldsmith, Stephen King, from King's short story. PH: Raoul Lomas. M: Jonathan Elias; with Peter Horton, Linda Hamilton, John Franklin, Courtney Gains.

Firestarter. USA. P: Frank Capra, Jr. D: Mark L. Lester. SP: Stanley Mann, from Stephen King's novel. PH: Giuseppe Ruzzolini; with David Keith, Drew Barrymore, Fred Jones, Martin Sheen.

The Company of Wolves. Great Britain. P: Chris Brown, Stephen Woolley. D: Neil Jordan. SP: Angela Carter, Neil Jordan, from a story by Angela Carter. PH: Bryan Loftus. M: George Fenton; with Angela Lansbury, Sarah Patterson. A child on the threshold to sexual awakening dreams of ancient fairytale motifs which, in this context, assume a veiled erotic connotation.

1985   Cat's Eye. USA. MGM. P: Dino de Laurentis. D: Lewis Teague. SP: Stephen King; with Drew Barrymore, Patty Lupon, Joe Cortese. The frame story centers upon a cat which, possessed by a demon, kills its owner, a small girl. After the demon has left the pet chases the actual murderer, while the girl's ghost defends the animal from her parents' wrath.

Joey. Germany. Filmverlag der Autoren. D, SP: Roland Emmerich. PH: Egon Werdin; with Joshua Morell, Eva Kryll, Tammy Shields, Jerry Hall. A small boy maintains contact with his deceased father via telephone and develops supernatural powers. He animates the dolls in his nursery and plays with them until he succumbs to the evil influence of a ventriloquist's dummy.

NOTES

INTRODUCTION

1.   Muriel G. Shine, The Fictional Children of Henry James (Chapel Hill: University of North Carolina Press, 1969), p. 3.

2.   Ibid., p. 3.

3.   Judith Wilt, Ghosts of the Gothic (Princeton, N.J.: Princeton University Press, 1980), p. 20.

4.   Ibid., p. 20.

5.   Bram Stoker, Dracula (1897; Harmondsworth: Penguin, 1979), p. 53.

6.   Ulrich Suerbaum, Ulrich Broich, and Raimund Borgmeier, Science Fiction (Stuttgart: Reclam, 1980), pp. 164-65.

7.   In an edition by Sam Moskowitz with the meaningful title Science Fiction by Gaslight (Westport, Conn.: Hyperion Press, 1974) one comes across a contribution on sea-monsters.

8.   In his study What is the Fantastic? (Was ist Phantastik?, trans. Reinhard Fischer; Berlin: Das neue Berlin, 1977) Julij Kagarlizkij wisely refrains from a definition of fantastic literature; examining the constituent traits he mentions, however, one can (for once) be positive that he has pure science fiction in mind, or, as it is also called, "scientific science fiction."

9.   Rein Zondergeld (who does see a connection between the fantastic and the supernatural) takes this fact into account when he declares that horror stories must not generally be mixed up with fantastic literature (Lexikon der phantastischen Literatur; Frankfurt a.M.: Suhrkamp, 1983, p. 282). Marie-Claire Bancquart points out that not every "conte cruel" (the French equivalent of the horror story) is a "conte fantastique," whereas every fantastic story is horrifying (Maupassant conteur fantastique; Paris: Minard, 1976, p. 51).

10.   Ray Bradbury's story "The Night" is an excellent example: it contains almost no action but focuses on a human being's sensory perceptions during an average summer night. Like an impressionistic painter, the author succeeds in re-creating the overall nocturnal atmosphere without sacrificing the realistic basis to the expression of emotional experience.

11.   Rosemary Jackson, Fantasy: The Literature of Subversion (London: Methuen, 1981); Bancquart, Maupassant conteur fantastique, p. 50.

12.   Dorothea Schurig-Geick, Studien zum modernen "conte fantastique" Maupassants und ausgewählter Autoren des 20. Jahrhunderts (Heidelberg: Winter, 1970), p. 11.

13.   Franz Hellens, Documents Secrets (Paris, 1958), p. 158.

14.   Roger Caillois, Images, Images (Paris: Corti, 1966).

15.   Tzvetan Todorov, Introduction à la littérature fantastique (Paris: Seuil, 1970); see also The Fantastic: A Structural Approach to a Literary Genre (Cleveland, 1973). Stanislaw Lem, "Tzvetan Todorovs Theorie des Phantastischen," in: Rein Zondergeld, ed., Phaicon I (Frankfurt a.M.: Insel, 1974), pp. 92-122.

16.   Schurig-Geick, Studien zum modernen "conte fantastique", p. 9.

17.   Ibid., p. 10.

18.   According to Schurig-Geick, the main problem of modern man consists in the disintegration of the human nature in its liberty and identity, a disintegration which is final and irrevocable and which occurs "against the background of a dissolved world of values;" Studien zum modernen "conte fantastique", p. 22.

19.   Stephen King, Danse Macabre (New York: Berkley, 1982), p. 258.

20.   This term is taken from a story by Maureen O'Hara with the same title.

21.   See Hermann Hamann, Die literarischen Vorlagen der Kinder- und Hausmärchen und ihre Bearbeitung durch die Gebrüder Grimm (Berlin: Mayer & Müller, 1906). The critic concentrates on the collectors' predilection for embellishment and artistic "enrichment."

22.   Max Lüthi, Das europäische Volksmärchen (1947; München: Francke, 1974), pp. 16-19; hereafter, references to this volume are put in parentheses.

23.   Instead of attempting such a definition, Dieter Petzold employs a pattern which is distinguished from the traditional fairytale as a comparative factor and not restricted in any other direction (Das englische Kunstmärchen im 19. Jahrhundert; Tübingen, 1981, p. 3).

24.   Jens Tismar, Das Kunstmärchen (Stuttgart: Metzler, 1977), p. 1.

25.   Hans Christian Andersen, for his part, employs countless realistic details in his description of children's play and power of imagination; he thus creates an idiosyncratic "Wirklichkeitsphantasie." Walter Berendsohn states that especially these references to real life endow Andersen's fiction with a human (and humane) element which strongly appeals to the reader's emotions (Phantasie und Wirklichkeit in den "Märchen und Geschichten" H. C. Andersens; Wiesbaden, 1973).

26. Karl Eimermacher, ed., <u>Vladimir Propp: Die Morphologie des Mär-chens</u> (München: Hanser, 1972), pp. 157-80.

27. Peter Penzoldt, <u>The Supernatural in Fiction</u> (New York: Humanities Press, 1965), pp. 146-91.

28. See, for instance, the chapter "Les themes sociologiques et psy-chologiques" in: Igor and Grichka Bogdanoff, <u>La Science-fiction</u> (Paris: Seghers, 1976); Dieter Wessels, <u>Welt im Chaos</u> (Frankfurt a.M.: Akademische Verlagsgesellschaft, 1974), pp. 86-88; on the "Icon of the Monster": Gary K. Wolfe, <u>The Known and the Unknown</u> (Kent: Kent State University Press, 1979).

CHAPTER ONE

1. John Saul, <u>Suffer the Children</u> (New York: Dell, 1977), p. 7.

2. Henry James, <u>The Turn of the Screw</u> (London: Dent & Sons, 1957), p. 16; hereafter, references to this volume are put in parentheses.

3. Herbert van Thal, ed., <u>The Fourth Pan Book of Horror Stories</u> (London: Pan, 1963), p. 25.

4. Ray Bradbury, <u>The Small Assassin</u> (Frogmore: Granada, 1976), pp. 9-10; hereafter, references to the story are put in parentheses.

5. Guy de Maupassant, <u>Contes et Nouvelles</u> (Paris: Larousse, 1974), II, 77; hereafter, references to the story are put in parentheses.

6. Irenäus Eibl-Eibesfeldt, <u>Grundriß der vergleichenden Verhaltens-forschung</u> (München: Piper, 1965), pp. 495-502.

7. John Coyne, <u>The Searing</u> (London: Fontana, 1981), p. 16; here-after, references to this volume are put in parentheses.

8. John Saul, <u>Suffer the Children</u>, p. 266.

9. John Coyne, <u>The Searing</u>, p. 150.

10. Ray Bradbury, <u>The Small Assassin</u>, p. 9.

CHAPTER TWO

Social Constellations

The Solitary Child

1.   Ambrose Bierce, Collected Works (New York: Gordian Press, 1966), III, 193.

2.   John Saul, Suffer the Children, p. 100.

3.   Stephen King, Firestarter (New York: New American Library, 1981), p. 371; hereafter, references to this volume are put in parentheses.

4.   F. J. van der Molen, ed., Het Kind in de Literatuur (Zeist: J. Ploegsma, 1920), p. 243.

5.   Graham Greene, Twenty-One Stories (London: Heinemann, 1970), p. 9; hereafter, references to the story are put in parentheses. Although Philip's gradual withdrawal is depicted in its entire logical course, the author's overall image as a "Catholic" writer leads Gerald E. Silveira to the absurd interpretation that the boy, being "at the age when a child is supposed to be capable of mortal sin," damns himself for eternity by rejecting responsibility ("Graham Greene's 'The Basement Room,'" Explicator, 15, 1956, p. 13).   Arthur W. Pitts, on the contrary, recognizes the true source of evil. The "unholy trinity" the boy is exposed to consists of adult human beings; "his gradual withdrawal is in proportion to his increasing fear...represented by his violent dreams of the French Revolution and Siberian wolves" ("Greene's 'The Basement Room,'" Explicator, 23, 1964, p. 17).

6.   Erich Trunz, ed., Goethes Werke (Hamburg: Wegner, 1948), I, 154.

7.   Ray Bradbury, Dark Carnival (London: Hamish Hamilton, 1948), p. 155; hereafter, references to the story are put in parentheses.

8.   Guy de Maupassant, Contes et Nouvelles, I, 104; hereafter, references to the story are put in parentheses.

9.   Peter Haining, ed., Great British Tales of Terror: Gothic Stories of Horror and Romance 1765-1840 (London: Gollancz, 1972), I, 252-53.

10.   Robert A. Wiggins, Ambrose Bierce (Minneapolis: University of Minnesota Press, 1964), p. 27.

11.   Ambrose Bierce, Collected Works, III, 190; hereafter, references to the story are put in parentheses.

12.   Robert Wiggins, Ambrose Bierce, p. 6.

13.   Thomas E. Connolly, ed., Nathaniel Hawthorne: The Scarlet Letter and Other Stories (Harmondsworth: Penguin, 1970), p. 25; hereafter, references to this volume are put in parentheses.   See also Gerhard

Friedrich, "A Note on Quakerism and Moby Dick: Hawthorne's 'The Gentle Boy' as a Possible Source," Quaker History, 54 (1965), 94-102.

14.   Elements of horror and the supernatural in connection with the tale under discussion are repeatedly referred to in: Harry Levin, The Power of Blackness: Hawthorne, Poe and Melville (New York: Alfred Knopf, 1958).

15.   The particular importance of Christian imagery is explained in detail in: Agnes McNeill Donohue, ed., A Casebook on the Hawthorne Question (New York: Crowell, 1963), in the editor's article "'The Fruit of that Forbidden Tree': A Reading of 'The Gentle Boy,'" pp. 158-70.

16.   See Frederic J. Masback, "The Child Characters in Hawthorne and James," Dissertation Abstracts, 21 (1960), p. 338.

17.   A child's extreme aversion to living parents and foster parents is the main subject of the story "My Very Best Friend" by Ronald Chetwynd Hayes. Here the small protagonist has a real guardian angel to protect him from (as Bierce puts it) "a multitude of parents" between him and the "woeful state" of being an orphan. Whenever any of the successive candidates for parentage rouses the boy's indignation, the angel simply deals him/her a lethal "judo chop on the back of the neck" (Cradle Demon; London: Kimber, 1978, p. 102).

18.   Terry Carr, ed., New Worlds of Fantasy (New York: Ace, 1967), p. 98; hereafter, references to the story are put in parentheses.

Brother and Sister

1.   Rohan O'Grady (June Skinner), Let's Kill Uncle (London: Longmans, Green, 1964), p. 136.

2.   The development of the island novel is dealt with in detail in: William Nelson, ed., William Golding's 'Lord of the Flies': A Source Book (Indianapolis: Odyssey Press, 1963); John S. Whitley, Golding: Lord of the Flies (London: Arnold, 1970).

3.   William Golding, Lord of the Flies (London: Faber & Faber, 1954), p. 28; hereafter, references to this volume are put in parentheses.

4.   Rohan O'Grady, Let's Kill Uncle, p. 83; hereafter, references to this volume are put in parentheses.

5.   James Thurber, The Thurber Carnival (New York: Harper & Row, 1944), p. 247.

6.   Apart from the fairytale, another famous source has probably influenced the plot of the novel: the 16th-century black-letter ballad of the Babes in the Woods, turned into a play by Robert Yarrington in 1601. In this drama, The Cruel Uncle, the children's wicked tutor leads them into the wood to dispose of them and inherit their money.

7.   Davis Grubb, The Night of the Hunter (1953; Harmondsworth: Penguin, 1977), p. 24; hereafter, references to this volume are put in parentheses.

8.   Irving Malin, New American Gothic (Carbondale: Southern Illinois University Press, 1962); hereafter, references to this volume are put in parentheses. David Punter, The Literature of Terror: A History of Gothic Fictions (London: Longman, 1980), pp. 373-401.

9.   Leslie Fiedler, Love and Death in the American Novel (New York: Criterion Books, 1960), p. 65.

10. David Punter, The Literature of Terror, p. 385.

11. Edward Albee, The American Dream and The Zoo Story (New York: New American Library, 1961), p. 100.

12. Ibid., p. 9.

13. Edward Albee, Who's Afraid of Virginia Woolf? (London: Jonathan Cape, 1964), p. 145; hereafter, references to this volume are put in parentheses.

14. Roger Vitrac, Victor ou Les Enfants au pouvoir (Paris: Gallimard, 1946), p. 11; hereafter, references to this volume are put in parentheses.

15. Jean Cocteau, Les Enfants terribles (Paris: Grasset, 1981),

p. 115; hereafter, references to this volume are put in parentheses.

16.   Jean-Jacques Kihm, Elizabeth Sprigge, and Henri C. Béhar, Jean Cocteau: L'homme et les miroirs (Paris: édition de la table ronde, 1968), pp. 164-66.

17.   Ray Bradbury, The Illustrated Man (Frogmore: Granada, 1952), p. 15.

18.   Guy de Maupassant, Contes et Nouvelles, I, 96-97.

Peer Groups

1. Ray Bradbury, <u>The Small Assassin</u>, p. 149.

2. Herbert van Thal, ed., <u>The Eighth Pan Book of Horror Stories</u> (London: Pan, 1967), p. 29; hereafter, references to the story are put in parentheses.

3. Gerald W. Page, ed., <u>The Year's Best Horror Stories Series VI</u> (New York: Daw, 1978), p. 147; hereafter, references to the story are put in parentheses.

4. Sir James George Frazer, <u>The Golden Bough: Spirits of the Corn and of the Wild</u> (London: Macmillan, 1955), II, 34; hereafter, references to this volume are put in parentheses.

5. Frazer, <u>The Golden Bough: The Dying God</u>, pp. 160-95.

6. Robert Graves, ed., <u>The Greek Myths</u> (Harmondsworth: Penguin, 1960), II, 227-31.

7. Seven years earlier, in 1953, an atomic explosion is already chosen as the starting-point for the development of a new race: in the science fiction novel <u>Children of the Atom</u> by Wilmar Shiras a number of superhuman children use their master minds to protect mankind from further scientific disasters. In 1959, a comparable incident leads to the extinction of adult mankind and the survival of a group of children. In Harold Mead's novel <u>Mary's Country</u> two opposing great powers have developed a virus which spreads without the agency of military forces. After the apocalypse the children are educated in special institutions by teachers whose aim is their pupils' total emotionlessness. Despite their efforts the children do develop emotions and set out for "Mary's Country," their dream of Eden.

8. Ronald Chetwynd-Hayes, <u>Cradle Demon</u>, p. 61; hereafter, references to the story are put in parentheses. Cf. Tom Reamy's "Beyond the Cleft" (1979): in this repulsive tale all children under eleven start running amuck in the same minute, devour the adults they meet and leave their homes to dig burrows in the river bank. Moving with silent determination like a single entity, they resemble vermin rather than human beings. The children, referred to as "they" by their parents, are naked and prematurely developed; their offspring are monsters, too, just like the children their elders give birth to after D-day. As the main reason for the sudden degeneration incest is suggested: the rich and fertile valley their forefathers settled in lies "at a dead end," and they have "prospered by their own standards."

9. John Wyndham, <u>The Midwich Cuckoos</u> (Harmondsworth: Penguin, 1960), p. 122; hereafter, references to this volume are put in parentheses.

10. Hans-Joachim Alpers, et al., eds., <u>Lexikon der Science Fiction-Literatur</u> (München: Heyne, 1980), pp. 690-92.

11.   Wolfgang Jeschke, ed., <u>Science Fiction Story-Reader 14</u> (München: Heyne, 1980), p. 222.

12.   Arthur Machen, <u>Tales of Horror and the Supernatural</u> (1949; Frogmore: Granada, 1965), II, 74; hereafter, references to this volume are put in parentheses.

13.   Machen's story "Out of the Earth" may be taken into consideration as an elucidative counterpart of the tale under discussion: in another English village the children have "gone quite out of hand" since the war and disquiet the inhabitants. In this case, however, they are not holy beings but "a swarm of noisome children, horrible little stunted creatures with old men's faces," worse than "a brood of snakes or a nest of worms." In connection with these goblin-like beings the narrator's friend also refers to the infant victims of the war: "'Read about Belgium...and think they couldn't have been more than five or six years old.'" These children emulate their victimizers (Ibid., pp. 14-15).

14.   The "musical construction" of the narrative was indeed obvious enough to attract the attention of one of Schwob's contemporaries, the musician Pierné, for whom, in 1905, the author wrote a libretto based on his original story. The composition was performed at the Concert Colonne and celebrated by the critics. Camille Bellaigue wrote to Schwob: "Vous avez fait une oeuvre de poésie, vous avez suscité par elle, et pour elle, une oeuvre de musique." Pierre Champion, <u>Marcel Schwob et son temps</u> (Paris: Grasset, 1927), p. 119.

15.   Marcel Schwob, <u>Oeuvres</u> (Paris: Mercure de France, 1921), II, 59; hereafter, references to this volume are put in parentheses.

16.   Considering works like Brecht's <u>Hauspostille</u> (1927), however, which includes poems such as "Apfelböck, oder Die Lilie auf dem Felde" (based on the authentic story of a twelve-year-old parricide), one becomes aware how deeply the author's work is rooted in the sinister tradition of the <u>Moritatensänger</u>. The poem shows the unique mixture of irony and horrifying matter-of-fact style that is typical of the genre. Nonetheless one must admit that the gruesome effect of the "Kinderkreuzzug" is based on pathos rather than irony.

17.   Mary Hottinger, ed., <u>Kindergeschichten</u>, trans. Marta Hackel (Zürich: Diogenes, 1978), p. 207; hereafter, references to the story are put in parentheses.

18.   Julian Gloag, <u>Our Mother's House</u> (1963; Harmondsworth: Penguin, 1982), p. 13; hereafter, references to this volume are put in parentheses.

Friends, Foes, and Allies

Children and Beasts

1.   Hector Hugh Munro, The Complete Works of Saki (London: The Bodley Head, 1980), p. 137.

2.   Ibid., p. 136; hereafter, references to the story are put in parentheses.

3.   Patricia Highsmith, The Animal-Lover's Book of Beastly Murder (Harmondsworth: Penguin, 1979), p. 192; hereafter, references to this volume are put in parentheses.

4.   Herbert van Thal, ed., The Seventh Pan Book of Horror Stories (London: Pan, 1966), p. 35; hereafter, references to the story are put in parentheses.

5.   Peter Haining, ed., The Midnight People (London: Everest, 1968), p. 163; hereafter, references to the story are put in parentheses.

6.   Hector H. Munro, The Complete Works of Saki, p. 423; hereafter, references to this volume are put in parentheses.

7.   Lester Del Rey, ed., The Best of Robert Bloch (New York: Ballantine, 1977), p. 305; hereafter, references to this story are put in parentheses.

8.   Herbert van Thal, ed., The Fifteenth Pan Book of Horror Stories (London: Pan, 1974), p. 116; hereafter, references to this story are put in parentheses.

9.   Giles Gordon, ed., Prevailing Spirits (London: Hamish Hamilton, 1976), p. 10; hereafter, references to this story are put in parentheses.

10.   Gerald Page, The Year's Best Horror Stories, p. 80; hereafter, references to this story are put in parentheses.

11.   Herbert van Thal, ed., The First Pan Book of Horror Stories (London: Pan, 1959), p. 186.

12.   Hector H. Munro, The Complete Works of Saki, p. 375.

13.   See Konrad Lorenz, Paul Leyhausen, Antriebe tierischen und menschlichen Verhaltens (München: Piper, 1968), pp. 388-407.

14.   Ray Bradbury, The October Country (Frogmore: Granada, 1976), p. 77; hereafter, references to this story are put in parentheses.

15.   Stephen King, Cujo (New York: New American Library, 1981), p. 17; hereafter, references to this volume are put in parentheses.

Children and Dolls

1.   Algernon Blackwood, Tales of the Uncanny and Supernatural (Feltham: Hamlyn, 1977), pp. 17-18.

2.   Ibid., p. 15; hereafter, references to the story are put in parentheses.

3.   James Herbert, The Dark (Sevenoaks: New English Library, 1980), p. 15; hereafter, references to this volume are put in parentheses.

4.   J. W. Lambert, ed., The Bodley Head Saki (London: The Bodley Head, 1963), p. 363; hereafter, references to this volume are put in parentheses.

5.   Kingsley Amis, Patricia Highsmith, Christopher Lee, eds., The Times Anthology of Ghost Stories (London: Cape, 1975), p. 72; hereafter, references to the story are put in parentheses.

6.   A. da Mosto, I dogi di Venezia nella vita pubblica e privata (Milano, 1960), pp. 132-36.

7.   John Saul, Suffer the Children, p. 113; hereafter, references to this volume are put in parentheses.

8.   See, for instance, William W. Atkinson, Reincarnation and the Law of Karma (1908; rptd. London: Fowler, 1965), chapter VII.

9.   Brenda Brown Canary, The Voice of the Clown (New York: Avon, 1982), p. 10; hereafter, references to this volume are put in parentheses.

10.   The relationship between the artist and his creation and the interaction between the work of art and its human model, topics which were greatly favored in Romanticism, also form the basis of the story in question. In many respects it may be compared to 19th-century works. The artist's "divine" creative/destructive potency is pointed out in Hawthorne's "Birthmark," the vital interdependence between painting and original reminds the reader of Wilde's Picture of Dorian Gray, Poe's "Oval Portrait," and to some extent of Robert L. Stevenson's "Ollala" or Sheridan LeFanu's "Schalken the Painter."

11.   Kingsley Amis, et al., eds., The Times Anthology, p. 19; hereafter, references to the story are put in parentheses.

12.   See J. M. Salgado, Le culte africain du Vodou et les baptisés en Haiti (Rome, 1964).

13.   Arthur Machen, Tales of Horror and the Supernatural, I, 68-69; hereafter, references to the story are put in parentheses.

14.   Gerald Page, ed., <u>The Year's Best Horror Stories</u>, p. 12; here-after, references to the story are put in parentheses.

15.   Herbert van Thal, ed., <u>The Fourth Pan Book of Horror Stories</u>, p. 52; hereafter, references to the story are put in parentheses.

CHAPTER THREE

The Child as a Victim of Parents and Tutors

1.   William H. Davies, The Complete Poems of W. H. Davies (London: Jonathan Cape, 1963), p. 233.

2.   Guy de Maupassant, Contes et Nouvelles, I, 49; hereafter, references to the story are put in parentheses.

3.   Herbert van Thal, ed., The First Pan Book of Horror Stories, p. 177; hereafter, references to the story are put in parentheses.

4.   Ray Bradbury, The Small Assassin, p. 81; hereafter, references to the story are put in parentheses.

5.   V. Andrews, Flowers in the Attic (New York: Pocket Books, 1979), p. 80; hereafter, references to this volume are put in parentheses.

6.   Gustav Meyrink, Der violette Tod (Frankfurt: Fischer, 1976), pp. 83-84 (my translation).

7.   Ray Bradbury, Long After Midnight (Frogmore: Granada, 1978), p. 229; hereafter, references to the story are put in parentheses.

8.   Popular superstition alleges that witches celebrate their annual gatherings on Halloween, when their evil power has reached its peak.

9.   Ruth Rendell, The Fallen Curtain (London: Arrow Books, 1980), p. 123; hereafter, references to the story are put in parentheses.

10.   Herbert van Thal, ed., The Third Pan Book of Horror Stories (London: Pan, 1962), p. 76.

11.   Bram Stoker, Dracula, p. 87.

12.   Herbert van Thal, ed., The Eleventh Pan Book (1970), p. 185.

13.   Herbert van Thal, ed., The First Pan Book, p. 300.

14.   D. H. Lawrence, The Complete Short Stories (London: Heinemann, 1964), III, 790; hereafter, references to the story are put in parentheses.

15.   The mother tends to be a threatening figure in most of Lawrence's fiction. She is depicted as a cold, egocentric creature who, as expressed in "The Lovely Lady," puts a sucker into one's soul, feeding on her children's essential life. The beautiful hard-hearted lady, a figure from the children's story, is perceived as "cannibalistic" by Kingsley Widmer (The Art of Perversity; Seattle, 1962, p. 95).

16.   See John F. Turner, "The Perversion of Play in D. H. Lawrence's 'The Rocking-Horse Winner,'" D. H. Lawrence Review, 15 (1982), 249-70.

The Child as a Victim of Its Environment

1.   Terrel Miedaner, The Soul of Anna Klane (New York: Ballantine, 1977), p. 48.

2.   Klaus Lindemann, Jeremias Gotthelf: Die schwarze Spinne (München: Blütenburg, 1983), p. 9. See also pp. 102-13.

3.   Jeremias Gotthelf, Die schwarze Spinne (Stuttgart: Reclam, 1976), pp. 63-64 (my translation).

4.   John Hayward, ed., Swift: Gulliver's Travels and Selected Writings (New York: Random House, 1949), p. 512; hereafter, references to this work are put in parentheses.

5.   Ambrose Bierce, In the Midst of Life and Other Stories (New York: New American Library, 1961), p. 27; hereafter, references to the story are put in parentheses.

6.   Stuart C. Woodruff, The Short Stories of Ambrose Bierce (Pittsburgh: University of Pittsburgh Press, 1964), pp. 39-40.

7.   Terrel Miedaner, The Soul of Anna Klane, p. 31; hereafter, references to this volume are put in parentheses.

CHAPTER FOUR

The Possessed Child

1. William Peter Blatty, The Exorcist (London: Corgi, 1972), p. 109.

2. See, for instance, C. B. Ives, "James's Ghosts in The Turn of the Screw," Nineteenth-Century Fiction, 17 (1963), 183-89; Hans-Joachim Lang, "The Turns in The Turn of the Screw," Jahrbuch für Amerikastudien, 9 (1964), 110-28.

3. Muriel G. Shine, The Fictional Children of Henry James, p. 63.

4. The Governess's subconscious sexual inhibitions and their fatal effect are explained in: George Knox, "Incubi and Succubi in The Turn of the Screw," Western Folklore, 22 (1963), 122-23; see also Robert B. Heilmann, "The Freudian Reading of The Turn of the Screw," Modern Language Notes, 62 (1947), 433-45.

5. Henry James, The Turn of the Screw, p. 148.

6. Muriel Shine, The Fictional Children of Henry James, p. 89.

7. Theodus Carroll, Evil is a Quiet Word (New York: Warner, 1975), p. 87.

8. Graham Masterton, The Revenge of Manitou (New York: Wieslava, 1975), p. 104; hereafter, references to this volume are put in parentheses.

9. John Coyne, The Searing, p. 113; hereafter, references to this volume are put in parentheses.

The Child as Catalyst or Medium

1. Stephen King, The Shining (London: New English Library, 1977), p. 348.

2. Ibid., p. 283; hereafter, references to this volume are put in parentheses.

3. Edmund Crispin, ed., Best SF IV (London: Faber & Faber, 1961), pp. 95-96; hereafter, references to the story are put in parentheses.

CHAPTER FIVE

The "Classic" Monsters--Homemade Monsters--The Seed From Outer Space--The Unholy Infant--The Everyday Monster

1. Herbert van Thal, ed., _The Fourth Pan Book_, p. 30.

2. See Basil Copper, _The Vampire in Legend, Fact, and Art_ (London: Hale, 1973).

3. Herbert van Thal, ed., _The Fourth Pan Book_, p. 25; hereafter, references to the story are put in parentheses.

4. Ronald Chetwynd-Hayes, _Cradle Demon_, p. 131; hereafter, references to the story are put in parentheses.

5. Anne Rice, _Interview With the Vampire_ (New York: Ballantine, 1976), p. 75; hereafter, references to the volume are put in parentheses.

6. Stephen King, _'Salem's Lot_ (New York: Doubleday, 1975), p. 380; hereafter, references to the volume are put in parentheses.

7. Ray Bradbury, _The October Country_, p. 74; hereafter, references to the volume are put in parentheses.

8. Herbert van Thal, ed., _The Fifteenth Pan Book_, p. 61.

9. Ronald Chetwynd-Hayes, _Cradle Demon_, p. 73; hereafter, references to the story are put in parentheses.

10. See Montague Summers, _The Werewolf_ (New York, 1933); B. J. Frost, _Book of the Werewolf_ (London, 1973).

11. Robert Stallman, _The Orphan_ (New York: Pocket Books, 1980), p. 13; hereafter, references to this volume are put in parentheses.

12. Stephen King, _Pet Sematary_ (New York: New American Library, 1983), p. 38; hereafter, references to this volume are put in parentheses.

13. G. A. McCluskey (OMD), "Genetic Engineering" (London: Virgin Music Publ. Ltd., 1983).

14. Kate Wilhelm, _Where Late the Sweet Birds Sang_ (London: Arrow, 1974), p. 4; hereafter, references to this volume are put in parentheses.

15. John Wyndham, _The Midwich Cuckoos_, p. 35; hereafter, references to this volume are put in parentheses.

16. David Galloway, ed., _The Other Poe: Comedies and Satires_ (Harmondsworth: Penguin, 1983), p. 82.

17.   Ray Bradbury, The Illustrated Man, p. 178; hereafter, references to the story are put in parentheses.

18.   John Wyndham, The Midwich Cuckoos, p. 156.

19.   During the Black Mass, an orgiastic feast meant as a mockery of the Christian Holy Mass, the participants worship the Devil or witches, performing obscene, cruel rituals determined by sexual and religious perversions. As a religious phenomenon the Greek bacchanal feasts are considered a precursory form of the Black Mass; in the early 19th century the Black Mass became a topic of interest in literature (de Sade, Baudelaire).

20.   See Jeffrey Burton Russell, The Devil: Perceptions of Evil from Antiquity to Primitive Christianity (Ithaca: Cornell University Press, 1977); Richard Woods, The Devil (Chicago: Thomas More Press, 1974).

21.   Ira Levin, Rosemary's Baby (London: Michael Joseph, 1967), p. 134.

22.   David Seltzer, The Omen (London: Futura, 1976), p. 16; hereafter, references to this volume are put in parentheses.

23.   John Shirley, Cellars (New York: Avon, 1982), p. 204.

24.   Stephen King, Danse Macabre, p. 373; hereafter, references to this volume are put in parentheses.

25.   Ludwig Hirsch, "Die gottverdammte Pleite" (Vienna: Edition Scheibmaier, 1979).

26.   Ian Craig Marsh (The Human League), "Crow and a Baby" (London: Virgin Music Publ. Ltd., 1980).

27.   Herbert van Thal, ed., The Fourth Pan Book, pp. 89-90; hereafter, references to the story are put in parentheses.

28.   Terry Carr, ed., New Worlds of Fantasy, p. 229.

29.   Herbert van Thal, ed., The Fourth Pan Book, p. 227.

30.   Isaac Asimov, ed., Tomorrow's Children (London: Macdonald Futura, 1966), p. 310; hereafter, references to the story are put in parentheses.

A la recherche du temps perdu

1.   Mark Schorer, ed., Truman Capote: Selected Writings (London: Hamish Hamilton, 1963), p. 127.

2.   Herbert van Thal, ed., The Fifteenth Pan Book, p. 89.

3.   Herbert van Thal, ed., The Seventh Pan Book, p. 29; hereafter, references to this story are put in parentheses.

4.   Herbert van Thal, ed., The Fourth Pan Book, p. 45; hereafter, references to this story are put in parentheses.

5.   Herbert van Thal, ed., The Seventh Pan Book, p. 157; hereafter, references to this story are put in parentheses.

6.   Terry Carr, ed., New Worlds of Fantasy, p. 104; hereafter, references to this story are put in parentheses.

7.   Ray Bradbury, Dark Carnival , p. 65; hereafter, references to this story are put in parentheses.

8.   Ray Bradbury, The Illustrated Man, p. 191; hereafter, references to this story are put in parentheses.

CONCLUSION

1.   Judith Wilt, Ghosts of the Gothic, p. 7; hereafter, references to this volume are put in parentheses.

2.   Ray Bradbury, The Small Assassin, p. 88.

3.   Oscar Wilde, The Picture of Dorian Gray (1891; Harmondsworth: Penguin, 1978), p. 5.

4.   Alfred Bader, ed., Geisteskrankheit, bildnerischer Ausdruck und Kunst: Zur Psychopathologie des Schöpferischen (Bern: Hans Huber, 1975), p. 104; hereafter, references to this volume are put in parentheses. The final translation is my own.

APPENDIX I

1.   Robert Moss, _Karloff and Company: The Horror Film_ (New York: Pyramid Publications, 1973), p. 3.

2.   Donald Willis, _Horror and Science Fiction Films_ (Metuchen, N. J.: Scarecrow Press, 1972), p. 281.

3.   Ibid., p. 136.

4.   Dennis Gifford, _The British Film Catalogue 1895-1970_ (New York: McGraw-Hill, 1973).

5.   Countless anecdotes about the "magician" among the pioneers, Georges Méliès, suggest that he was led to some of his original plots and devices by way of technical accidents. See Jerzy Toeplitz, _Geschichte des Films 1895-1928_ (Munich: Rogner & Bernhard, 1973), p. 22.

6.   Ivan Butler, _Horror in the Cinema_ (London: Zwemmer, 1970), p. 72.

7.   Lawrence Hammond, _Thriller Movies_ (London: Octopus, 1974), p. 63.

8.   David Pirie, _A Heritage of Horror_ (London: Fraser, 1973), p. 137.

9.   John Baxter, _Science Fiction in the Cinema_ (New York: Barnes, 1970), p. 129.

10.   David Pirie, _A Heritage of Horror_, p. 135.

11.   Roy Huss and T. J. Ross, eds., _Focus on the Horror Film_ (Englewood Cliffs, N. J.: Prentice Hall, 1972), p. 150-51.

12.   Karl Weber, "Teufelsaustreibung made in Hollywood," _ZOOM_, 26 (1974), pp. 2-5.

SELECTED BIBLIOGRAPHY

PRIMARY SOURCES

    1. Novels

Adams, Richard. <u>The Girl in a Swing</u>. Harmondsworth: Penguin, 1980.

Andrews, Virginia. <u>Flowers in the Attic</u>. New York: Pocket Books, 1979.

Blatty, William Peter. <u>The Exorcist</u>. London: Corgi, 1972.

Canary, Brenda Brown. <u>The Voice of the Clown</u>. New York: Avon, 1981.

Carroll, Theodus. <u>Evil is a Quiet Word</u>. New York: Warner, 1975.

Cocteau, Jean. <u>Les Enfants terribles</u>. Paris: Grasset, 1929.

Coyne, John. <u>The Searing</u>. London: Fontana, 1981.

Cronenberg, David. <u>The Brood</u>. London: Granada, 1979.

Gloag, Julian. <u>Our Mother's House</u>. Harmondsworth: Penguin, 1982.

Golding, William. <u>Lord of the Flies</u>. London: Faber & Faber, 1954.

Gotthelf, Jeremias. <u>Die schwarze Spinne</u>. Stuttgart: Reclam, 1976.

Grubb, Davis. <u>The Night of the Hunter</u>. Harmondsworth: Penguin, 1977.

Herbert, Frank. <u>The Dark</u>. Sevenoaks: New English Library, 1980.

James, Henry. <u>The Turn of the Screw</u>. London: Dent & Sons, 1957.

King, Stephen. <u>Cujo</u>. New York: New American Library, 1981.

_____. <u>Firestarter</u>. New York: New American Library, 1981.

_____. <u>Pet Sematary</u>. New York: New American Library, 1983.

_____. <u>'Salem's Lot</u>. New York: Doubleday, 1975.

_____. <u>The Shining</u>. London: New English Library, 1977.

Lawrence, H. L. <u>Children of Light</u>. London: Macdonald, 1965.

Levin, Ira. <u>Rosemary's Baby</u>. London: Michael Joseph, 1967.

Masterton, Graham. <u>The Revenge of Manitou</u>. New York: Wieslawa, 1975.

Miedaner, Terrel. <u>The Soul of Anna Klane</u>. New York: Ballantine, 1977.

O'Grady, Rohan. _Let's Kill Uncle_. London: Longmans, Green, 1964.

Rice, Anne. _Interview With the Vampire_. New York: Ballantine, 1976.

Saul, John. _Comes the Blind Fury_. New York: Dell, 1980.

———. _Cry For the Strangers_. New York: Dell, 1979.

———. _Suffer the Children_. New York: Dell, 1977.

Seltzer, David. _The Omen_. London: Futura, 1976.

Shirley, John. _Cellars_. New York: Avon, 1982.

Smiley, Virginia K. _High Country Nurse_. London: Mills & Boon, 1974.

Stallman, Robert. _The Orphan_. New York: Pocket Books, 1980.

Wilhelm, Kate. _Where Late the Sweet Birds Sang_. London: Arrow, 1977.

Wyndham, John. _The Midwich Cuckoos_. Harmondsworth: Penguin, 1960.

2. Anthologies

Amis, Kingsley, Highsmith, Patricia, and Lee, Christopher, eds. _The Times Anthology of Horror Stories_. London: Cape, 1964. ("Marius the Doll;" "The Doll Named Silvio;" "The Locket")

Asimov, Isaac, ed. _Tomorrow's Children_. London: Macdonald, 1966. ("When the Bough Breaks;" "The Father-Thing")

Bierce, Ambrose. _Collected Works_. New York: Gordian Press, 1966. ("A Baby Tramp;" "Chickamauga")

Blackwood, Algernon. _Tales of the Uncanny and the Supernatural_. Feltham: Hamlyn, 1977. ("The Doll")

Bradbury, Ray. _Dark Carnival_. London: Hamish Hamilton, 1948. ("The Lake;" "The Night")

———. _Long After Midnight_. Frogmore: Granada, 1978. ("The October Game;" "The Miracles of Jamie")

———. _The Illustrated Man_. Frogmore: Granada, 1980. ("The Veld;" "Zero Hour;" "The Playground")

———. _The October Country_. Frogmore: Granada, 1976. ("The Traveler;" "Uncle Einar;" "Homecoming;" "The Emissary")

———. _The Small Assassin_. Frogmore: Granada, 1976. ("Jack-in-the-Box;" "The Lake;" "The Night;" "Let's Play 'Poison'")

Brecht, Bert. _Kalendergeschichten_. Hamburg: Rowohlt, 1953. ("Kinderkreuzzug 1939")

Carr, Terry, ed. New Worlds of Fantasy. New York: Ace Books, 1967.
    ("The Other;" "The Evil Eye;" "A Red Heart and Blue Roses")

Chetwynd-Hayes, Ronald. Cradle Demon. London: Kimber, 1978. ("Why?;"
    "The Brats;" "My Mother Married a Vampire")

Crispin, Edmund, ed. Best SF IV. London: Faber & Faber, 1961. ("It's
    a Good Life")

Davis, Richard, ed. The Year's Best Horror Stories. 2 vols. London:
    Sphere Books, 1973. ("The Problem Child;" "David's Worm;" "The
    Silent Game")

Del Rey, Lester, ed. Best of Robert Bloch. New York: Ballantine,
    1977. ("The Funnel of God")

Gordon, Giles, ed. Prevailing Spirits. London: Hamish Hamilton, 1976.
    ("Holiday")

Greene, Graham. Twenty-One Stories. London: Heinemann, 1970. ("The
    Basement Room")

Haining, Peter, ed. The Midnight People. London: Everest Books, 1968.
    ("Drink My Blood")

Handke, Peter, ed. Der gewöhnliche Schrecken. München: DTV, 1971.
    ("Entlarvung der flüchtig skizzierten Herren")

Highsmith, Patricia. The Animal-Lover's Book of Beastly Murder.
    Harmondsworth: Penguin, 1979. ("Hamsters vs. Websters")

Lawrence, D. H. The Complete Short Stories. London: Heinemann, 1964.
    ("The Rocking-Horse Winner")

Machen, Arthur. Tales of Horror and the Supernatural. 2 vols. Felt-
    ham: Hamlyn, 1977. ("The Happy Children;" "The White People")

Maupassant, Guy de. Contes et Nouvelles. 2 vols. Paris: Larousse,
    1974. ("L'Orphelin;" "Madame Hermet;" "Le Baptême")

Meyrink, Gustav. Der violette Tod. Frankfurt: Fischer, 1976. ("Die
    Urne von St. Gingolph;" "Das Wachsfigurenkabinett")

Munro, Hector H. The Complete Works of Saki. London: The Bodley Head,
    1980. ("Sredni Vashtar;" "Morlvera;" "Hyacinth;" "The Penance")

Page, Gerald W., ed. The Year's Best Horror Stories Series VI. New
    York: Daw, 1978. ("Children of the Corn;" "The Horse Lord")

Reamy, Tom. San Diego Lightfoot Sue and Other Stories. New York:
    Berkley, 1983. ("Beyond the Cleft")

Rendell, Ruth. The Fallen Curtain. London: Arrow Books, 1980. ("The
    Vinegar Mother")

Schorer, Mark, ed. _Truman Capote: Selected Writings_. London: Hamish
     Hamilton, 1963. ("Miriam")

Schwob, Marcel. _Oeuvres_. Paris: Mercure de France, 1921. ("La Crois-
     ade des enfants")

van Thal, Herbert, ed. _The First Pan Book of Horror Stories_. London:
     Pan Books, 1959. ("Raspberry Jam;" "Oh, Mirror, Mirror")

_____. _The Third Pan Book_. 1962. ("The Last Night;" "Special Diet")

_____. _The Fourth Pan Book_. 1963. ("The Pale Boy;" "Guy Fawkes
     Night;" "Harry;" "The Little Girl Eater;" "The Attic Express")

_____. _The Seventh Pan Book_. 1966. ("The Bats;" "The Return;" "Street
     of the Blind Donkey")

_____. _The Eighth Pan Book_. 1967. ("The Children;" "Playtime;" "The
     Brindle Bull Terrier;" "The Benefactor;" "Sugar and Spice")

_____. _The Eleventh Pan Book_. 1970. ("The Babysitter;" "Dear Jeffy;"
     "Oysters;" "The Market-Gardeners")

_____. _The Fifteenth Pan Book_. 1974. ("Under the Flagstone;" "Wally;"
     "'Quieta Non Movere;'" "A Problem Called Albert")

_____. _The Sixteenth Pan Book_. 1975. ("The Evil Innocent")

3. Drama and Poetry

Albee, Edward. _Who's Afraid of Virginia Woolf?_ London: Cape, 1964.

_____. _The American Dream and The Zoo Story_. New York: New American
     Library, 1961.

Anderson, Maxwell. _The Bad Seed_. New York: Dramatist's Play Service,
     1957.

Davies, William H. _The Complete Poems of W. H. Davies_. London:
     Jonathan Cape, 1942. ("The Inquest")

Hirsch, Ludwig. "Die gottverdammte Pleite." Vienna: Edition Scheib-
     maier, 1979.

McCluskey, G. A. (OMD). "Genetic Engineering." London: Virgin Music
     Publ. Ltd., 1983.

Marsh, Ian Craig (The Human League). "Crow and a Baby." London:
     Virgin Music Publ. Ltd., 1980.

Vitrac, Roger. _Victor ou Les Enfants au pouvoir_. Paris: Gallimard,
     1946.

SECONDARY SOURCES

1. Children in Literature

Avery, Gillian. Nineteenth Century Children. London: Hodder & Stough-
ton, 1967.

Babenroth, A. Charles. English Childhood. New York, 1922.

Borgmeier, Raimund. "Welt im Kleinen: Kinder als Zentralcharaktere in
der modernen englischen short story." Poetica, 5 (1972), 98-120.

Buckroyd, Peter. "More Children in Tragedy 1695-1750." Restoration
and 18th-Century Theatre Research, 12 (1973), 49-51.

Cambon, Glauco. "What Maisie and Huck Knew." Studi Americani, 6
(1960), 203-20.

Coveney, Peter. The Image of Childhood. Harmondsworth: Penguin, 1967.

_____. Poor Monkey: The Child in Literature. London: Barrie & Rock-
liff, 1965.

Garber, Marjorie. "Coming of Age in Shakespeare." The Yale Review,
66 (1977), 517-33.

Haney, Charles W. "The Garden and the Child: A Study of Pastoral
Transformation." Dissertation Abstracts, 26 (1965), 2212.

Kazin, Alfred. "A Procession of Children." The American Scholar,
Spring 1964, 173.

Kohli, Devindra. "Dream Drums: The Child as an Image of Conflict and
Liberation." The Malahat Review, 35 (1975), 75-100.

Shine, Muriel G. The Fictional Children of Henry James. Chapel Hill:
The University of North Carolina Press, 1969.

2. Gothic/Horror/Fantasy/Science Fiction

Alpers, Hans-J., et al. Lexikon der Science Fiction-Literatur. München: Heyne, 1980.

Barclay, Glen St. John. Anatomy of Horror: The Masters of Occult
Fiction. London: Weidenfeld & Nicolson, 1978.

Birkhead, Edith. The Tale of Terror: A Study of the Gothic Romance.
New York: Russell, 1963.

Bogdanoff, Igor and Grichka. La Science-Fiction. Paris: Seghers, 1976.

Fiedler, Leslie. Love and Death in the American Novel. New York:
Criterion Books, 1960.

Jackson, Rosemary. <u>Fantasy: The Literature of Subversion</u>. London:
    Methuen, 1981.

King, Stephen. <u>Danse Macabre</u>. New York: Berkley, 1982.

Lovecraft, H. P. <u>Supernatural Horror in Literature</u>. New York:
    Abramson, 1945.

Malin, Irving. <u>New American Gothic</u>. Carbondale: Southern Illinois
    University Press, 1962.

Penzoldt, Peter. <u>The Supernatural in Fiction</u>. New York: Humanities
    Press, 1965.

Punter, David. <u>The Literature of Terror: A History of Gothic Fictions
    from 1765 to the Present Day</u>. London: Longman, 1980.

Quinn, Patrick F. <u>The French Face of Edgar Poe</u>. Carbondale: Southern
    Illinois University Press, 1957.

Summers, Montague. <u>The Gothic Quest</u>. New York: Russell, 1938.

Todorov, Tzvetan. <u>The Fantastic: A Structural Approach to a Literary
    Genre</u>. Cleveland: Case Western Reserve University Press, 1973.

Tymm, Marshall B., ed. <u>Horror Literature: A Core Collection and
    Reference Guide</u>. London: Bowker, 1981.

Wilt, Judith. <u>Ghosts of the Gothic</u>. Princeton, N. J.: Princeton
    University Press, 1980.

3.   The Horror Film

Baxter, John. <u>Science Fiction in the Cinema</u>. New York: Barnes, 1970.

Blatty, William Peter. <u>The Exorcist: From Novel to Film</u>. New York:
    Bantam Books, 1974.

Butler, Ivan. <u>Cinema in Britain</u>. New York: Barnes, 1973.

_____. <u>Horror in the Cinema</u>. London: Zwemmer, 1970.

Frank, Alan. <u>The Horror Film Handbook</u>. London: Batsford, 1982.

Gifford, Dennis. <u>Movie Monsters</u>. London: Studio Vista, 1969.

_____. <u>The British Film Catalogue 1895-1970: A Reference Guide</u>.
    New York: McGraw-Hill, 1973.

Hammond, Lawrence. <u>Thriller Movies</u>. London: Octopus, 1974.

Huss, Roy, and Ross, T. J. <u>Focus on the Horror Film</u>. Englewood
    Cliffs, N. J.: Prentice Hall, 1972.

Moss, Robert. _Karloff and Company: The Horror Film_. New York: Pyramid Publications, 1973.

Pirie, David. _A Heritage of Horror_. London: Gordon Fraser, 1973.

Toeplitz, Jerzy. _Geschichte des Films 1895-1928_. München: Rogner & Bernhard, 1973.

Willis, Donald C. _Horror and Science Fiction Films_. Metuchen, N. J.: Scarecrow Press, 1972.

INDEX

About the Author

Sabine Büssing is a research assistant at Ruhr University in Bochum, West Germany.